Also by Jon Meacham
Available from Random House Large Print

The Soul of America

IMPEACHMENT

IMPEACHMENT

AN AMERICAN HISTORY

Jeffrey A. Engel

Jon Meacham

Timothy Naftali

Peter Baker

RANDOM HOUSE
LARGE PRINT

Published in the United States of America by Random House Large Print in association with Modern Library, an imprint of Random House, a division of Penguin Random House LLC, New York.

Cover Design: Oliver Munday
Cover Photographs: National Archives/Getty Images (Andrew Johnson), The Washington Post/Getty Images (Richard Nixon), Associated Press (Bill Clinton)

The Library of Congress has established a Cataloging-in-Publication record for this title.

ISBN: 978-1-9848-4350-0

www.penguinrandomhouse.com/large-print-format-books

FIRST LARGE PRINT EDITION

Printed in the United States of America

10 9 8 7 6 5 4 3 2 1

This Large Print edition published in accord with the standards of the N.A.V.H.

CONTENTS

INTRODUCTION

It is rare, and for good reason. Impeaching a president is no small thing. Designed to check tyrants or oust corrupt leaders, the process of impeachment outlined in the United States Constitution nonetheless constitutes what Thomas Jefferson called "the most formidable weapon for the purpose of a dominant faction that was ever contrived." It means, let us be blunt, nullifying the will of voters, and with it the basic foundation of legitimacy for all representative democracies. Hence its rarity. Only twice in two-plus centuries has the House of Representatives approved articles of impeachment against a sitting president, sending his and the nation's political fate for trial in the Senate. A third time, certain impeachment and likely conviction were averted only at the eleventh hour by the resignation of a president who realized he'd run out of options.

And that is it. Only three times in American history has a president's conduct led to such political outrage or disarray as to warrant his potential removal from office, transforming a political crisis into a constitutional one. None has yet seen the process end in a president's ouster. Andrew Johnson was impeached in 1868 for undermining Reconstruction and failing to kowtow to congressional leaders—and, in a large sense, for failing to be Abraham Lincoln—yet survived his Senate trial by the thinnest of margins. A vice president elevated following tragedy, he nonetheless made the office his own, bringing racial sensibilities and an idea of how to bring Confederate states back into the fold following the Civil War—a process broadly termed Reconstruction—far different from that the man he replaced likely would have pursued, and most surely at odds with the Republican majority in Congress. They wanted him out, but it was not clear he'd done anything wrong or illegal, save not hewing to the party line. Trial in the Senate ensued. Then haggling, bribery, threats, and soul searching, and acquittal by a single vote. Unpopular in Washington—albeit increasingly popular throughout the defeated South, whose ideals he sympathized with—Johnson remained to the end of his term, defiant, despised, and despicable. But still the president.

The same cannot be said for Richard Nixon, who, under fire for two years, ultimately resigned in August 1974 after the House Judiciary Committee approved three articles of impeachment for contempt of Congress, obstructing justice, and employing his executive power for personal and political gain. The scandal began with a bungled, politically inspired break-in at the Watergate office complex and blossomed as proof of Nixon's complicity ultimately overtook his denials and dissembling. Upon reviewing the charges, one London newspaper quipped that in the time since George Washington first took the presidential oath in 1789 the office had progressed from a man who could not tell a lie, to one who could not tell the truth.

Even for a nation contemporaneously beset during the early 1970s by racial tensions, energy shortages, economic woes, and a military and humanitarian debacle in Vietnam, newly sworn-in president Gerald Ford's assessment of Watergate's broad impact was only partly true: "Our long national nightmare," he told Americans the day Nixon left office, "is over." Its legacy lingered. Respect for journalists initially flourished in Watergate's wake, given the central role investigative writing had played in unraveling the scandal, but it did not last. The public's overall faith in the fourth estate weakened in the longer term as the cancer injected into the national consciousness by months of partisan slander and Nixon's lamentations of the "witch hunt" waged against him slowly metastasized. Nixon's supporters preferred to blame his ouster less on his own crimes than on those who reported them.

"Watergate, by process of indignation," Republican senator Jesse Helms proclaimed, "became the lever by which embittered liberal pundits have sought to reverse the 1972 conservative judgment of the people." Like-minded publisher Henry Regnery perceived an even deeper conspiracy. "The most ominous thing about Watergate," he wrote, "is that it clearly demonstrates that the press and the bureaucracy, working together, can destroy the president, and from now on, every president is going to have to take this fact into account."[1]

Two generations later these charges still ring true in conservative circles. "The Richard Nixon I knew had almost nothing to do with the Richard Nixon as portrayed in the media," columnist Ben Stein explained fully forty-one years after Nixon's resignation, describing a wise but misunderstood man hounded from office by an urban and elitist news media determined to undermine his presidency and the traditional American values he espoused. "Like the schoolyard bullies they are," Stein said, "the media went after him for his vulnerability."

This is historical tripe, but effective when delivered to a receptive audience. Lies told often enough form a reality of their own, and Americans of all stripes struggled in the decades after Watergate to simultaneously process a president's unprecedented resignation alongside broader changes in their nation's economy, global role, and even ethnic and religious makeup. Conspiratorial explanations flourished in the combative political ecosystem that followed, with partisan critique ultimately proving more persuasive—and certainly better for ratings, first on radio and then on cable television—than the unraveling of complex facts. Small wonder, then, that the public's overall trust in journalists as the watchdogs of democracy has never again reached pre-Watergate levels.[2]

Faith in government plummeted over the same period. "In the broadest sense," one well-respected polling group concluded, "public confidence in America's leaders hasn't been the same since" Nixon's resignation. Before Watergate, more than half of Americans polled trusted their public officials to "do the right thing." Never again would more than half of respondents say the same. There is a reason we apply "-gate" to any and all public outrages since: the maelstrom that consumed Nixon's White House shattered public confidence in a manner impossible to ever again fully repair, setting the standard by which all ensuing scandals are measured.[3]

Public faith in the presidency in particular plummeted to 40 percent after Nixon's resignation. Gerald Ford, an honest public servant, though the only president never featured on a winning national ticket, lost his ensuing bid to remain in office in part because voters could not countenance retaining the man who had pardoned his criminal predecessor. Ford's Democratic challenger served only a single term, leading to the conclusion that but for Watergate, Republicans may well have held the White House from the end of the 1960s to the beginning of the 1990s. Public confidence in presidential reliability—that is, faith that their president most often or always told the truth—slowly rebounded over time, ahead of their faith in other public institutions (all, in fact, save for the military), with nearly two-thirds of Americans polled during Bill Clinton's second term believing they could once more trust their president's basic honesty.[4]

Then Clinton lied, too. His sexual affair with a one-time White House intern primarily during his first term came to light during his second, but he was impeached ostensibly not for that prurient act but for trying to hide it during a civil sexual harassment lawsuit brought against him by another woman, and then for later lying under oath when pressed on the matter. By the time he came clean, he had already lied about his affair to the American people, and his own family, for seven months.

Unlike Nixon, however, Clinton refused to resign in shame, launching instead an orchestrated push to save his presidency by undermining his accusers' credibility. He ultimately won this third presidential campaign of his two terms when the required supermajority of senators declined to convict him of perjury and obstruction of justice. He thus avoided joining Nixon as only the second president to be driven from office by scandal. He could not, however, evade the dubious distinction of joining Johnson as one of the only two presidents ever impeached. Neither could his accusers elude a wave of investigations into their own personal lives that produced a series of embarrassing revelations and resignations. In particular, each of the three men who led House Republicans during Clinton's impeachment would ultimately face ridicule, ouster, and even prison for their infidelities and sexual crimes. For the majority of Americans who believe to this day that Clinton was impeached for sexual impropriety, his political adversaries committed the even worse sin of hypocrisy.[5]

Impeachment thus disrupts the American political landscape as few other events do, leaving scars for generations while dimming the political careers of all involved. Clinton was not only the second president impeached; he was also the first impeached after having been elected president, a stain his two-term vice president and would-be Democratic successor found impossible to wash away during his subsequent razor-tight campaign for the presidency in 2000. Al Gore's promise to continue Clinton's nearly eight years of peace and prosperity, without mentioning Clinton's name at all if possible, paled in the end against George W. Bush's pledge to "restore honor and dignity to the Oval Office." Everyone knew what he meant.

Similarly, 1999's legacy played out in real time during the 2016 election, as a presidential candidate with a well-documented record of womanizing (and worse) rebuffed those charges by pointing out that his opponent's husband had done much the same. Just as Nixon's resignation opened the door for a Democrat to claim the White House in 1976, Bill Clinton's impeachment thus directly contributed to the election of the two subsequent Republican presidents in 2000 and 2016, respectively. But for his behavior, the twenty-first century might have unfolded completely differently.

Impeachments undermine national unity as well. Americans are today more politically divided than before Nixon's resignation and Clinton's trial, each side of the aisle more comfortable demonizing the other and better trained at retreating into their own camps when rifts arise. Not unrelated, citizens born after Watergate are less trusting of their government than those born before. The same is true of Americans who came of age before and after 1999. More ominously, faith in information itself mimics the same pattern, with a source's tribal affiliation carrying more weight for the typical voter than their evidence.

Nixon's and Clinton's defenders and accusers believed their own rightness and righteousness with equal fervor. They thus each thought their opponents not just wrong but depraved, and the ensuing tone of our national civil discourse—and willingness to seek or accept bipartisan solutions—has today fallen to levels unseen since before the Civil War. Andrew Johnson's presidency fell prey to that conflict's lingering partisan divide, his impeachment becoming what Jon Meacham calls another battle in the North-South conflict. While presidential impeachments are not wholly to blame for more recent political fissures, it is hard to argue that Americans living in their long shadow enjoy the "domestic tranquility" their Constitution promises.

—

These three political crises do not comprise the full history of presidential impeachments, merely its most consequential cases. President John Tyler beat back an impeachment resolution by a vote of 127 to 83 in the House of Representatives in 1843, for example, prevailing in large measure over his own Whig Party, who'd grown dissatisfied with his fulfillment of William Henry Harrison's short-lived presidency. Harrison's principal advisers suggested that as "acting president" he should govern by the group's consensus and fulfill his predecessor's agenda. He'd run as Harrison's vice president, after all. "I am the president," Tyler reminded them instead. "I shall be pleased to avail myself of your counsel and advice. But I can never consent to being dictated to as to what I shall or shall not do."

Tyler's unexpected presidency set a series of new precedents. The first time a vice president had taken office following a president's death and the youngest person to yet hold the office, he was also the first president to see a cabinet nominee formally rejected by the Senate, the first to veto congressional legislation because he believed it bad policy and not just unconstitutional, and then the first to see his veto overridden by enraged legislators. He also faced the first notable threat of impeachment, though his opponents ultimately failed to win a majority in the House of Representatives, in large measure because they could not demonstrate that the man they derisively termed "his accidency" had committed any crime other than fulfilling his oath of office the way he saw fit. Unpopular yet unvanquished, Tyler left the White House in 1845 after failing to gain either the Whig or the Democratic Party's nomination for a second term (unloved by either, he'd tried for both), retiring to his native Virginia before in his final act winning election to the Confederate Congress.

Tyler endured the closest failed impeachment attempt in the House of Representatives, but was not the only other president confronted by its possibility. A House committee investigating James Buchanan found evidence of corruption but not enough to warrant impeachment, a charge Ulysses S. Grant endured as well. Neither ever faced a formal vote on the matter. Representatives twice submitted impeachment resolutions against Herbert Hoover during the long interval between Franklin Roosevelt's election and his inauguration, but amid the Great Depression ultimately showed little interest in adding a short-lived constitutional crisis to the nation's overwhelming economic misery. Neither did impeachment resolutions gain traction when submitted to punish Harry Truman for his unpopular firing of General Douglas MacArthur during the Korean War; Ronald Reagan after news of the Iran-Contra scandal pointed toward direct White House involvement; or George W. Bush following his ill-fated invasion of Iraq in 2003.

None ever reached a vote, though the specter of impeachment is never far from Oval Office considerations. George H. W. Bush privately vowed to go to war to liberate Kuwait from Iraqi occupation even if Congress denied its consent, alluding to impeachment in his diary five times between November 1990 and January 1991. Barack Obama's aides similarly feared military strikes against Syria without congressional approval might generate impeachment hearings. There can be no doubt that impeachment indeed hangs as the Constitution's architects intended: as an omnipresent reminder that even presidents might face a higher authority.

Today the word "impeachment" once again echoes throughout American national politics, less a distant specter than an omnipresent reality. Donald Trump's unprecedented presidency has generated unprecedented pleas for his removal from across the political spectrum. His words rankle and excite as few politicians' before him, as does his eager rejection of his office's traditions. "I can be presidential," he explained in 2016, though it would be "boring as hell." A year later he proclaimed a different standard: "With the exception of the late great Abraham Lincoln," Trump told supporters, "I can be more presidential than any president who has ever held this office. That I can tell you."[6]

He was certainly not a traditional presidential candidate, refusing to open his tax records to public scrutiny, something every presidential candidate since Nixon—or, more accurately, because of Nixon—had done, emboldening critics to question his financial propriety even before he assumed office. The number of Americans who could define the word "emolu-ments," the term used in the Constitution to denote the profit gained from holding office, rose dramati-cally as his inauguration neared.

More ominously for Trump's political standing, ac-cusations of foreign influence in his electoral victory and ties between his campaign and foreign actors (Russian, specifically), catalyzed by the rabid vehe-mence of his all-caps "NO COLLUSION" denials, erupted a mere four months into his presidency fol-lowing his firing of James Comey, the FBI director charged with investigating those claims. "When I de-cided to just do it [fire Comey], I said to myself, I said, 'You know, this Russia thing with Trump and Russia is a made up story,'" the president immedi-ately explained in words that caused advisers to wince. "It's an excuse by the Democrats for having lost an election that they should have won."[7]

Little more than a week later, former FBI director Robert Mueller was appointed special counsel to take over the investigation into Russia's interference in the election and any possible collaboration with Trump's campaign, including whether the president had sought to impede the investigation. Suddenly, Trump confronted a degree of scrutiny typically unseen dur-ing a president's first term, and almost never during his first year in office.

Such scrutiny can be understood only in historical terms: "Will Comeygate Lead to Impeachment?" read one news journal's headline. Firing an FBI director is a president's prerogative. Firing the nation's chief lawman to affect an investigation into one's own potential wrongdoing, if proven, would be something else entirely. "Our system is designed so that impeachment is the remedy" for such a blatant abuse of presidential authority, University of Texas law professor Robert Chesney noted. But Congress would require a pattern of abusive behavior, "something more Nixonian" rather than a single example of executive overreach, before the case for impeachment would likely gain political traction.

Something like an insider to the conspiracy coming clean? A Watergate-like whistle-blower, or what Trump recently dubbed with derision, "John Dean–type RAT," who aided Nixon's downfall from the inside. Or something like further firings, perhaps? Personnel problems contributed to each major impeachment case in history. Andrew Johnson's attempt to fire his secretary of war—in fact, Lincoln's secretary of war—roused his congressional critics to seek his removal. A century later, the resignations of Nixon's attorney general and deputy attorney general, who were unwilling to execute his orders terminating the Watergate special prosecutor—the oft-called "Saturday Night Massacre"—similarly fueled calls for **his** impeachment. Fears of a president's ability to shape or even eliminate criminal inquiries through personnel changes led Congress in Watergate's wake to strip chief executives of the ability to fire their investigators. Presidents then regained this prerogative following the perceived partisan vehemence of Clinton's inquisitors, who explored if the president or his surrogates had improperly used his office to secure his paramour federal employment.

Trump is thus empowered to act Nixonian in a way Clinton was not, though his supporters have warned that even legal use of this authority might be unwise. "It would be the end of Trump's presidency if he fired Robert Mueller," current Trump ally Senator Lindsey Graham of South Carolina said several months after the special counsel's appointment. Trump's approval ratings were too low, and his margin of error too thin, to survive the political backlash. Nothing that has occurred in the months since has altered this reality. On the contrary, calls for Trump's removal have only grown in number and volume. A year into his presidency, even before his widely condemned Helsinki meeting with Russian president Vladimir Putin, where Trump refused yet again to accept his own government's conclusion that Moscow had interfered in the 2016 election, one poll found only 38 percent of Americans queried expected to vote for his reelection in 2020; 41 percent favored impeachment hearings instead.[8]

Stop and consider those numbers. For such a drastic course to be in the minds of so many citizens is astounding, even granting the era's hyper-partisan tribalism. So, too, was it remarkable, again unprecedented, for discussion of a president's potential treason—siding with a foreign government over his own—to so widely enter mainstream political discussion. The point here is not if Trump was indeed treasonous, but rather that so many Americans considered it a question worth pondering. Rejecting their fellow citizen's electoral choice—or at least the choice of the electoral college—four in ten Americans consequently believe the next election cycle too long to wait for a change at the top. The percentage of American voters who favored Nixon's impeachment, by comparison, didn't top the percentage of those in favor of impeaching Trump until a few short weeks before his resignation. And, no more than a third of Americans polled at the time favored Clinton's impeachment by the House of Representatives. Indeed, Clinton's approval rating actually spiked (topping out at 73 percent) as his trial unfolded, making his conviction in the Senate politically difficult no matter the facts of the case.

These are more than merely interesting factoids, especially for Trump's current legal team. Instead they point to lessons to be learned and applied. Channeling Nixon, albeit with newer technology, Trump tweeted the term "witch hunt" three times as often during the first six months of 2018 as during the previous year, for example, undermining public faith in his investigators. By the same token, his advisers appreciate the way Clinton's popularity helped save his presidency. "Nobody is going to consider impeachment if public opinion has concluded this is an unfair investigation," Rudolph Giuliani, one of President

Trump's principal legal advisers, noted, "and that's why public opinion is so important."[9]

Just as contemporary Washington insiders are looking to the past for answers, it is no secret why you are reading this book. The word "impeachment" resonates throughout the political ecosphere today as rarely before in American history, and never so soon in a presidency. Andrew Johnson reigned for two tumultuous years before his critics rallied enough votes to seriously threaten his removal. Nixon and Clinton each won reelection by healthy margins before succumbing in their second terms to the scandals that remain their greatest popular legacies. Trump, conversely, finished his first year with the lowest voter approval rating ever recorded for a president after an equivalent time in office, despite historically low unemployment and a sustained bull market on Wall Street.

Talk of impeachment, moreover, is no longer just a theoretical exercise or a means of venting partisan frustration. Democratic Party activists and funders have called for Trump's impeachment since his election, though without any realistic hope that the House of Representatives would begin the process so long as Republicans controlled the chamber. That may soon change. Even if impeached, Trump's prospects for conviction appear slim at best, barring some tectonic change in the current political landscape, given his own party's current majority in the Senate and the difficult if not impossible path to the supermajority required for his ouster. Any Democratic majority in the House may, nonetheless, prompt a groundswell of support for at least impeachment hearings, speeding revelation of Mueller's findings, no matter how much the party's current leadership fears the long-term electoral consequences of beginning the process.

Impeachment never just affects the person impeached. "It's not someplace I think we should go," House Minority Leader Nancy Pelosi recently said. Impeachments are invariably divisive, she argued, consuming all the available political oxygen the capital can muster. "I believe whatever we do," she suggested instead, "we have a responsibility to first and foremost unify the nation."[10]

Impeachments never do that. The word's mere invocation catalyzes partisan passions, something Alexander Hamilton predicted two centuries ago. "The prosecution [of impeachments], will seldom fail to agitate the passions of the whole community," Hamilton wrote, "and to divide it into parties more or less friendly or inimical to the accused." Democrats in the age of Trump are clearly divided on the issue. So, too, Republicans. A small but growing chorus of GOP strategists would welcome the chance to put their political fortunes into a President Mike Pence's hands, he being more reliably conservative and certainly less volatile than their current leader. Others employ impeachment's specter to rally supporters to the polls.

"It's very simple," onetime Trump adviser Steve
Bannon opined in mid-2018. "November 6th, up or
down vote . . . up or down vote on the impeachment
of Donald Trump."

The president apparently agrees. "We have to keep
the House," he told a 2018 campaign-style rally in
Michigan, because if they fail, Democrats are already
vowing "We will impeach him."[11]

You are most likely reading this book because of
impeachment's contemporary salience, and also because you realize history matters. You know that the
old aphorism "Those who do not study history are
destined to repeat it" is, in fact, wrong. Those who
study history are also destined to repeat it. But we are
less surprised. An accurate understanding of the past
makes one more thoughtful about the present, and,
while not perfect, at least better able to make informed judgments of what may come next. Very little
stated above about the American political landscape
in the Age of Trump is likely surprising, but impeachment's fascinating history is less well understood.
With a chance that this issue overwhelms American
politics before long—and, make no mistake, if the
issue rises to the fore it will eclipse all others from
view—the time is ripe to renew our understanding of
the thing that binds even divided Americans most:
our shared past.

What follows, therefore, are four chapters designed
to equip citizens with a better appreciation of a past
that may well become intrinsically relevant again. In-

deed, one need not read this book with President Trump in mind. None of our chapters mention him by name, and we recommend putting him out of your thoughts until his presidency is invoked again in the book's conclusion. Read these histories of presidential impeachments as history first, beginning with a discussion of how the Constitution's architects considered the issue and provided their posterity with this political tool; then explore in chronological order the impeachment of President Andrew Johnson in 1868, the likely impeachment of Richard Nixon in 1974, and the impeachment of Bill Clinton twenty-four years later.

Answers for our own day lie within. "No man is above justice," George Mason preached at the Constitutional Convention in 1787. That sentiment still rings true, yet competes with the political reality offered by then-representative Gerald Ford, who quipped in 1970 that "an impeachable offense is whatever a majority of the House of Representatives considers it to be at a given moment in history." Both these statements may be simultaneously true, but if we are to consider impeachment in our own political era we should at least debate with a clear and impartial reading of history on our side.

Facts do matter, after all, and are central to our national heritage. In 1776, American revolutionaries declared their independence only after noting that "a decent respect to the opinions of mankind requires that they should declare the causes which impel them to the separation." Whether keen to separate a president from his office or to retain him some two-plus centuries after those words were first published, we offer this book to impeachment's potential proponents and detractors so that they might follow that example, doing each other the decent respect of familiarizing themselves with their nation's past before taking actions likely to impact its future.

—JEFFREY A. ENGEL

IMPEACHMENT

THE CONSTITUTION
Jeffrey A. Engel

Their government was failing by 1787, which hadn't taken long. A mere decade after declaring independence, and only four years after winning a bloody Revolution fought to prove that point, Americans found the Articles of Confederation that bound the states together wholly inadequate. Designed during the war by representatives of thirteen independent states who longed to stay that way as much as possible, it denied federal officials the ability to effectively regulate the new nation's trade, orchestrate a unified foreign policy, or even maintain basic civil order. State power ruled instead of federal control, and it proved incapable of coping with a steady barrage of economic blows, diplomatic insults, and widespread popular unrest.

"Our situation is becoming every day more and more critical," James Madison lamented in early 1787. Frustrated by representing Virginia in a federal congress powerless to change the nation's course, he found "thoughtful observers unanimously agree that the existing confederacy is tottering to its foundation." Calls for disunion multiplied, with "many individuals of weight" increasingly "leaning towards monarchy" for salvation.

Monarchy was what the thirteen colonies had rebelled against in the first place only a decade before—a tyrannical monarchy that had threatened their liberties, but at least had been able to provide order, which seemed increasingly appealing as an alternative to their current woes. Madison worried, as their problems grew—with seemingly little their government could do in response—that Americans were "losing all confidence in our political system" which "neither has nor deserves advocates."[1]

They could, at least, attempt something better, which is why delegates gathered in Philadelphia throughout the summer of 1787 in hope of repairing their fatally flawed constitution. If they failed to find a better way, or even a replacement powerful enough to tackle the nation's problems yet constrained enough to ensure liberty's survival, the United States would likely become little more than a footnote in history.

Therein lay the real problem, and the reason the Articles had constrained federal power in the first place. Power was dangerous. Americans in this era widely agreed it poisoned any who wielded it with an insatiable desire for more, its steady accumulation engendering corruption and injustice. Freed from Britain's powerful grip, they'd tried doing without a strong federal government of their own, and in particular without a national executive empowered to keep the peace and enforce the nation's laws, but soon found they couldn't live without either. What form of government could therefore be trusted with the power it required, without simultaneously employing that power to undermine liberty? More specifically, in whose hands could such power possibly be trusted?

The question defined their entire epoch. "Show me that age and country where the rights and liberties of the people were placed on the sole chance of their rulers being good men without a consequent loss of liberty," Virginia's famed orator Patrick Henry subsequently challenged when the Constitutional Convention delegates were done forging a new government. "I say that the loss of that dearest privilege has ever followed, with absolute certainty, every such mad attempt." Their proposed salvation might ultimately prove their undoing, he charged. The new constitution forged in Philadelphia "winked towards monarchy," with a presidency and legislature empowered not so much to ensure popular freedom and prosperity as to guarantee their own.[2]

Henry was right, at least about one thing: It had never worked before. The new American republic lived in a world of monarchies, and no republic in history had ever been attempted over such a wide expanse and vast citizenry. Neither had any managed to retain the liberties proclaimed at its birth, as the virtuous rulers chosen to safeguard their people's security instead came to value their pocketbooks and powers more. Rome had fallen in this way. So, too, Athens and every other example from the classical age that the delegates to the 1787 convention studied, finding to their dismay that even the most virtuous republic proved vulnerable to this same unavoidable flaw.

"There is scarce a king in a hundred who would not, if he could, follow the example of Pharaoh," Pennsylvania's scientist and statesman Benjamin Franklin reminded his fellow delegates. "Get first all the people's money, then all their lands, and then make them and their children servants forever." This was simply the natural order of things. "It will be said, that we don't propose to establish Kings" in our new government, he continued. Yet "I am apprehensive," indeed "perhaps too apprehensive, that the Government of the States, may in future times, end in a Monarchy."[3] Franklin's was no isolated fear, which extended well beyond a simplistic if ominous fear of one day living under a new American king. Leaders charged with protecting liberty, the founders believed, might one day prove its demise.

That last sentence should hurt your eyes, or at least make them roll. Sweeping assertions about the unified beliefs of the nation's "framers" or "founders"—or, worse yet, "founding fathers"—are almost invariably misleading. Most fail to appreciate the generation's diversity and divisiveness out of ignorance. Others intentionally obscure those qualities to bolster some faulty contemporary argument. Reality was more complex. The ranks of those who contributed to the American Revolution and the independent country that followed included merchants and landowners, politicians and preachers, slave owners and those appalled by the practice, each part of a national palette so vast that few residents could reliably claim to have visited its wide expanse or even met someone from each of its thirteen states.

The Revolution's length further complicates broad assessments of its participants. Nearly a decade separated Britain's despised 1765 Stamp Act and the new taxes it imposed on its North American colonies from the 1773 Boston Tea Party those policies ultimately inspired. More than a decade, in turn, passed between the latter and the nation's first presidential inauguration. Indeed, the entire period's two signature events—literally so, as each produced documents whose endorsements were, in the moment, as important as their text—occurred eleven years apart, and the men who debated the radical and revolutionary Declaration of Independence in 1776 were far different in temperament and experience than those who composed the much more conservative 1787 Constitution. Only six signed both, a mere 5 percent of total participants, though they, too, had been changed by the intervening years of bloodshed, anxiety, loss, and triumph.

The collective variety and extended chronology of those who revolted and those who constructed makes for colorful history, but it muddies the average citizen's ability to discern the era's applicability for their own lives. Specifically, the founding generation's ideological and political diversity, coupled with the self-evident differences between the eighteenth and the twenty-first centuries, makes any contemporary understanding of the Constitution's binding language difficult at best. This is more than mere inconvenience or academic concern. The Declaration is inspiring, but the Constitution's specific wording—the result both of political compromise over issues specific to the era, as well as severe editing—continues to guide our politics today.

We may choose, as a matter of legal philosophy or political practicality, to employ the text for broad guidance as we rethink and relitigate new and old problems alike. That is the unassailable right of every ensuing generation, who in the words of retired Supreme Court justice Anthony Kennedy can "invoke its principles in their own search for greater freedom." Others may care only for its words as originally intended. "The Constitution, as you know, contains a number of broad provisions, which are necessarily vague in their application," Kennedy's court colleague Antonin Scalia countered. "Originalism gives to those terms the meaning they were understood to have when the people adopted them.[4]

No matter one's preferred methodology for interpreting the Constitution, whether celebrated as a living document or venerated as what Scalia called "the good old dead Constitution," we should at least offer its authors the respect of asking why they wrote and thought what they did. This is especially important when putting their eighteenth-century words and thinking into contemporary effect, pondering in the context of this book meaningful yet potentially debatable terms such as "treason, bribery, or high crimes and misdemeanors." To understand the history of presidential impeachments, we must start with both the office and that process as its designers initially conceived them.[5]

The presidency did not arise by accident. Delegates to the federal convention met for months behind closed doors, shuttered and sealed to immunize their debates from public pressure, hammering out a government with overlapping spheres of power. None might grow too large or powerful, they reasoned, if coequal legislative, judicial, and executive branches were aligned against one another. Lawmakers could see their legislation vetoed by an executive who considered their work unwise, for example; judges could invalidate legislators' statutes or a president's actions if counter to the Constitution's prescripts; and presidents required Congress's approval before spending a dime or concluding treaties with foreign lands. Because none held unlimited power, the Constitution's framers reasoned, none would be able to attain it at the expense of the others.

Then they added one more additional restraint on the executive, the branch most like the monarch they'd just rejected but whose stability and authority they nonetheless desired, inserting into their new constitution a means of ejecting any president who threatened to employ the powers at his disposal to harm the general welfare or to profit too greatly at its expense.[6] A president could be impeached, though even this was not wholly enough to alleviate their ingrained fear of concentrated executive power. One thing did. Or rather, one man did. Indeed, the entire convention would likely not have succeeded but for him.[7]

Which leads back to one of those few things this complex generation overwhelmingly agreed upon: George Washington would be first. Consequently the best way to understand what they collectively envisioned a president should be is to consider the degree of duty and sacrifice that made him their unanimous ideal. Conversely, when asking what sort of president might warrant impeachment, a useful first step is to envision one wholly lacking these critical virtues.

The Constitution's framers never expected subsequent presidents would replicate George Washington precisely. They were not fools, nor deluded into thinking him flawless or beyond reproach. Many in the room had personally seen him stumble, lose his temper, or choose the wrong course. Yet none had ever seen him put his own needs above the nation's. Consequently, any future chief executive who demonstrated the opposite—placing personal aggrandizement or malfeasance above their sense of duty to the people at large, perhaps even damaging the republic's future in the process—would be so unlike the president they envisioned as to warrant removal and dishonor. When considering what the Constitution's authors thought about which acts or defects might warrant a president's impeachment, therefore, one shorthand explanation can be found in asking what would George Washington **not** have done?[8]

—

The United States were, in truth, more coalition than country by the mid-1780s. Independence had brought peace but neither stability nor prosperity, especially as victory eliminated the one thing that truly bound the thirteen together. Without a common foe, they instead acted more like sovereign countries than as parts of a broader whole, providing ample hope in European capitals that the new American union might yet break apart. Washington feared as much. Long an unwavering advocate of a strong national government after eight years in command of the Continental army, he worried as the war ended in 1783 that Americans were destined in its absence to become little more than "the sport of European politics."[9]

Time seemed to prove him right, and with remarkable speed. British forts and colonies lined the borders to the north and northwest as the 1780s progressed, as did potentially hostile and certainly wary Indian nations. Britain's peerless fleet meanwhile controlled the Atlantic to the east and the Caribbean to the south. Spain dominated the continent's central arteries, strategically positioned to make good on its repeated threats to curtail American access to the critical Mississippi River, New Orleans, and the markets beyond. Denied easy access to Britain's markets at war's end, or confidence in the long-term availability of new customers and goods, all the while rebuilding from the war itself, American per capita production and earnings by mid-decade fell to merely half what they had been before the war, resulting in what some experts consider the nation's worst economic crisis until the Great Depression a century and a half later.

"Our commerce is almost ruined," a Massachusetts congressman lamented, and the country's weak federal government seemed incapable of altering their course. Federal currency was untrusted and frequently unaccepted, its value varying from state to state and questioned abroad, leaving central authorities unable to repay hefty wartime debts. To accomplish anything under the Articles required consent from three-fourths of the state delegations to Congress present for any vote, something impractical in the best of circumstances yet largely impossible, given that spotty attendance typically made even fielding a quorum difficult enough. Recalcitrant (and frequently absent) Rhode Island rejected every effort to retire the federal debt; as the smallest state it was wholly uninterested in sharing the load with its larger brethren. Georgia habitually and politely voted yes, then refused to pay. Others simply declined to voice an opinion.[10]

This was not unusual. Congressional resolutions were frequently ignored under the Articles. Six requisitions on the states passed Congress between 1781 and 1786. Only a third brought any revenue at all.[11] The last netted a mere $663 dollars, less than 2 percent of the total requested.[12] "No money is paid into the public treasury," Madison lamented, and "no respect is paid to the federal authority." Washington fumed from Mount Vernon at the news, and at those who continued to support a federal government too impotent to warrant any concern over its tyrannical possibilities. "To be fearful of vesting Congress, constituted as that body is, with ample authorities for national purposes," he lamented to fellow colonial leader John Jay, "appears to me the very climax of popular absurdity and madness."[13]

The time had come for their union to either draw closer together or disband. Their postwar regime was "a half-starved, limping government," Washington lamented as 1786 drew to a close, and if Americans could not conceive of themselves as one people with one set of shared priorities because it was right, they'd have to be forced to cooperate for their own good. "We have probably had too good an opinion of human nature in forming our confederation," he commiserated once more to Jay. "Experience has taught us, that men will not adopt & carry into execution, measures the best calculated for their own good without the intervention of a coercive power. I do not conceive we can exist long as a nation, without having lodged somewhere a power which will pervade the whole Union."[14]

Not everyone approved of this remedy, however. In small and large states alike politicians and editors rehashed and recycled traditional warnings against concentrated power. "In the debilitated condition of the federal government," a fellow Virginia planter warned Washington that year, "it is unwise to risk the offense of any part of the empire" lest it break away to pursue its own destiny. In every state, Virginia congressman Henry Lee worried, calls for "amplification of the powers of the union has too many enemies" to survive the attempt.[15]

Opponents and skeptics of increased centralized power wielded a powerful card beyond generic fears of tyranny. Any strengthening of federal power would first require states to relinquish some of their own. The Articles of Confederation explicitly guaranteed each state "its sovereignty, freedom and independence," which, given the general anti-monarchical sentiment of the day, many state legislatures took as license to experiment without executive power at all. Pennsylvania's wartime constitution did away with one entirely; New Jersey placed an executive council in charge; while most simply allowed their governors only the means to execute the legislature's will, nothing more. Severing "the monarchical part" of government, "we vainly imagined that we had arrived at perfection," a South Carolinian lamented in 1784, "and that freedom was established on the broadest and most solid basis that could possibly consist with any social institution."[16]

Sadly, he conceded, "we have in some points been mistaken." Legislative rule proved largely inefficient, and in a real sense too democratic, producing less its promised equality and justice and more often something closer to mob rule. "It was supposed that what is called the executive part of government was the only dangerous part," influential essayist Thomas Paine wrote of Pennsylvania's regime. Internationally famous following his 1776 critique of British monarchical rule titled **Common Sense,** a decade later Paine grudgingly admitted that "quite as much mischief, if not more, may be done, and as much arbitrary conduct acted, by a legislature." New York's Alexander Hamilton and Virginia's Thomas Jefferson, whatever their subsequent disputes, agreed. For legislators the "inquiry constantly is what will please, not what will benefit the people," the former lamented, producing "nothing but temporary expedient, fickleness and folly." The latter noted bitterly of Virginia's hidebound governor and all-consuming legislature that "an elective despotism was not the government we fought for."[17]

Despotism had indeed been what they had been trying to avoid in the first place, though sense of the term evolved in American minds in subtle though profound ways during the transatlantic strife that followed the end of the Seven Years' War in 1763 and which culminated in the ensuing revolution. Colonists initially associated little of their growing frustration with British rule with their sovereign, King

George III, who remained in the early 1770s widely respected and often beloved. Considered by most above partisanship and perhaps even the details of day-to-day policymaking, he appeared instead a benevolent father to them all, empowered to oversee his subjects' general welfare.

"Eighteenth-century America became more overtly monarchical than England itself" during the bulk of the eighteenth century, historian Brendan McConville has concluded, with kings widely considered the principal defender in the "ongoing struggle between pan-European Protestantism and Catholicism, absolutism, and popery." One of King George III's American subjects stated the same more plainly: "The brightest gem which the King of England wears in the British Crown is that majesty, trust, and confidence, which the Americans invest him with, as the King and Guardian of their Rights and Liberties."[18]

His ministers were another matter. Even as they consistently praised the king's good graces, colonial political observers of the day frequently considered nefarious cabals within his orbit, bent on profiting from the erosion of American liberties, the root cause of transatlantic strife. Conspiracy theories flourished throughout the period and were afforded much weight. As one American pamphleteer of the early 1770s put it, "the cause of all that distresses the people in England or in America," was "a kind of fourth power that the [English] constitution knows nothing of, or has not provided against." This was an "overruling arbitrary power, which absolutely controls the King, Lords and Commons."[19]

Fear of these ill-defined cabals permeated American circles as the 1770s progressed, infecting even the Continental Congress, which was called in response to the growing rift between Britain and its colonies and which, in 1774, joined the chorus of those who appealed to the king for justice. "Your Royal indignation, we hope, will rather fall on those designing and dangerous men," they pleaded, "who . . . employed to dissolve the bonds of society by abusing your Majesty's authority" in order to perpetuate "the most desperate and irritating projects of oppression." Appealing to the king as the "loving father to all your peoples," they verily begged for his intervention.[20]

To no avail. Congress's formal plea "came down among a great Heap of Letters of Intelligence from Governors and Officers in America, Newspapers, Pamphlets, Handbills, &c from that Country," Benjamin Franklin reported from London, where he served as a colonial representative. "Undistinguished" amid the flurry of paper, and unremarked upon by the king's ministers for his benefit, "I do not find that it has had any further notice taken of it yet, than that it has been read as well as the other Papers."[21]

King George's real reply came in the dispatch of troops and a growing sense that he, too, could no longer be trusted to protect American liberties. Open revolt erupted the following year in Massachusetts, though it took yet another year for delegates gathered in Philadelphia to fully break not only from the king's authority, but with him personally. Once their paternal source of safety and security, George III by 1776 had in their eyes instead become part of the problem itself, "a prince, whose character is thus marked by every act which may define a tyrant," the Declaration of Independence concluded.

Yes, this was political rhetoric designed to persuade potential foreign allies and further arouse an already agitated population at home, but the manner in which Americans shook off their once-beloved monarch stamped their political culture from the start with a healthy disdain for disreputable sovereigns and the profound suspicion that even the most trusted leader could one day turn despotic. The Declaration of Independence was, in short, an indictment, proving guilt that demanded punishment. "I could hardly own the King and fight against him at the same time," one patriot explained after first hearing its words, "but now these matters are cleared up. Heart and hand shall move together."[22]

The Declaration's indictment drove more Americans than ever to take up arms, but importantly, its basic underlying charge did not surprise. George III, whom they once thought different, had simply fallen victim like all the rest to something virtually impossible to avoid: power's appeal. It was a sad truism of the "depravity of mankind," Boston's revolutionary firebrand Sam Adams explained, though a plethora of similar examples abound, "that ambition and lust of power above the law predominate passions in the breasts of most men." Power was too "intoxicating" to resist, he continued, invariably converting "a good man in private life to a tyrant in office." Democratic elections wouldn't solve this problem alone, one constitutional framer subsequently feared. An "elective king" would undoubtedly first seek to expand his office's reach, then likely entrench himself for life, only to then "lay a train for the succession of his children." Either that, another predicted, or establish "a corrupt, tyrannical aristocracy."[23]

Having evicted their king and devalued all measures of executive authority in his absence, the people throughout the thirteen newly liberated states were therefore in charge as never before by the mid-1780s, and yet they were not happy. Open rebellion loomed in several states, as the sputtering postwar economy prompted state legislatures to respond alternatively with new taxes and protections for creditors. Pennsylvania, South Carolina, and New Hampshire each saw armed protestors respond by sporadically shutting down local courthouses in 1785 and 1786, thus preventing foreclosures on farms and homes of those unable to simultaneously pay their arrears and their assessments. Similar revolts sprang up in a half dozen states overall, each evaporating without widespread bloodshed when confronted by organized militias and the threat of deadly force.[24]

Massachusetts proved different. Violence exploded during the winter of 1786–87 only a few days' march from the Revolution's first battlefields. Disgruntled hinterland debtors, many sporting their wartime uniforms and carrying muskets last fired in anger against the British, shut down courthouses in five counties before marching on Springfield's federal armory in search of supplies and weapons to sustain their revolt. Private militias, largely funded by the Boston elites who held the loans those near-bankrupted farmers refused to pay, routed them instead.

"Only recently independent," historian David O. Stewart has observed, "Americans were slaughtering each other on the field of battle" over the same basic issues as had led to the political rupture a decade before: who had the right to impose taxes, and who had the power to collect them. More fundamentally, where did real power in American society reside, and how much was required to provide both liberty and order? Was there no middle ground between anarchy and tyranny, between the chaos of mob rule and the desperation of a tyrant's grip? Perhaps they'd indeed been better off under Britain's unjust rule, a Massachusetts legislator simultaneously wondered. At least then they had order. "I cannot give up the idea that monarchy in our present situation is to become absolutely necessary to save the states from sinking into the lowest abyss of misery."[25]

The bloodshed in Massachusetts further catalyzed calls for strengthening national authority, especially as the federal government operating under the Articles had not even proved capable of contributing to the uprising's demise. "Insurgency and rebellion may pervade more states," a Pennsylvania congressman worried, while a counterpart from Virginia believed "the period seems to be fast approaching when the people of these United States must determine to establish a permanent capable government, or submit to the horrors of anarchy and licentiousness."[26]

Washington endorsed the drumbeat of calls for a national convention to rethink their federal government, though he hoped it might proceed without him. He was tired. And retired. Away from home for almost all of the eight years he'd commanded the Continental army, he'd resigned his commission in 1783 as the war reached its close, in his mind closing the door on any further public service as well. "I am now become a private citizen on the banks of the Potomac," he wrote his companion the Marquis de Lafayette, "under the shadow of my own vine and my own fig tree . . . not only retired from all public employments, but I am retiring within myself."[27]

More than simply retired, he perceived little to personally gain from further participating in national politics and much to lose. His personal stock could hardly go higher. "Washington, the Saviour of His Country," The Connecticut Journal had already dubbed him. In New York they wondered "Who is more WORTHY our LOVE and ESTEEM, than the GUARDIAN and SAVIOUR of his Country!" Yale College's president declared "O WASHINGTON! How do I love thy name . . . upheld and protected by the Omnipotent, by the Lord of Hosts." In Virginia and Maryland festivals already marked his birthday. He was the closest thing to a unifying national figurehead they had. "Equally renowned with the most celebrated Worthies of Antiquity," one typical letter to Mount Vernon called him, "unrivaled by any Patriot, or Hero, of the present Age & whose Memory will be perpetuated thro' the loud Trump of Fame."[28]

He had nowhere to go but down, which was no trifling matter given how much Washington cared for his reputation, which he termed in 1785 "the principle thing which is laudable in my conduct." That sentiment deserves unpacking to be fully appreciated. He'd been carefully cultivating his public image his entire life, and one might easily say it was his life's work. As historian Gordon Wood sagely noted, "in modern eyes Washington's concern for his reputation is embarrassing; it seems obsessive and egotistical." And yet, "his contemporaries understood. All gentlemen tried scrupulously to guard their reputations, which is what they meant by their honor." Fellow historian Joanne Freeman put it this way: "A man without honor" during this period was "no man at all." Yet "a man of honor was defined by the respect he received in public," for this most precious commodity to elite gentlemen like Washington "did not exist unless bestowed by others."[29]

Honor consequently colored his every decision, and its pursuit his every act, however monumental or trifling. "How would this matter be viewed then by the eye of the world," he'd said of one decision, though the question permeated his thinking, "and what would be the opinion of it?"

Honor dictated he could not summarily reject his nomination to represent Virginia at the proposed Philadelphia convention, even though his name had been put forth without his knowledge or consent. Neither could he readily accept unless, at the least, he could be assured that delegates would be empowered to do more than just point out the current government's flaws. Mere talk did little good. They must be allowed to "probe the defects of the [current] Constitution to the bottom," he believed, "and point out radical cures." He'd not join otherwise.[30]

Washington thus dithered throughout the early months of 1787 as the date for the proposed convention neared, pleading from Mount Vernon first minor ailments and then scheduling conflicts as reasons to demur, even as wartime brethren and younger associates begged him to attend, or at least to allow them to use his name to encourage others. There seemed no way the meeting would succeed without his participation, a trusted friend advised, and no way the country would accept its result unless it came with his endorsement. "The unbounded confidence the people have of Your tried patriotism, and wisdom, would exceedingly facilitate the adoption of any important alteration that might be proposed by a convention of which you were a member," another confidant advised, or perhaps even its . . . "president."

Indeed, if under his leadership the convention some-how managed to develop an "energetic and judicious" system to replace the current catastrophe, he'd go down in history unrivaled for the "glorious republican epithet—The Father of Your Country."[31]

His indispensability was precisely Washington's concern. For most delegates the decision to travel to Philadelphia for a new federal convention meant a few weeks or, at most, months of service. Washington feared participation meant a permanent return to public life. The convention, and ultimately any new government it forged, would require a new leader, one well-endowed with sweeping powers if he and like-minded delegates got their way. He knew they'd look to him first. He was the one man they universally respected, and the only one they'd universally follow. His approval more than any other on their final product ensured even a chance of its success. "The signature of his name to whatever act shall be the result of [its] deliberations will secure its passage through the union," James Monroe wrote Jefferson in Paris. But only if he served.[32]

Washington's sense of duty eventually overcame his desire for tranquility. "The pressure of the public voice was so loud, I could not resist the call to a convention of the states which is to determine whether we are to have a government of respectability under which life—liberty, and prosperity secured to us," he explained. "Or whether we are to submit to one which may be the result of chance or the moment, springing perhaps from anarch Confusion, and dictated perhaps by some aspiring demagogue who will not consult the interest of his country so much as his own ambitious views." Aware he could no longer sit idly under his own fig tree and vine as the nation he'd fought for threatened to break apart, he reluctantly began the long trip to Philadelphia.[33]

—

Washington arrived in May to a hero's welcome, his carriage escorted into the city by cannon salutes and a military honor guard. It was how he entered most cities those days if residents were forewarned of his arrival. Other delegates arrived to far less fanfare— most none at all—and the convention opened later that month. Its first order of business? His election as its chairman and president, a vote that only confirmed his fear that his retirement was no more. "It was not until after a long struggle with myself," he wrote a confidant, that "I could obtain my own consent to appear again in a public theater."[34]

Delegates quickly sketched the rough outlines of a government with three equal branches, whose legislature and judiciary would serve alongside an executive endowed with what Madison termed the "energy" required to maintain order and implement national plans. They initially found it difficult to even discuss this office candidly with Washington in the room, however, as he'd so obviously soon wield any power they granted the office. Similarly, any limitation on executive power, or fear of executive excess, even if only theoretical, proved naturally awkward to debate in his presence. An uncomfortable silence therefore ensued when delegates first addressed the matter of the executive's role and responsibilities, what Madison dubbed "a considerable pause." This was not a group typically lacking for words. Only Franklin's gentle chiding that they "deliver their sentiments" on this "point of great importance," shook the discussion forward.[35]

Why was Washington their logical and obvious choice? Because he'd already done what many considered impossible, twice, in a manner revealing of the convention's ultimate sense of a president's fundamental purpose. The first was lead a successful military revolt against the world's most powerful empire, binding his army together at times with little more than his force of will. The second was then relinquishing the power derived from the first. For a people innately suspicious of military power, for whom standing armies in particular threatened liberty, Washington's willingness to forgo the power that so many others in the past had employed on their way to the throne particularly impressed. "Tis a conduct so novel," a well-connected American wrote home from London at the news of Washington's initial withdrawal from public life, "so inconceivable to People who, far from giving up powers they possess, are willing to convulse the empire to acquire more."[36]

Most historical figures in his position had done just that. Julius Caesar offered a more typical example for the classically obsessed delegates, his ascent to political power at the head of an army considered a key milestone in Rome's long road from republican glory to tyrannical collapse. A more recent illustration loomed as well. Oliver Cromwell had turned command of his revolutionary army into a license to rule during the previous century's English Civil War, whose bloody reverberations could still be felt. "A Cromwell" might "arise in this country" if similarly given more power than any one man could reasonably control, South Carolina's Pierce Butler warned. "In all countries" both past and present, he reasoned, "the executive power is in a constant course of increase."[37]

Washington reminded them of a different historical figure. First dubbed America's Fabius for his prudent avoidance of battle, by war's end he'd become a new Cincinnatus—the general from Rome's glorified republican era, called to lead an army whenever his country required, given sweeping powers to solve its crises, yet content to return to his farm when that duty was done. It was an image at once real and cultivated, repeatedly cited by writers, evoked by artists, and employed even by those who saw him during his retirement not as a mythical figure from afar but in the flesh. "I should prefer seeing you Cincinnatus-like following your plow," a wartime associate wrote Washington, who read the note approvingly. "Your services are of that nature as to demand the approbation and admiration of succeeding generations, but cannot be rewarded by money."[38]

There is today simply no comparably unifying figure in American politics, what one historian called
"the moving emblem of legitimacy in unsettled
times." It was little wonder that proponents of a more
vigorous federal government believed his presence so
vital. "In 1775, we beheld him at the head of the
armies of America, arresting the progress of British
tyranny," one Philadelphia newspaper proclaimed.
"In the year 1787, we behold him at the head of a
chosen band of patriots and heroes, arresting the
progress of anarchy."[39]

Oft-compared to a hero or demigod of old, Washington was, however, quite human, a reality whose
consequence captivated delegates as debate over their
prospective national executive unfolded. He could
not rule forever, and not every leader could be
expected to be as trustworthy. Some subsequent
executive—they did not begin referring to the position as "president" until months into the convention—
might even prove too dangerous to allow to complete
his term in office, his very presence too much a cancer on the republic to withstand.

"General Washington would in all probability be
the first president under the new constitution," one
of its initial detractors wrote during the critical period between the document's publication and its ultimate ratification by the states. "In that case all might
be well, but perhaps after him General Slushington
might be the next or second president." The apocry-
phal Slushington might prove himself capable even

of undoing all that Washington had provided. "The first man put at the helm will be a good one," Franklin similarly mused to his fellow delegates. Yet "nobody knows," he continued, "what sort may come afterwards."[40]

This was no isolated fear. With Washington in mind, they wrote a constitution that gave the president significant control over foreign policy and the military, influence over all manner of appointments including to the federal judiciary, and a powerful veto over congressional legislation. "Many of the members cast their eyes towards General Washington and shaped their ideas of the powers to be given to a president by their opinions of his virtue," a delegate from South Carolina reported.

Concern for a weaker man's use of these tools led delegates simultaneously to limit a president's veto authority, subjecting his diplomatic and military policies to congressional oversight, and exposing his most senior appointments to the Senate's scrutiny and approval. The Senate could not explicitly tell a president whom to place in his government, for example—an issue soon to arise in our next chapter—but could deny him the advisers of his choice.

Washington gave them comfort, but Slushington gave them pause, though at least they knew which would hold the office first and set presidential standards. Of course, the same South Carolina delegate noted with trepidation, he could not set them forever, and a subsequent executive might abuse the very powers placed safely in Washington's hands. In this way the "man, who by his patriotism and virtue contributed largely to the emancipation of his country, may be the innocent means of its being, when he is laid low, oppressed."[41]

Discussion of the executive's role and responsibilities consequently initially produced more questions than consensus, with delegates debating his selection, term and tenure of office, and critical relationship with the other two branches.[42] They also pondered if a president could be removed from office before the proscribed end of his term. Given their broad expectation that some future executive would inevitably seek to expand his power or even make permanent his position, this was a seismically important question indeed.

"Some mode of displacing an unfit magistrate is rendered indispensable by the fallibility of those who choose, as well as by the corruptibility of the man chosen," Virginia's George Mason vigorously argued. Washington's neighbor and friend, Mason more than most felt comfortable outlining a president's potential ills even in the presence of the presumptive first. The question of an executive's removal was "so important that no man ought to be silent or reserved," Pennsylvania's John Dickinson added in another enjoinder to his colleagues to discuss the matter frankly.[43]

North Carolina's Hugh Williamson offered the first real solution, arguing that the words "and to be removable on impeachment & conviction of malpractice or neglect of duty" be added to any subsequent description of the new executive. The concept of impeachment itself, by which they meant a trial whose purpose was to determine an officeholder's continued employment, was well known to the group, deriving from the process employed to remove corrupt judges or nefarious ministers in recent British history, and in the colonies as well. Some dated it to the fourteenth century, though moribund for extended periods since, as part of the long and circuitous formation of Britain's constitution. It offered an elegant and lawful solution to dangerous leaders, though not to despots.

Removing a king born to office risked revolution or civil war, hardly perils to be undertaken save for the direst circumstances. Yet through a formal impeachment process, the king's subjects could at least rid themselves of their monarch's more dangerous appointments. Given that their new president would not hold a king's divine right to rule, impeachment thus seemed precisely what they required if a similarly malicious executive came to hold their new office, and delegates approved Williamson's motion to include an impeachment clause on June 2, 1787. So the matter lay for more than a month, with agreement on an impeachable executive, though with little in the way of detail or process worked out.[44]

However popular as an idea, impeachments nonetheless remained relatively rare in the seventeenth and eighteenth centuries, and with good reason, being at their most basic designed to undo the sovereign's will, or, in the case of a republic, the people's choice or their selection's own appointment. In most cases time proved a less confrontational remedy for a poor or controversial administrator than his trial and potential punishment or ejection. The worst ministers could be simply waited out, in other words, until the sovereign came to his senses or the next election cycle brought a new one to power. Yet not every nefarious actor could be grudgingly endured, and as Virginia's George Mason, one of the Constitution's framers, explained in later debate: "No point is of more importance than that the right of impeachment shall be continued," even and especially for someone given as much power as the new president. "Shall any man be above justice?" he asked.[45]

Other questions beckoned first, and delegates only subsequently returned to discussion of the presidency, and of impeachments, the following month. Debate began with a rousing endorsement of a powerful executive—and an equally powerful argument against an impeachment clause—by Pennsylvania's Gouverneur Morris. At once one of the convention's youngest delegates, he was also among its most vocal. Morris reminded his colleagues that "one great object of the Executive is to control the legislature," a point that required little further evidence, given recent experience.

Congress most closely embodied the people's collective will, but not necessarily its best judgment. Someone above the fray was required to keep legislative despotism at bay. "The legislature will continually seek to aggrandize & perpetuate themselves," Morris argued. He thus desired the president to be "a guardian of the people, even of the lower classes, against Legislative tyranny." He wanted, in effect, a benevolent sovereign like the one they once had—or thought they did—in Britain's king, empowered to think of the public's broad welfare, even as legislators strove to defend their more parochial interests.[46]

But not impeachable. Fearing legislative power already, Morris argued that providing this branch of government the ability to forcefully remove a president enfeebled the latter. "It will hold him in such dependence that he will be no check on the legislature," he explained, and "will not be a firm guardian of the people and of the public interest." Morris also reasoned that impeachments, more than unwise, were also unnecessary. A good executive would retain the people's trust and be retained, he argued. A bad one would be turned out at the next election. Better to employ shorter terms of office and thus frequent popular referendums on his trustworthiness, Morris said, than to make the president beholden to ongoing legislative approval.[47]

Morris made a compelling case for doing away with presidential impeachments entirely, yet we know the Constitution ultimately included just such a process. His objections should not be hastily dismissed, however, as they subtly reveal what many delegates considered their new executive's true role. The office existed to make the government more efficient—and, of course, to keep legislative tyranny in check—but also because, for most of the delegates present, a future executive's prerogative, like a sovereign king's, was the country as a whole. "A firm guardian of the people and of the public interest," in Morris's words, the chief executive was their "great protector." Yes, an executive was necessary to execute the legislature's will, but there was something more, something almost mystical—or royal—in the way a sovereign should care for his subjects, and his sense of duty to them. An honorable leader would put their welfare above his own.[48]

Morris's continued objections to the inclusion of any process for presidential impeachment, and the counters they provoked, similarly provide greater clarity for what sort of troubles the Constitution's authors feared a future president might commit, and what might therefore warrant his impeachment. They took up the matter directly on July 20, 1787, debating the resolution that a president "should be removable on impeachment and conviction for malpractice or neglect of duty."

Most supported the proposition at the start of discussion, and even more did so by the end. If unimpeachable, North Carolina's William Davie warned, a thusly immunized president would "spare no efforts or means whatever to get himself re-elected." A president who came to power under questionable circumstances—a flawed or tampered election for example—would no doubt be further incentivized to retain office by the same means.

Mere reelection or popular approval would therefore be neither proof of such a president's innocence or a proper illustration of the people's will if they'd in fact been duped into the choice, despite what Pennsylvania's Morris suggested. Continued victory might instead be merely the result of recurring collusion or deception. Electors could be bribed or coerced as well, Virginia's irascible Mason added, thus the ballot alone could not fully protect against an overreaching executive. "The man who has practiced corruption & by that means procured his appointment in the first instance," he argued, might otherwise "be suffered to escape punishment, by repeating his guilt." If he continued the deception until his death, there being no limit to the number of terms a president could serve in the original constitution, he might never receive the justice he deserved.[49]

Tensions mounted as impeachment's supporters parried with its detractors, providing Franklin reason to reroute the discussion. He favored making executives impeachable, but not for the reason others suggested. Any who aspired to the office should embrace the opportunity an impeachment trial provided, he offered. The alternative was worse. "What was the practice before this in cases where the chief Magistrate rendered himself obnoxious?" Franklin asked. "Why recourse was had to assassination." However effective in transferring power, he noted that such a drastic measure did not provide an innocent executive opportunity to defend his record, or his honor. Or for that matter, to survive.

Franklin's interjection carried more substantial meaning, as was so often the case with his remarks, as a steady and stable republic could not ultimately be built on such a violent foundation. Assassinations were of their nature beyond the law. Impeachments, meanwhile, required respect for a formal process, enabling a functioning regime to continue even after it had taken the drastic step of removing its executive. Justice rendered through violence would irreparably corrode any republic, while proscribed procedures for impeachment reinforced the rule of law. One could assassinate a despot, Franklin's message emphasized, but doing so would doom their hopeful republic to a violent end.[50]

Notes from the meeting do not record how or even if delegates responded to Franklin's observation, but do note that Morris immediately after conceded a critical point. Upon reflection, he granted, a president should face impeachment for "corruption and some few other offenses." But at the same time political opponents couldn't simply have a free hand to oust any president they disagreed with. Rather, for such a drastic remedy as impeachment, "the cases ought to be enumerated & defined."[51]

Morris's call for specificity prompted the most illuminative aspect of the entire debate for our contemporary purposes. Initial language for an impeachment clause had employed the word "malpractice" to describe a president whose actions proved himself unfit, yet the term and the synonym delegates subsequently employed more often, "maladministration," offered significant space for interpretation and thus for legislative chicanery. If Congress could remove a president merely by judging his performance poor, a purely subjective metric, any president they did not enjoy or even like, even the most competent, could be ejected at their whim. Madison therefore offered a more precise list. A president "might lose his capacity after his appointment," he suggested, or "might pervert his administration into a scheme of peculation or oppression." (An unusual word to modern ears, "peculation" described the embezzlement of public funds.) A despicable soul might even succumb to bribes while in office, or, worse yet, Madison added, "betray his trust to foreign powers." Any such corruption or loss of capacity would provide reason enough to impeach, Madison argued. "Either of them might prove fatal to the republic."[52]

A president who posed any of these threats, Massachusetts's Elbridge Gerry agreed, employing his office for personal profit or conspiring with foreign foes, should—indeed **must**—be removed. One of the few delegates who had signed the Declaration of Independence in that very building more than a decade before, he knew a thing or two about how delegates should handle tyrants. "A good magistrate will not fear" impeachments, Gerry argued. "A bad one ought to be kept in fear of them." He furthermore "hoped the maxim would never be adopted here that the chief magistrate could do no wrong."

Morris came around. One reason for the secrecy imposed on the convention's debates was so delegates might enjoy this precise ability to change their minds without suffering public embarrassment. He "was now sensible of the necessity of impeachments," Morris offered upon hearing his colleagues out, especially as presidents were unlike kings, whose expenses were typically guaranteed for life. A president "may be bribed by a greater interest to betray his trust," he explained, "and no one would say that we ought to expose ourselves to the danger of seeing the first Magistrate in foreign pay." As head of state, and in this real sense like a monarch devoid of hereditary rule, the president's chief concern should be the people's broad welfare. Yet Morris now could see that "this magistrate is not the king but the prime-minister. The people are the king." He therefore conceded the necessity of an impeachment process, yet still hoped for "some mode that will not make him [a president] dependent on the legislature."[53]

Having now formally and for a second time agreed upon impeachment's necessity, the group once again postponed further discussion of its practical mechanics. Yet they'd critically honed the issue, moving the criteria for impeachment away from the ambiguity of "maladministration," a term that undoubtedly came naturally to those in the room—five states already employed this criteria for impeaching a governor. New York's constitution offered the similarly vague "malconduct," while North Carolina's cited "misbehavior." Madison had suggested "incapacity, negligence, or perfidy" as reasons for removal, which the convention's committees for style and detail—so named because they molded the majority's consent into usable language—revised by September 4 to read: "He shall be removed from his office on impeachment from the House of Representatives, and conviction by the Senate, for treason, or bribery."[54]

They were getting closer to finding the right words, but this criteria still seemed lacking. Mason argued on September 8, 1787, now nearly four months since the convention began and as patience wore thin throughout, that while their language on impeachment had once been too vague, now it seemed to his ears too limited. "Why is the provision restrained to Treason and bribery only?" he wondered. There were many "great and dangerous" offenses that might not reach the level of treason, and in Britain a celebrated case was even then ongoing whereby a chief royal administrator in India was currently on trial after impeachment for poor administration. "Attempts to subvert the constitution may not be Treason" if narrowly defined, Mason added, but they may be reason enough to fear a president's continued tenure. He therefore moved to reinsert the once-banished word "maladministration" to the list of potential impeachable offenses.[55]

Madison considered this matter already settled, and with good reason. "So vague a term would be equivalent to a tenure during pleasure of the Senate," he quickly countered his fellow Virginian, noting once more that if the legislature were given the right to remove a president on such subjective grounds they would wield power to make that determination based on political sentiment alone. An excellent president might find himself in that case impeached merely for being unliked, a characteristic that might justify defeating him in the next election but not his summary ejection from office. To Madison's mind, being poor at one's job or unpopular were not impeachable offenses. One needed malevolency as well. Better to let the people deal with merely lousy presidents, Morris concurred, returning once more to his notion that plebiscites could solve all presidential problems. "An election every four years will prevent maladministration."[56]

Evidently convinced by Madison's reasoning, Mason withdrew his suggestion of "maladministration" as a cause for impeachment, though he still found "bribery and treason" too narrow. He suggested inserting "other high crimes and misdemeanors" in place of "maladministration." Mason's motion and definition being quickly approved so the group could move on to more pressing matters, the delegates said nothing further on the nature of impeachment before their convention closed. Their final result brought all branches of the government together. According to Article I of the Constitution, articles of impeachment could be brought up in the House of Representatives, and if approved by a majority, a president would then face trial in the Senate in sessions overseen by the chief justice. But, Article II, Section 4, of their hopeful constitution matters most: "The President, Vice President and all civil Officers of the United States, shall be removed from Office on impeachment for, and Conviction of, Treason, Bribery, or other high Crimes and Misdemeanors."

"High crimes and misdemeanors," the new addition alongside bribery and treason as impeachable offenses, has puzzled readers ever since, providing modern ears hardly more clarity than "maladministration." "Bribery" seems clearer, and had real and clear meaning to those in the room, especially when considered alongside Washington's looming presence. "It was read both actively and passively" by the Constitutional Convention, one leading scholar of the crime noted, including the acts of "bribing someone and being bribed." Of particular concern, no doubt, was the potential bribing of electors, but then as now the simplest definition suffices. Someone who would stoop to putting money above country could not be trusted, and indeed was no Washington, who'd not even accepted payment for his wartime service.

"Only an unprincipled monster would insinuate a thing so vile" as to suggest Washington's loyalty could be swayed or bought, one newspaper replied to a potential critic, describing him as a man "who, for eight years . . . fought and struggled to obtain to you freedom and independence." Recalling our simple test of impeachable offenses, bribery was clearly something Washington would not do.[57]

"Treason," too, sounds clear to our modern ears, and is explicitly defined elsewhere within the Constitution. "Treason against the United States," Article III, Section 3, reads, "shall consist only in levying war against them, or in adhering to their enemies, giving them aid and comfort." It is the crime of actively undermining one's own state, whose heinous nature and likely severe punishment upon conviction prompted the further constitutional stipulation that "no person shall be convicted of Treason unless on the Testimony of two witnesses to the same act, or on confession in open court." A single voice alone could not convict someone for treason, though at the risk of belaboring the point when considered in the context of impeachment, it is hard to conceive of anyone seriously lodging such an accusation against the man already dubbed "father of his country." Washington would never turn traitor. A successor, however, might not prove so loyal, and might even combine treason with bribery in the most unconscionable way. "No man," Gouverneur Morris reminded his fellow delegates—who required no convincing on this point—would say "an Executive known to be in the pay of an Enemy should not be removable."[58]

However less clear to our ears than treason or bribery, the term "high crimes and misdemeanors" offered no puzzle to the Constitution's authors. Their use of the term was not a cop-out or the result of fatigue. Words mattered to the framers, who appreciated that the ones they employed would be parsed and critiqued not only by future generations, but more immediately by their peers once their convention closed. Whatever they produced in Philadelphia required ratification by the states to take effect, a reality delegates never forgot. Their honor was thus at stake not only in the document's intent, but in its clarity as well. As Massachusetts's Rufus King explained to his state's ratifying convention, "It was the intention and honest desire of the Convention to use those expressions that were most easy to be understood and least equivocal in their meaning."[59]

"High crimes and misdemeanors" therefore spoke clearly in their minds, and its acceptance without debate strongly suggests a shared general understanding of the phrase. It certainly was not new. A similar term, "high treasons and offenses and misprisions," appeared in English law as early as 1386, and evolved over the ensuing centuries along a common thread: "High" offenses were those committed against the sovereign's state, or against the people in republics where the people held sovereignty on their own. The adjective is the key. A "crime" occurred when one citizen or subject harmed another. "High crimes" were conversely those committed against the crown in a monarchy, or the people in a democracy. The term says nothing about the severity of the crime, or its consequent penalty, merely its type as one that surpassed mere criminal law, being a more fundamental assault against the body politic. Such "public wrongs," William Blackstone, the leading legal scholar of the day, argued in 1792, "are a breach and violation of the public rights and duties, due to the whole community." They "strike at the very being of society."[60]

Put in even clearer terms, "high" crimes warranting impeachment were those a president might commit against the entire American people, a point the Constitution's authors and their contemporaries reinforced repeatedly, in Madison's case as a means of "defending the Community" from a corrupt or dangerous leader. "Impeachments are confined to political characters, to political crimes and misdemeanors, and to political punishments," James Wilson lectured in 1801. One of the handful of foreign-born signers of the Constitution, Wilson subsequently served on the Supreme Court as well, during which time he argued that impeachable offenses did not reside "within the sphere of ordinary jurisprudence." They were of a particular nature, and a preponderance of evidence supports his analysis of the framers' sense of the term. As legal historian Cass Sunstein has noted, North Carolina's Hugh Williamson, a key contributor to the convention's debates on impeachment, no doubt drew his understanding of the political nature of impeachable offenses from his state's constitution, which dubbed them "offenses against the public interest which need not be indictable under the criminal law."[61]

To the Constitution's authors, therefore, a "high crime and misdemeanor," need not violate an extant law or statute, and neither would a president who commits a common violation be guilty of a "high" offense. An impeachable offense need not be illegal at all. "Lying to the American people might be impeachable," Yale Law School professor Akhil Amar has recently noted, "but it might not be a crime on the statute books." The same notion holds true for the term "misdemeanor," as the Constitution's editors thought it unnecessary to repeat the adjective "high" twice in the same clause. Typically desirous of precision, they longed for a bit of style as well, and understood the term to mean not necessarily a felony or a misdemeanor in the narrow sense, but rather like bribery or treason as an assault against civil order and governance itself. "High crimes and misdemeanors" were, another early Supreme Court justice argued, "offences which are committed by public men in violation of their public trust and duties," and represent "injuries to the society in its political character." As is so often the case, Alexander Hamilton made the point as clearly as any. "They are of a nature which may with peculiar propriety be denominated POLITICAL," he wrote, "as they relate chiefly to injuries done immediately to the society itself."[62]

At last we can fully appreciate what sort of president the founders feared, and wished to ensure could be pried from office. Impeachable offenses were those perpetuated with sinister intent to harm the republic for personal gain. The House should not impeach, nor the Senate convict, a president merely because the majority in the former or a supermajority in the latter disagree with his policies or dislike him personally. Voters had made their choice, and would have the chance to remedy it in four years' time.

As Virginia's Edmund Randolph explained the clause to his state's ratifying convention, "No man ever thought of impeaching a man for an opinion," or even for making a mistake, so long as the error came while in honest search of an ideal course. Merely being bad at the job did not demand one's impeachment. Undesirable yes; despicable perhaps; but not impeachable. Neither were proof of clear mistakes cause for impeachment. "It would be impossible to discover whether the error in opinion resulted from a willful mistake of the heart," Randolph elaborated, "or an involuntary fault of the head."

Future Supreme Court justice James Iredell similarly argued in North Carolina's ratification convention that impeachment required "wicked motive." Should further confirmation of this point be needed we might look to the presidential oath detailed in the original Constitution, which required officeholders to act only "to the best of my abilities." So long as a president is, as his oath of office demands, performing "to the best of my abilities," voters should be his ultimate judge.[63]

One that intentionally does his worst is another matter indeed. Malfeasance, scheming to harm the republic or to place one's own interest above the people's—the direct opposite of a Washingtonian virtue—was the true basis of an impeachable offense. As the closest thing Americans would have to a sovereign, that paternal protector role played by a benevolent guide and guardian, presidents needed to be above petty local concerns.

"Under this Constitution" the president will be the leader "of the whole union," James Wilson argued, "and will be chosen in such a manner that he may be justly styled THE MAN OF THE PEOPLE; being elected by the different parts of the United States, he will consider himself not particularly interested in any of them, but will watch over the whole with paternal care and affection." This broad view carried an equal measure of responsibility. "The President," Iredell further argued, is to be "personally responsible for any abuse of the great trust reposed in him." Any breach of that trust was reason enough to seek impeachment.[64]

There was one final question to address—or loophole to close, really. No man was above the law, as Mason had argued, and none more so than the president. But their new constitution afforded the president broad powers to pardon crimes and offenses. Might this not provide a guilty president means of escape? What if he chose to "pardon crimes which were advised by himself," Mason subsequently asked in Virginia's ratification debate, or to "stop inquiry and prevent detection" of a crime he or an associate had committed? What if a president employed the power of his office to purposefully slow investigations or halt the wheels of justice from turning? "It may happen at some future day," Mason warned, and thus "he will establish a monarchy, and destroy the republic."[65]

Madison offered an unequivocal reply. "If the President be connected, in any suspicious manner, with any person" who schemed to harm the republic, "and there be grounds to believe he [the president] will shelter him," he explained, "the House of Representatives can impeach him; they can remove him if found guilty." The president did not necessarily have to personally commit a high crime in order to be impeached, but could merely have made way for its commission, or have failed to halt it once he learned of it.

Crimes that did not harm the republic he thought a different matter. A president could thus commit common crimes (though this the framers would neither have recommended nor desired), but remain in office so long as those transgressions did not damage the prospects for widespread liberty itself. A jaywalking president, to cite a modern example, need not worry the offense might somehow violate the public's trust. Jaywalking is not impeachable. Purposefully hindering an investigation of his jaywalking, however, could be.[66]

This is not to say a president need not worry about basic aspects of the criminal code entirely. Presidents could face the consequences of those acts once they departed office. The aforementioned jaywalking president would still be required to pay the normal fine once his term ended, when his rights as a former commander in chief ranked precisely the same as the lowest citizen. Neither does the Constitution specifically require an impeached president be removed from office, though that remains the most likely result of conviction. He could be impeached and found guilty, and then be given a lesser punishment by the Senate if they chose.

For a group like the Constitution's authors, for whom personal honor held real meaning, there were deeper stains than mere unemployment. "Judgements in Cases of impeachment shall not extend further than to removal from Office," the Constitution ultimately read, "and disqualification to hold and enjoy any Office of honor, Trust or profit under the United States." As judgments could not extend "further," they also by extension could easily comprise lesser penalties—a formal rebuke, for example. More important to their eyes was that once convicted of violating the public's trust, a disgraced president would never be so trusted again.

Even to be impeached by the House, though not convicted by the Senate, would doom a president to "infamy," Hamilton subsequently wrote. "The punishment, which may be the consequence of conviction upon impeachment, is not to terminate the chastisement of the defender." He would instead face "the perpetual ostracism from the esteem and confidence, and honors and emoluments of his country." This is why a president's pardon power, also outlined in the Constitution, does not extend to cases of impeachment. Someone so thoroughly dishonored could never be fully rehabilitated, even by subsequent presidential decree. Some stains cannot be pardoned away.[67]

To the Constitution's framers the greatest dishonor a president could suffer would be not the criminal consequences of nefarious acts, but rather the judgment of his peers that he had violated the people's trust. This, above all else, Washington would not do, as both duty and, to an even greater extent, pursuit of honor and reputation (which duty provided), were central to his very core, and why impeachable acts are those contrary to his being. This is why delegates in 1787 felt so comfortable with him as their ideal president, and their first. "George Washington has already been destined, by a thousand voices, to fill the place of the first President," **The Pennsylvania Gazette** proclaimed soon after the delegates at long last departed Philadelphia in September. "If anything," historian Edward Larson notes, "the **Gazette**'s count was far too low."[68]

Our nation's first president thus reveals all we need to know about what the Constitution's framers considered an impeachable one, but we should neither consider that George Washington was therefore perfect, nor that the founders expected his successors to be so. Washington made mistakes. Yet at every major and minor fork in his personal journey, in office or as a private citizen, he took care to consider two essential and intertwined questions: first, how his response might affect his honor, and second, if his response prioritized public good. He ultimately made decisions that inadvertently harmed both, and his record as a battlefield commander in particular leaves military historians and armchair strategists to this day frustrated over his performance. But at worst these were examples of maladministration more than malice, and no one who ever worked with him could doubt that he strove to better the common good, and thus his own, no matter the personal sacrifice required.

No, he was not perfect, even as histories of his life frequently approach an uncomfortable degree of hagiography. He was vain, struggled his entire life to contain his violent temper, and rarely saw his plantation turn a profit. Debt was his constant companion. He could be stiff and impersonal even to close friends, so concerned with maintaining propriety that he often denied himself or those around him mirth or the pleasure of relaxation. Worst of all, he owned other human beings, buying and selling them and their families for profit or to pay off lenders, and lived almost entirely off the fruit of enslaved lives and labor. Famously afflicted by poor dental health, he even wore teeth implanted in his jaw only after having been ripped from the mouths of his slaves. This unpleasant procedure was not uncommon, and surgeons typically paid the unfortunate contributors for their "donations," albeit for slaves like Washington's, only one-third the going rate for a free person's tooth. Such facts make us squirm, as should the ever-present reality that the constitutional freedoms we extend to all citizens today were denied to most by its authors.

Their flaws embedded in the "good old dead Constitution" remain in the "living Constitution" still in use, making their words less sacred scriptures than prescriptions, including most especially their sense of duty and public service. This is why looking back to the eighteenth century to understand more fully the possibility of a presidential impeachment in the twenty-first matters. The Constitution's framers trusted Washington not because they considered him perfect in 1787, but because they never doubted his integrity. Any ensuing president who met that standard earned the right, indeed the privilege, of serving until dismissed by his fellow citizens. Any who failed to live up to Washington's standard, not of performance but of devotion to the community's needs, could be impeached.

States ratified the Constitution the following year, and electors made him their unanimous choice a year later. Abigail Adams, who as his vice president's emotional and political partner knew him well, perhaps said it best: "If he was not really one of the best-intentioned men in the world," she wrote during Washington's first term as president, during which time his every act served as precedent for those who would follow, "he might be a very dangerous one."

This is ultimately why Washington's peers thought of him when they hoped for a leader who might display virtue enough to withstand the lure of tyranny. This is also why the absence of virtue—evidenced by a president's concern for his own welfare above and beyond the public's, whose fate he is entrusted to preserve—is the best sign we have that the founders would have wanted him impeached.[69]

ANDREW JOHNSON
Jon Meacham

The peace seemed to be collapsing. In the wake of the four-year struggle that had claimed hundreds of thousands of lives, the nation that had survived what Abraham Lincoln had called the "fiery trial" of the Civil War was ready, many believed, to fight again. "We are to have another war," Tennessee governor William G. Brownlow predicted in the summer of 1866.[1] The conflict between President Andrew Johnson and the Republican-controlled Congress over post–Civil War Reconstruction policies, **The New York Herald**'s James G. Bennett wrote in August 1867, "trembles on the brink of open war."[2]

In a disturbing February 1868 letter, a Massachusetts state senator, Benjamin Pratt, told U.S. senator Charles Sumner that Johnson needed to be removed by any means necessary—including the force of arms. "The crisis is at hand," Pratt wrote. "If delayed, or deferred again, the golden opportunity may be forever lost, and the traitor President, the representative of Jeff Davis, may have the reins so strong that Congress may be broken up and dispersed. . . . Arrest him before he takes another step. One step more, and he may have gone so far that he will resort to arms. We have been through one war, but rather than to have treason and traitors triumph, we will fight again . . . if the cause demands it."[3]

And so the aftermath was proving in some ways as chaotic as the war itself, for the Confederate surrender at Appomattox on Palm Sunday 1865 turned out to be as much a beginning as an end. "We may say," the poet-novelist-critic Robert Penn Warren wrote a century later, "that only at the moment when Lee handed Grant his sword was the Confederacy born; or, to state matters another way, in the moment of death the Confederacy entered upon its immortality."[4]

Warren was right, and the years of Andrew Johnson, who filled the remainder of the assassinated Lincoln's term, repay our consideration. In Johnson's tumultuous and troubled reign we can find elements of public life that resonate in our own time: an obstinate president; a divided Congress; a nation that seemed intractably tribal; fears that the grand American experiment in democracy was coming to an end; and, as a capstone, a battle over the legitimacy of the president amid impeachment proceedings that went to the very final hour before resolution.[5]

The consuming debate of the era was what the victorious North should do in relation to the vanquished South. "Reconstruction" is a catchall term for a multiplicity of political and cultural conflicts that roiled the nation as the militarily triumphant federal government tried to compel a defeated region to accept the implications of the Union victory, particularly in terms of equality.[6] Republicans controlled much of the North and held the strongest of hands in Congress. Though Republican opinion was hardly unanimous, the main thrust of the party, which had come into being in the 1850s to oppose slavery, was now to reconstruct the former Confederate states into political entities in which black Americans enjoyed constitutional protections. The battles between Johnson and the Republican Congress over the nature of life in the South would define the age—and lead to the showdown over impeachment.

As I wrote in **The Soul of America: The Battle for Our Better Angels,** my 2018 history of contentious moments in American politics, Republicans were hopeful Johnson would follow their lead and, like Lincoln, stand up to largely unrepentant Southern states. "Johnson, we have faith in you," Republican senator Benjamin F. Wade said on Johnson's ascension to the presidency. "By the Gods, there will be no trouble now in running the government."[7] The great Charles Sumner himself remarked that Johnson was "the sincere friend of the negro and ready to act for him decisively."[8]

The Republicans would quickly come to see that their initial optimism about Johnson was unfounded. Many in the Party of Lincoln were eager to force the former slave states to extend political and civil rights to the newly emancipated rather than allow them to return to the Union with a legally free but functionally persecuted black populace.

Johnson, at heart a Democrat, disagreed: "White men alone must manage the South," Johnson remarked in 1865.[9] Later, he claimed black people could not manage their own governance. "No independent government of any form has ever been successful in their hands. . . . On the contrary, wherever they have been left to their own devices they have shown a constant tendency to relapse into barbarism."[10] It was, the historian Eric Foner observed, "probably the most blatantly racist pronouncement ever to appear in an official state paper of an American president."[11]

Johnson was quick to give the white South the leeway to prevent advances in civil rights. Though emancipated from slavery, black Americans were finding that citizenship did not end oppression. "Every political right which the State possessed under the Federal Constitution [before the Civil War] is hers today, with the single exception relating to slavery," Alabama governor Lewis E. Parsons said.[12] Johnson vetoed the 1866 civil rights bill and the Freedmen's Bureau bill. Against the civil rights bill, he argued "the distinction of race and color is by the bill made to operate in favor of the colored and against the white race."[13]

Under Johnson, the presidency had become a force for reaction, not transformation.[14] He vetoed the Civil Rights Act of 1866 and Reconstruction legislation in 1867 that created military districts in the

South and guaranteed black suffrage. (An insistent Congress overrode those vetoes.) He unsuccessfully opposed the Fourteenth Amendment, which granted citizenship to former slaves and guaranteed equal protection under the law, at least on paper.

For his obstructionism Johnson was eventually impeached (but not convicted) by a Republican majority in Congress that had come to see him as an impediment to the work of the nation. His impeachment illustrates a fundamental truth about the American system: The process of removing a president from office is as much political in nature as it is legal. Republicans held overwhelming majorities in both chambers throughout Johnson's term—a six-fold margin in the Senate and almost a four-fold advantage in the House. And many of them wanted Johnson out. After much searching they finally found a pretext for it in 1867–68: a purported violation of the uninterestingly titled Tenure of Office Act.

The tenure legislation, which in essence required that federal officials confirmed by the Senate could be dismissed by the president only with the permission of the Senate, had been passed in early 1867 to protect Republican influence in the Age of Johnson. The law, which Johnson unsuccessfully vetoed, was of dubious constitutionality, but the passions of the era were such that Congress believed it needed all the weapons it could muster to combat the president's lenient attitude toward the South. By insisting on the Tenure of Office Act, the Republican majority hoped that it could protect the power of men such as Secretary of War Edwin Stanton, who held a Republican, not a Johnsonian, view of Reconstruction.[15]

The purported violation of the Tenure of Office Act was only the occasion, not the cause, of Johnson's 1868 impeachment by the House and trial in the Senate. Indeed, there were no fewer than four separate efforts to remove him from office in the nearly four years he served as president.[16] The first, from December 1866 to June 1867, was begun by Representative James Ashley, Republican of Ohio, and failed in the House Judiciary Committee; it mainly concerned unproven charges that Johnson had been involved in Lincoln's assassination. The second, from July to December 1867, focused (as did all the rest) on the removal of Stanton and other federal officers, but was defeated on the floor of the House. The third, from January to February 13, 1868, also died in committee. It was only the fourth, which unfolded from February 21 to May 26, 1868, that reached a final vote in the Senate.

In the story of Johnson and his showdown with the Republicans of the day, we can see how impeachment is a weapon of politics—and that any era can find itself amid a crisis over the removal of a president if the passions of the hour are ferocious enough.

To understand Johnson's particular moment—with its threat of renewed violence, its significance in the enduring debates over freedom and equality, and its lessons for an age in which impeachment is in the air—we must begin in the war years themselves, with the most perennial of forces: a politician's anxieties about the judgment of the voters.

—

Abraham Lincoln was worried.[17] It was 1864, and the president, facing reelection amid the Civil War, fretted that the Union's electorate, tired of the conflict and ready for a change of commander in chief, might choose to cast its lot with George B. McClellan, the Democratic Party nominee. In 1860 Lincoln had run on the Republican ticket with Hannibal Hamlin of Maine. Now, four years later, concerned about appearing solely the party of the North, Lincoln weighed his options as the 1864 election approached. One thought: Replace Hamlin with someone who could broaden the Republicans' appeal beyond their base.

Andrew Johnson was one possibility. In the vernacular of the age, Johnson was a member of what Henry Clay had called the great company of "enterprising and self-made men."[18] Born in Raleigh, North Carolina, in 1808, Johnson was the child of illiterate parents.[19] His father, Jacob, was a porter in a bank; the elder Johnson died after rescuing some town notables from a capsized boat. Johnson's mother, Polly, was a seamstress and laundress who eked out a living for her and her two sons (Johnson had one older brother) before apprenticing both children to a tailor, James Selby.[20]

They belonged to the lowest precinct of white society, a state of affairs that most likely shaped Johnson's later views on race and class. "The idea of white supremacy gave people in the Johnsons' social position a sense of identity that softened the reality of their downtrodden existence," wrote the historian Annette Gordon-Reed.

> While there is no question that as a free person Andrew was legally better off than an enslaved boy, and would have thought of himself as superior to any black person, the question of actual racial superiority was more problematic. . . . What beyond their white skin did poor whites have to show for being better than blacks? The closer they came to blacks, in terms of the way they lived, their lack of social standing, independence, and putative lack of virtue, the more anxious they grew. Having nothing themselves, they claimed superiority by asserting that a common skin color linked them to the talents, actions, and accomplishments of others who looked like them.[21]

As Johnson rose in the world, learning to read, fleeing James Selby, and eventually moving to Tennessee, he made a place for himself as a tailor in Greeneville, in the upper eastern part of the state. In the Age of Andrew Jackson, young Johnson won elections as an alderman, mayor, state legislator, U.S. congressman, governor, U.S. senator, and, finally, during the Civil War, served as the Union's military governor of Tennessee. A Democrat who was devoted to the rights of the common white man, Johnson was a relentless foe of advances for blacks. Frustrated by the emphasis on slavery in national politics, Johnson once joked that "if the Ten Commandments were to come up for consideration [in Congress], somebody would find a Negro in them somewhere and the slavery question would be raised."[22]

A powerful and elemental orator, Johnson was adept at moving crowds—white crowds, to be sure—with raw appeals. As the Union disintegrated and war came, he preached a gospel of nationalism, viewing the elite planter class as an impediment to the aspirations of lower-class white folk. "Damn the Negroes," Johnson remarked. "I am fighting those traitorous aristocrats, their masters."[23] He despised the secessionists who had broken the United States in two, though not the way of life white Southerners were seeking to protect. "I am," he said, "for a white man's government in America."[24]

In Johnson's worldview, then, both the richest of men (the slave owners) and the enslaved themselves were to be faced down and conquered by the broad white populace. It was a kind of Hobbesian understanding of the universe: the war of all against all. Johnson, who had known only strife in his own life, projected that drama onto the larger national enterprise. Conflict was the natural state of things, and Johnson, who had mastered the world around him through willfulness, raising himself from illiteracy and servitude to power and place in a republic riven by the crisis over freedom and slavery, conducted himself as though such conflict was inevitable and perpetual.

When, in his term as military governor of Tennessee, Confederate troops threatened Nashville, Johnson told his Union officers: "I am no military man, but anyone who talks of surrendering I will shoot."[25]

This intransigence was a Johnsonian hallmark, and where others saw obstinance and stubbornness, President Lincoln, facing a difficult reelection in 1864, saw strength that the Republican ticket badly needed. The war had not gone well; there had been nearly three years of epic bloodletting on both sides. Voters throughout the North were frustrated and restless. In August 1864, just a few months before the November balloting, the Republican Thurlow Weed was despondent. "I have told Mr. Lincoln," Weed wrote Secretary of State William Seward, "that his re-election was an impossibility."[26]

That same month, in a private memorandum, Lincoln wrote: "This morning, as for some days past, it seems exceedingly probable that this Administration will not be re-elected. Then it will be my duty to so co-operate with the President-elect, as to save the Union between the election and the inauguration."[27]

Nominated for vice president in the hope that his bellicosity and Democratic credentials might help put Lincoln over the top once more, Johnson was demagogic in campaign speeches, wandering off into perilous territory as he played to crowds. Speaking to a largely black audience during the election season, Johnson heard someone shout that Johnson himself might prove to be a Moses-like figure.[28] Flush with excitement in the moment, and quite willing to entertain heroic visions of himself, the vice-presidential nominee said: "Humble and unworthy as I am, if no better be found, I will indeed be your Moses, and lead you through the Red Sea of war and bondage!"

It was not to be. Sober observers saw Johnson more clearly than he ever saw himself. Carl Schurz, the Union general, wrote that he found no "sunlight" in Johnson, but "rather something sullen, something betokening a strong will inspired by bitter feelings. I could well imagine him leading with vindictive energy an uprising of a lower order of society against an aristocracy from whose lordly self-assertion he had suffered, and whose pride he was bent on humbling."

Buoyed by a series of military victories in the fall of 1864, the Lincoln-Johnson ticket won, and the self-made man from the poor white South was now the vice president of the United States. Things, however, did not begin well on Inauguration Day 1865. "It must be said," the journalist Noah Brooks reported, "that upon that momentous and solemn occasion, where were assembled the good, the brave, the beautiful, the noble of our land, and the representatives of many foreign lands, Andrew Johnson, called to be Vice President of the United States, was in a state of manifest intoxication."[29]

Supporters claimed he was ill, but sick or no, those who were there agreed that he was drunk: "The Vice President Elect was too drunk to perform his duties & disgraced himself & the Senate with a drunken foolish speech."[30] Lincoln tried to dismiss the talk. "I have known Andy Johnson for many years," the president told Secretary of the Treasury Hugh McCulloch. "He made a bad slip the other day, but you need not be scared; Andy ain't a drunkard."[31]

But he was a racist. Frederick Douglass, the great American writer, orator, and activist who had been born into slavery, left a damning account of his impressions of Johnson from the inaugural festivities. "There are moments in the lives of most men, when the doors of their soul are open, and unconsciously to themselves, their true characters may be read by the observant eye," Douglass wrote. "It was at such an instant when I caught a glimpse of the real nature of this man, which all subsequent developments proved true."[32] Lincoln, Douglass reported, pointed Douglass out to Johnson. "The first expression which came to [Johnson's] face, and which I think was the true index of his heart, was one of bitter contempt and aversion. Seeing that I had observed him, he tried to assume a more friendly appearance, but it was too late; it is useless to close the door when all within had been seen. His first glance was the frown of the man; the second was the bland and sickly smile of the demagogue." Douglass turned to a neighbor and remarked: "Whatever Andrew Johnson might be, he is no friend of our race."

Which might not have mattered, much, had it not been for the events of Friday, April 14, 1865, when John Wilkes Booth shot Lincoln during a performance of **Our American Cousin** in Washington. Johnson and Seward were to have been killed the same night, but the assassin who was supposed to have attacked Johnson failed to show up, and Seward survived an assault.

The vice president had turned in early that evening.[33] A boarder at the Kirkwood House hotel at Twelfth Street and Pennsylvania Avenue in Washington, he was in bed in Suite 68 when the news came. Taking the oath of office from Chief Justice Salmon P. Chase the next day, Johnson listened as the jurist offered a kind of benediction: "You are President," Chase told Johnson. "May God support, guide, and bless you in your arduous duties."[34] As it turned out, even the Lord Himself could not (or would not) do much to aid the seventeenth president.

—

After a brief interlude of appearing open to accepting the implications of the Union victory in the Civil War on race, liberty, and power, Johnson reverted to his white Southern origins. This pivot set the president at odds with Republicans in Congress, who believed that the North's triumph had indeed amounted to what Lincoln had, at Gettysburg, called a "new birth of freedom." Before his murder, Lincoln had struck conciliatory notes toward the South in both early policy moves and in his Second Inaugural.[35] "With malice toward none, with charity for all," Lincoln had said, the nation should look to bind up the wounds of war rather than aggravate them.

Yet Lincoln was forever evolving; his views on emancipation provide incontestable proof of that.[36] Historians have long noted that he would have likely shifted his perspective on Reconstruction as events warranted, almost certainly taking a firmer hand as white Southern recalcitrance became ever more evident. In his last public speech, delivered at the White House on Tuesday, April 11, 1865, Lincoln acknowledged the complexities ahead. "We simply must begin with, and mold from, disorganized and discordant elements," he said. "Nor is it a small additional embarrassment that we, the loyal people, differ among ourselves as to the mode, manner, and measure of reconstruction."[37]

Now that the task of managing those competing elements had fallen to a white Democrat from Tennessee, Johnson broke with the Republicans whose ticket he had joined less than a year before. On issue after issue, the new president sided with white Southerners, insisting that the national government did not have the right to impose its will on the defeated Confederate states. In this most complex of eras, after having lost perhaps its most complex and subtle president of all, America was being led by a man to whom nuance was a foreign concept. "His mind had one compartment for right and one for wrong, but no middle chamber where the two could commingle," wrote the historian Howard K. Beale.[38] Once Johnson decided on a course, he could be intractable. "There is nothing like starting out on principle," he once said.

"When you start out right with principles clearly defined you can hardly go astray."[39]

The problem was that the principle on which Johnson had embarked was one of white supremacy in the wake of a war fought not least to create a more inclusive national political order. He opposed Reconstruction legislation designed to protect the hard-won rights of blacks from the racist policies of the individual states.[40] Former Confederates were allowed to assume office in regimes that quickly enacted "Black Codes," a forerunner of Jim Crow.[41] That the federal government would reach over the state authorities to guarantee the civil liberties of the newly freed slaves was anathema to the president, who spoke in the language of states' rights. "In all our history . . . no such system as that contemplated by the details of this bill has ever before been proposed or adopted," Johnson wrote as he vetoed the civil rights bill of 1866. "It is another step, or rather stride, toward centralization and the concentration of all legislative powers in the National Government."[42]

Johnson was erratic and insecure. In a moment where he might have offered reassurance to an anxious, divided nation, he instead fiercely criticized his Republican opponents and chose to promote fears of conspiracy. To him, Republican efforts to federally guarantee and enforce equality—for the first time in the history of the United States—actually represented a dangerous centralization of power.

While trying to block their efforts, he played the

victim. "Who, I ask, has suffered more for the Union than I have?" Johnson said in a speech on Washington's Birthday in 1866.[43] He went so far as to suggest that he might soon be the target of Republican assassins. "If my blood is to be shed because I vindicate the Union and the preservation of this Government in its original purity and character," he said, "let it be shed; let an altar to the Union be erected, and then, if it is necessary, take me and lay me upon it, and the blood that now warms and animates my existence shall be poured out as a fit libation to the Union of these States." As Eric Foner observed, it was "Johnson at his worst—self-absorbed (in a speech one hour long he referred to himself over 200 times), intolerant of criticism, and out of touch with political reality."[44]

Johnson's were the words of an angry man, not unlike those who had argued most passionately against the ratification of the Constitution of 1787 for fear it might undermine liberty. And as in so many other eras of American life, the elements of anger and of fear were important parts of the story of the Johnson presidency.

For white Southerners, it was a fearful time, for life as they had long known it was ending. Their way of life was in ruins, the war lost, the future precarious. In an 1866 book entitled **The Lost Cause: A New Southern History of the War of the Confederates,** the Virginia Confederate and journalist Edward Alfred Pollard called on the white South to fight on in the face of loss. "The people of the South have surrendered in the war what the war has conquered"—slavery and secession—"but they cannot be expected to give up what was not involved in the war, and voluntarily abandon their political schools for the dogma of Consolidation."[45] The war, Pollard wrote, "did not decide negro equality; it did not decide negro suffrage; it did not decide State Rights. . . . And these things which the war did not decide, the Southern people will still cling to, still claim, and still assert in their rights and views."[46]

The fear of black equality, of a loss of a political, social, and economic power structure built on an unsustainable but persistent view of the innate inferiority of others, gave shape and substance to the postbellum universe. Fear, Aristotle wrote, is "caused by whatever we feel has great power of destroying us, or of harming us in ways that tend to cause us great pain"[47] and does not strike those who are "in the midst of great prosperity."[48] It did, however, strike defeated white Southerners intoxicated by nostalgia and driven by resentments. "No passion," Edmund Burke wrote, "so effectually robs the mind of all its powers of acting and reasoning as **fear**."[49] The stage was set for a conflict between a restive regional segment of the population, defeated but not yet conquered, and a more deliberative Congress, victorious but not yet fully in control.

The seventeenth president's frequently intemperate public remarks underscore the point. In political life, fear, which can be hidden, often manifests itself in detectable expressions of anger. Such anger was on display in the White House one day in August 1866, when Johnson, "in a loud voice"—an **angry** voice, it seems safe to say—denounced the Congress to a visiting group of citizens.[50] "So far as the Executive Department of the government is concerned," Johnson was reported to have said, "the effort has been made to restore the Union, to heal the breach, to pour oil into the wounds which were consequent upon the struggle, and, to speak in a common phrase, to prepare, as the learned and wise physician would, a plaster healing in character and co-extensive with the wound."[51] Turning his fire on Congress, he continued:

> We thought and we think that we had partially succeeded, but as the work progresses, as reconstruction seemed to be taking place, and the country was becoming reunited, we found a disturbing and moving element opposing it. . . . We have witnessed in one department of the government every endeavor to prevent the restoration of peace, harmony and union. We have seen hanging upon the verge of the government, as it were, a body called or which assumes to be the Congress of the United States, while in fact it is a Congress of only part of the States. We have seen this Congress pretend to be for the Union, when its every step and act tended to perpetuate disunion and make a disruption of States inevitable. We have seen

Congress gradually encroach, step by step, upon constitutional rights, and violate day after day, and month after month, fundamental principles of the government. We have seen a Congress that seemed to forget that there was a limit to the sphere and scope of legislation. We have seen a Congress in a minority assume to exercise power which, if allowed to be consummated, would result in despotism or monarchy itself.

He reveled in attacking his foes, particularly those in the Republican-controlled Congress. In Cleveland a few weeks later, he spoke again in that "loud voice," crying out that Congress "had taken much pains to poison the constituents against him" and was now, with its "factions and domineering," attempting "to poison the minds of the American people."[52]

At a subsequent stop in St. Louis, the president— yes, again with that "loud voice"—went even further, invoking the drama of the Passion:

I know that I have been traduced and abused. I know it has come in advance of me here, as elsewhere, that I have attempted to exercise an arbitrary power in resisting laws that were intended to be forced upon the government; that I had exercised that power; that I had abandoned the party that elected me, and that I was a traitor, because I exercised the veto power in attempting, and did arrest for a time, that which was called a "Freedmen's Bureau" bill. Yes, that I was a traitor. And I have been traduced; I have been slandered; I have been maligned; I have been called Judas Iscariot, and all that. Now, my countrymen, here to-night, it is very easy to indulge in epithets; it is easy to call a man a Judas, and cry out traitor, but when he is called upon to give arguments and facts he is very often found wanting. Judas Iscariot? Judas! There was a Judas, and he was one of the twelve Apostles. O, yes, the twelve Apostles had a Christ, and he never could have had a Judas unless he had twelve Apostles. If I have played the Judas who has been my Christ that I have played the Judas with? Was it Thad. Stevens? Was it Wendell Phillips? Was it Charles Sumner? They are the men that stop and compare themselves with the Savior, and everybody that differs with them in opinion, and tries to stay and arrest their diabolical and nefarious policy is to be denounced as a Judas. Well, let me say to you, if you will stand by me in this action, if you will stand by me in trying to give the people a fair chance, soldiers and citizens, to participate in these office, God be willing, I will kick them out. I will kick them out just as fast as I can. Let me say to you, in concluding, that what I have said is what I intended to say; I was not provoked into this, and care not for their menaces, the taunts and the jeers. I care not for threats, I do not intend to be bullied by enemies, nor overawed by my friends. But, God willing, with your help, I will veto their measures whenever any of them come to me.[53]

Republicans in Congress were listening, and they did not like what they were hearing. The next year, 1867, lawmakers passed a series of laws in an attempt to circumscribe Johnson's ability to translate his rhetorical fury into governmental reality, or at least to limit the ways in which he might hinder their agenda until they could elect a new president in 1868.

A Reconstruction Act designed to bring about black suffrage and the ratification of the Fourteenth Amendment, for example, included provisions that empowered federal military officials to enforce the letter and spirit of the law.[54] An army bill required the president, though the commander in chief, to route all orders through General Ulysses S. Grant and provided that the Senate had to approve any presidential attempt to remove Grant from the chain of command.[55] (The language in this legislation had originated with Johnson's secretary of war, Edwin Stanton, who had been placed in the post by Lincoln and who had told a Republican congressman that he was "more concerned about the nation's fate than he had been during the Civil War.")[56] Finally, Congress passed the more wide-ranging Tenure of Office Act to ban the president from dismissing any official confirmed by the Senate without Senate approval.[57]

The constitutionality of the measures, particularly the last two, was questionable, but Congress was determined to take a bold stand against Johnson's indulgence of the white South. Johnson had vetoed the first and third acts; both vetoes were overridden. He signed the second bill—concerning military orders and General Grant—but argued that he believed it unconstitutional.[58]

Confusion and controversy followed upon confusion and controversy. The basic political truth of the moment was this: Republicans in Congress wanted Johnson gone and were desperately seeking a cause of action to remove him legislatively rather than waiting for the presidential election of 1868. It's a measure of the fevered nature of the time that they turned to impeachment so early on, in late 1866. Ohio representative James Ashley tried to persuade the Judiciary Committee that Johnson, whom Ashley described as a "loathing incubus which has blotted our country's history," had had a hand in Lincoln's murder.[59] (Secretary of the Navy Gideon Welles dismissed Ashley as "a calculating fanatic.")[60] The lead witness, the detective Lafayette Baker, also reported, without evidence, that a Washington prostitute named Lucy Cobb had told him that she had helped Johnson arrange the sale of pardons for old Confederates.[61]

The early hearings were a fiasco. "No facts, no charges, no malconduct are known or preferred," Welles wrote in his diary. "A more scandalous villainy never disgraced the country."[62] In June 1867, the Judiciary Committee voted against recommending impeachment; Johnson, the historian David O. Stewart wrote, "had dodged the impeachment bullet."[63]

Not for long. At Johnson's request, Attorney General Henry Stanbery curbed the powers of the military district commanders in the South, ruling that, contrary to congressional Reconstruction legislation, officers need not enforce federal laws designed to give blacks civil and political rights.[64] "Johnson's use of the attorney general's opinions was daring and provocative," Stewart wrote, "undermining the plain intent of Congress."[65] Congress struck back with a new Reconstruction Act that restored the powers Stanbery had taken away; Johnson unsuccessfully vetoed it.[66] But he never truly gave up, making liberal use of his patronage powers, from postmasterships to regional military commanders, to remove Republicans and install those with Southern sympathies.[67]

By mid-1867, meanwhile, Johnson had decided (accurately) that Stanton was more sympathetic to the Republicans in Congress than to his president. According to the terms of the Tenure of Office Act, he suspended Stanton and appointed Grant in Stanton's place until the Senate convened late in the year.

"The President has usurped the power of Congress on a colossal scale," Charles Sumner said in early 1867, "and he has employed these usurped powers in facilitating a rebel spirit and awakening anew the dying fires of the rebellion."[68] Sumner was thinking not only of the suspension of Stanton (which was, after all, within the letter of the Tenure of Office Act; according to the legislation, which to this point Johnson was following, the president had the right to suspend an official and then await the Senate's reaction once it was back in session) but of Johnson's consistent attempts to soften Congress's efforts at subduing and remaking the South.

The fate of the president—and of Reconstruction—would hinge on whether Sumner's complaint would meet the definition of an impeachable offense, in the view of the necessary number of members of Congress and of senators. To Grant's dismay, Johnson also removed Philip Sheridan and Daniel Sickles, two Union generals who, as military governors, were more in line with the congressional vision of Reconstruction than they were with the president's.[69] Grant, though he was now the acting secretary of war, protested Johnson's maneuvers, telling the president that the removals would be seen "as an effort to defeat the laws of Congress."[70]

Johnson did not care. The Stanton suspension enraged Republicans, who were already under electoral siege in off-year elections, and when they, still a strong majority, gathered in Washington in December, they again pressed forward with impeachment, casting the widest of nets to find something that would be a convincing high crime or misdemeanor. As Chief Justice William H. Rehnquist (appointed by Richard Nixon and elevated to chief by Ronald Reagan) wrote in a history of the Johnson saga, the Republicans, through the House Judiciary Committee for the second time, grasped for whatever was at hand as they assembled "a record of miscellaneous charges against the president," a collection of rumors and grievances that included "letters addressed to Jefferson Davis with the president's signature (although the witness who testified about them was never able to produce the letters), misuse of patronage, wrongful use of the pardon power . . . and even the possible complicity of Johnson in the assassination of Lincoln. . . . The committee also examined Johnson's private financial dealings and bank accounts."[71]

At first the renewed effort, unfolding in the closing months of 1867, seemed likely to end as the first impeachment foray had just a few months earlier. James Ashley was still on the scene, testifying about what Chief Justice Rehnquist characterized as "his theory that every vice-president who had succeeded to the presidency had played a part in bringing about the death of his predecessor. This theory, of course, included such unlikely conspirators as John Tyler, who had succeeded William Henry Harrison in 1841, and Millard Fillmore, who had succeeded Zachary Taylor in 1850."[72] Rehnquist's dry verdict: "Ashley was unable to supply any concrete evidence to support his theory, and apparently neither he nor his theory was taken seriously."[73]

But this time, impeachment was. The key distinction between the first effort and this one lay with rising Republican anxiety about Johnson's substantive obstruction on Reconstruction. Credit for the successful vote in the Judiciary Committee goes to

Representative John Churchill, Republican of New York, who changed his vote and gave the articles the necessary majority to pass out of committee to the floor. Churchill detailed his thinking in a letter to **The New York Times:** He had voted against the president because of "Johnson's statements denouncing Reconstruction, the attorney general's opinions limiting Reconstruction statutes, Johnson's veto of the Third Reconstruction Act (the one passed to overturn Stanbery's eviscerating rulings), the suspension of War Secretary Stanton, and the ouster of Generals Sheridan and Sickles."[74]

The impeachment drama moved from committee to the broader House. The majority argued that a president could be impeached even if no specific indictable crime had been committed, a complicated arena of constitutional contention. The minority report from the Judiciary Committee was explicit on this point, saying outright: "Political unfitness and incapacity must be tried at the ballot box, not in the high court of impeachment."[75]

So there it was, framed starkly and unmistakably: Should Congress—**could** Congress—remove a president for political and temperamental reasons, or was impeachment to be reserved for unambiguous violations of established law? (The Stanton removal was not yet the focus of the effort.) This was the question of "maladministration" James Madison and others had feared when impeachment first arose at the Constitutional Convention. Now, eight decades later, the fate of Andrew Johnson offered the country its first test case at the highest levels.

Congressman George Boutwell, Republican of Massachusetts, spoke in favor of impeachment as a weapon to be used even in the absence of a particular legal offense. Addressing the House, Boutwell retold the history of Johnson and Reconstruction, listing the president's repeated concessions to the white South to undermine the rule of law and subvert the will of the majority as manifested in the actions of Congress. "It may not be possible, by specific charge, to arraign him of this great crime [of attacking Reconstruction legislation]," Boutwell said, "but is he therefore to escape? . . . Will you hesitate to try and convict him . . . knowing . . . that in this way, and this way only, can you protect the State against the final consummation of his crime?"[76]

Representative James F. Wilson, Republican of Iowa, an impeachment opponent, answered Boutwell with the case for a stricter interpretation of the removal power. "If we cannot arraign the President for a specific crime," Wilson said, "for what are we to proceed against him? For a bundle of generalities such as we have here . . . ? If we cannot state upon paper a specific crime how are we to carry this case to the Senate for trial?"[77]

Wilson, not Boutwell, carried the day in the waning weeks of 1867. Not enough lawmakers were convinced that impeachment could be used generally rather than specifically, and Johnson was rescued in the full House by a vote of 108 to 57.[78] The future was a force here, too: Had Johnson been removed from office, the president pro tempore of the Senate, Ben Wade, a hardline Republican, would have become president, thus giving him and his wing of the party an advantage over the more moderate (but still anti-Johnson) Ulysses S. Grant in the 1868 election.[79] Such calculations—and they are perennial calculations—led a sufficient number of Republicans to, as Stewart wrote, think it "better to keep Andrew Johnson in the White House for fifteen more months."

Even facing the existential threat of removal from office—there had now been three attempts to impeach him—Johnson, who had ambitions to become the Democratic nominee for a term of his own in 1868, gave no quarter. In his 1867 annual message, sent to Congress amid the impeachment proceedings in the first week of December, the president spoke, somewhat obliquely, of renewed national violence. "How far the duty of the President 'to preserve, protect, and defend the Constitution' requires him to go in opposing an unconstitutional act of Congress is a very serious and important question, on which I have deliberated much and felt extremely anxious to reach a proper conclusion," Johnson wrote. Speaking of "civil war," he added: "If Congress should pass an act which is not only in palpable conflict with the Constitution, but will certainly, if carried out, produce immediate and irreparable injury to the organic structure of the Government, and if there be neither judicial remedy for the wrongs it inflicts nor power in the people to protect themselves without the official aid of their elected defender . . . in such a case the President must take the high responsibilities of his office and save the life of the nation at all hazards."[80]

At all hazards: hence the very real anxieties that war was once more imminent and Republican fears that presidential tyranny was at hand. Following up on his removal of Sheridan and Sickles, Johnson dismissed two more military governors. "It is a misnomer to call this question in the South a political question," one of the generals wrote of the removals. "It is War pure and simple."[81]

—

The action in Washington was hardly less pitched. In the first weeks of 1868, the Senate reconvened and voted to reinstate the suspended Edwin Stanton. Determined to keep Stanton out of the department, Johnson went to great lengths to preclude the returning secretary from physically taking possession of his old office.[82] The president thought he had secured Grant's promise to keep Stanton at bay, but Grant surrendered the office to Stanton, who savored his return. A furious Johnson believed Grant had betrayed him, and the president decided to strike out at Stanton yet again.

The means of Johnson's vengeance was a man whose name is almost entirely lost to history: Union general Lorenzo Thomas, whom the president appointed to replace Stanton even though, according to the Tenure of Office Act (which heretofore Johnson had actually followed), Stanton was now the rightfully restored secretary of war. Stanton and Thomas faced off against each other in the War Department, both men claiming that he, not the other, was the official in charge of the nation's defense.[83] Stanton had a warrant issued for Thomas's arrest, and constables took the general—who was worse for the wear after an evening of drinking in the capital—into custody in the early morning hours. Determined to hold on to his position, Stanton moved into his office.

But at last, at last, the Republicans believed that the Thomas maneuver gave them a specific offense with which to charge the president. In the middle weeks of February 1868, the House majority was so eager to move forward that it voted for impeachment before it had drawn up actual articles.[84] In a visit to the floor of the Senate, Representative Thaddeus Stevens of Pennsylvania solemnly reported the news. "We do impeach Andrew Johnson, President of the United States, of high crimes and misdemeanors in office."[85] The specifics, he said, would come "in due time."[86] A striking sign of the times: Johnson's foes were so anxious to force him from power that they had impeached without specifics.

They quickly returned to the legislative spadework. Back in the House, the Republicans drafted eleven articles of impeachment to be sent to the Senate.[87] The first ten made painfully detailed and often repetitive charges based on the Stanton drama; the articles can read as though the House was trying to convince itself of the gravity of an episode that did not truly rise to the impeachable. The eleventh drew together both the allegations about the Tenure of Office Act and Johnson's attacks on Congress. Included in the articles were a series of quotations from Johnson's 1866–67 tirades against Congress, evidence for the charge, it was said, that the president, "unmindful of the high duties of his high office and the dignity and proprieties thereof, and of the harmony and courtesies which ought to exist and be maintained between the executive and legislative branches of the Government of the United States . . . did attempt to bring into disgrace, ridicule, hatred, contempt and reproach, the Congress of the United States." His speeches, the House claimed, had been designed "to excite the odium and resentment of all good people of the United States against Congress" with "intemperate, inflammatory and scandalous harangues, and . . . loud threats and bitter menaces . . . amid the cries, jeers and laughter of the multitudes then assembled."

This language is revealing, for it illuminates the political, as opposed to the legal, nature of the Johnson impeachment, for in these articles Congress was explicitly objecting to the president's tone rather than his actions. The fact that Johnson had so thunderously attacked Congress was perhaps unsettling, but it was more difficult to see how it might be impeachable unless the Senate, in its trial for conviction, chose to interpret impeachment in the way George Boutwell had done in December—as a broad means of removing a president.

The legal specifics, meanwhile, remained problematic. Though the Thomas appointment was a plausible violation of the Tenure of Office Act (though the underlying law itself would be repealed in 1887 and was finally declared unconstitutional by the Supreme Court), it was a tenuous ground on which to remove a president. The reasonable course would have been for Congress to await a Supreme Court ruling on the act, but the high court could not render a decision until the end of the year, and lawmakers did not want to wait.[88] The only other route to engage the judiciary in determining whether the Tenure of Office Act was even constitutional lay in the Lorenzo Thomas matter—he was still facing a suit from Stanton—but Stanton urged an end to the proceeding, precluding the case from going to the courts. Johnson would be judged in Congress, sooner rather than later.

—

The trial that began on the floor of the United States Senate on Thursday, March 5, 1868, was fascinating spectacle. Chief Justice Salmon P. Chase presided; hyperbole prevailed. "No event in the civil history of the country had ever before occurred to arouse public antipathies and public indignation against any man," Senator Edmund G. Ross, Republican of Kansas, recalled in a memoir.[89] Washington was particularly chaotic. "Its streets and all its places of gathering had swarmed for many weeks with representatives of every State of the Union," Ross wrote, "demanding in a practically united voice the deposition of the President."

Ross also took note of an especially vivid moment.[90] Congressman Boutwell, who was serving as a House manager, or prosecutor, in Senate, "ventured, in the course of his argument, upon a flight of imagination in depicting the punishment that should be meted out to Mr. Johnson for venturing to differ with Congress upon the constitutionality of an act of that body," Ross recalled. As Boutwell put it, "Travelers and astronomers inform us that in the Southern heavens, near the Southern cross, there is a vast space which the uneducated call the 'hole in the sky,' where the eye of man, with the aid of the powers of the telescope, has been unable to discover nebulae, or asteroid, or comet, or planet, or star, or sun. In that dreary, cold, dark region of space . . . the great author of celestial mechanism has left the chaos which was in the beginning."

The most fitting fate for Johnson, Boutwell went on, would be his banishment to just this region of darkness—"there forever to exist in a solitude eternal as life or as the absence of life, emblematical of, if not really, that outer darkness of which the Savior of mankind spoke in warning those who are enemies to themselves and of their race and of God."

The House dispatched seven managers: Stevens, Boutwell, Wilson, Benjamin Butler, John Bingham, John Logan, and Thomas Williams. Johnson appointed five lawyers for his defense: Stanbery (who resigned as attorney general to defend the president), Benjamin Curtis, William Evarts, William Groesbeck, and Thomas Nelson. The president had talked of going to the well of the Senate himself but was convinced otherwise. "Gentlemen," Johnson said to his lawyers in a White House meeting the evening before the trial, "my case is in your hands. I feel sure you will protect my interests."[91]

As the ten-week trial unfolded, he followed things from his end of Pennsylvania Avenue. "Well," he would ask of his staff each day, "what are the signs of the zodiac today?"[92]

The president and his team were hard at work beyond the floor of the Senate.[93] Edmund Cooper, a Tennessee ally, as well as political allies known as the Astor House group and a collection of businessmen called the Whiskey Ring, all trafficked in cash, patronage, and other favors to try to win votes for Johnson. The trial alternated between noble rhetoric on the floor and backroom deals; it was a remarkable mélange of high politics and low dealings. It was difficult then—and nearly impossible now—to determine the precise role money and influence played, but the president and his men did all they could to secure support for acquittal.

Conviction required a two-thirds vote, which meant that seven Republican senators could save Johnson from removal. (Of the fifty-four senators, twelve were Democrats and would all vote for the president.) The debate in the trial was by now familiar: pro-impeachment lawmakers argued that the president was a threat to the nation in his Reconstruction policies, the removal of Stanton, and his attacks on Congress, while anti-impeachment voices pressed the point that Johnson, however controversial and however out of sync with the majorities of Congress, had not in fact committed a convictable offense.

Speaking for the president, William Evarts (a future secretary of state under Rutherford B. Hayes) summarized the defense. "The Tenure of Office Act was unconstitutional," the historian Gene Smith wrote in characterizing Evarts's remarks. "The Congress had assigned to itself rights that it did not have under the Constitution. The President's sworn duty by the oath he took three hours after Lincoln's death forbade him to accept the Tenure of Office Act. As for the charge that he had defamed Congress . . . he stood on his rights of free speech, guaranteed by the Constitution."[94]

Rising for the prosecution, Benjamin Butler spared the president nothing. "By murder most foul he succeeded to the Presidency, and is the elect of an assassin to that high office!" Butler declared.[95] The House believed—or at least said it did—that Johnson had violated the Tenure of Office Act, but Butler argued that the senators had an even higher obligation under the circumstances: The president, in his view, was deleterious to the country and had to be removed. "Bound by no law," Butler told the Senate, "you are a

law unto yourselves, bound only by the natural principle of equity and justice." It was the broadest of
views of the power of the Senate in determining the
fate of a president, a call to vote less on the details of
the articles than on the more general question of the
president's fitness.

Outside of the Southern states, public opinion appeared to favor the president's removal by unmistakable margins. In an interview with the **New-York
Tribune,** General Grant, who worried that Johnson
was prone to usurpations of power that could extend
to using military force to pursue his policies and perhaps even to maintain himself in office, made his own
views clear. "He feels national security demands the
removal of the President. . . . When the General of
our armies entertains this conviction, there is no
room for doubt as to the duty of the Senate."[96] According to the historian Eric McKitrick, "There was a
deep psychological need to eliminate Johnson from
American political life forever, and it was principally
Johnson himself who had created it."[97] Joseph Me-
dill, the Republican publisher of the **Chicago Tribune,** wrote that "Like an aching tooth, everyone is
impatient to have the old villain out."[98]

The public pressure, however, did not change a reality on the floor of the Senate: The president's lawyers were having the better of the constitutional
arguments. "The [House] managers were overmas-
tered throughout in learning and ability," **The Nation** reported.[99]

As the trial neared its climax, the rhetoric remained unchanged from the early stages of the drama: Both sides claimed to hold the high ground. The matter was ending as it had begun. Stanbery, the former attorney general, closed Johnson's defense with a frank appeal to the raw power of the populace and to the hero who had first held the presidential office. "Yes, Senators, with all his faults, the President has been more sinned against than sinning," Stanbery said. "Fear not, then, to acquit him. The Constitution of the country is as safe in his hands from violence as it was in the hands of Washington. But if, Senators, you condemn him, if you strip him of the robes of office, if you degrade him to the utmost stretch of your power, mark prophecy: the strong arms of the people will be about him. They will find a way to raise him from any depths to which you may consign him, and we shall live to see him redeemed and to hear the majestic voice of the people: 'Well done, faithful servant; you shall have your reward!' "[100]

Answering Stanbery on behalf of the House managers, John Bingham of Ohio evoked the carnage of the Civil War, arguing Johnson had disgraced those who had died for the Union. "I ask you to consider that we stand this day pleading for the violated majesty of the law, by the graves of half a million of martyred hero-patriots who made death beautiful by the sacrifice of themselves for their country, the Constitution, and the laws," Bingham told the Senate, "and who, by their sublime example, have taught us that all must obey the law; that none are above the law."[101] His final cry: "Before man and God, he is guilty!"[102]

But was he guilty of an impeachable offense that justified conviction and removal from office? Everything hung on how two-thirds of the fifty-four senators chose to answer that question. A narrow view would likely lead to acquittal; a broad one to conviction. Edmund Ross of Kansas was one of the swing votes. "Well, Sprague," Ross had said to Senator William Sprague of Rhode Island when the matter came over from the House, "the thing is here; and, so far as I am concerned, though a Republican and opposed to Mr. Johnson and his policy, he shall have as fair a trial as an accused man ever had on this earth."[103]

As Ross saw it, the presidency was in the dock quite as much as Johnson was. He later recalled:

In a large sense, the independence of the executive office as a coordinate branch of the government was on trial. If the President must step down a disgraced man and a political outcast upon insufficient proofs and from partisan considerations, the office of President would be degraded, cease to be a coordinate branch of the government, and ever after subordinated to the legislative will. It would practically have revolutionized our splendid political fabric into a partisan Congressional autocracy. This government had never faced so insidious a danger control by the worst element of American politics. If Andrew Johnson were acquitted by a nonpartisan vote America would pass the danger point of partisan rule and that intolerance which so often characterizes the sway of great majorities and makes them dangerous.[104]

Seven Republicans chose to break ranks and vote "Not guilty" when called upon to convict the president, ensuring Johnson's survival in office for the remaining months of his term.[105] "Well, thank God, Mr. President," one of his lawyers, Thomas Nelson, told Johnson, "you are free again."[106] Johnson was pleased and celebrated his acquittal with what a contemporary described as "much whiskey drinking and jollification."[107]

It had been a narrow thing, with Ross himself casting the decisive ballot. Johnson had performed well during the trial, uncharacteristically remaining quiet, announcing that he would appoint an acceptable alternative, General John Schofield, to serve as Stanton's successor rather than Lorenzo Thomas, and most likely countenancing the spending of money and the promising of appointments.[108] In private moments, he promised wavering senators that he had "no thought of wrong or rash doings" if acquitted.[109]

The larger political atmosphere was also a key factor: Republicans were about to nominate Grant for president in 1868 (that would become official on May 24, the week after the May 16 Senate vote), and Johnson was to lose the Democratic nomination in July to Horatio Seymour. (The president was frustrated by the Democratic decision. "They profess to accept my measures: they say I have stood by the Constitution and made a noble struggle," Johnson remarked, but his White House years were ending.)[110]

For our purposes the essential lesson of the Johnson impeachment is how political passion and national division found expression in the attempt to remove a president while his term was still unfolding. In the articles the House sent to the Senate, Eric Foner wrote, "Nowhere were the real reasons Republicans wanted to dispose of Johnson mentioned—his political outlook, the way he had administered the Reconstruction Acts, and his sheer incompetence. In a Parliamentary system, Johnson would have long since departed, for nearly all Republicans by now agreed with Supreme Court justice David Davis, who described the President as 'obstinate, self-willed, combative,' and totally unfit for his office. But these, apparently, were not impeachable offenses."[111]

Taken all in all, the Johnson case suggested that impeachment could be undertaken for reasons of political conflict but would be pursued only along more technical grounds. It was as though the House had permission to act emotionally while the Senate would be expected to act rationally, giving future generations of presidents and lawmakers an impeachment precedent that was more daunting than inviting.

—

Things could very easily have been different. The successful removal of Johnson on the grounds available would have likely weakened the presidential office and enshrined congressional supremacy for a significant time to come. It would also have elevated a Republican, Ben Wade, to the office, and Wade was committed to the cause of using the federal government to pursue equality—the cause that was the true force behind the impeachment of the president.

To Edmund Ross, the tool of impeachment was "a two-edged sword, which must be handled with consummate judgment and skill."[112] To decline to use the weapon in the event of presidential lawbreaking would destroy the primacy of the rule of law. To deploy it in times of great political passion but without a clear violation of law, however, risked (and risks) pushing the American system in a parliamentary direction—a development that might have its virtues but which would be a definitive break from the original intent and the organic evolution of the constitutional order. For better or for worse, the framers intended America's to be a popular, not a legislative, government. The voters acting through the electoral process, not lawmakers in parliamentary setting, were to determine the occupant of the presidency.

As with so much else in American life and politics, this can be frustrating, infuriating, even maddening. In my view, Andrew Johnson's presidency marks the lowest of moments in our history. An unabashed white supremacist, he opposed the great work of more fully realizing the nation's fundamental premise: the assertion, if not always the realization, of human equality. Yet the broader national experiment endured, albeit tragically.

Andrew Johnson was no friend of what his predecessor had called "the better angels of our nature." Should he therefore have been impeached and removed from office? The verdict in his own time was no—the decision to push him from the presidential chair should, Congress decided, lie with the voters rather than with lawmakers. "This country is going to the devil!" Thaddeus Stevens grumbled when Johnson was acquitted. Perhaps. But such was the tragic nature of life in a fallen world—a world that will never be perfect, but which staggers forward, its ultimate fate in the hands not of the few, but of the many.

RICHARD NIXON
Timothy Naftali

It was Saturday, October 20, 1973, and President Richard Nixon had just fired the Watergate special prosecutor Archibald Cox. In a dramatic flexing of executive muscle, Nixon also ordered the Federal Bureau of Investigation, a part of the Justice Department, to seal the office of the Watergate Special Prosecution Force.

"We can't do that," said FBI agent Angelo Lano when FBI brass relayed the order at about 8:00 P.M. from the White House. For sixteen months, Lano had been heading up the Bureau's investigation of the break-in at the Democratic National Committee headquarters in the Watergate office complex. After Cox's appointment in May 1973, the FBI had also been assisting the Watergate prosecutor. Lano and his team of investigators had already concluded that President Nixon was implicated in a cover-up. "That man's going to jail," Lano told his boss. "You don't want to do this."[1]

But Lano and a second FBI special agent dutifully went over to the special prosecutor's headquarters.

"Traitor!" the lawyers who were still working in the office yelled at Lano.

"Look, I don't want to be here," replied the embarrassed FBI agent. "Do me a favor, lock your doors, lock the safes, just close everything up. We'll mind our business. . . . And if you continue working, fine, but don't take anything out tonight." Lano had no desire to get the FBI mixed up in what was clearly an effort by Nixon to obstruct the prosecutor's valid criminal investigation.

The FBI takeover was televised to a shocked nation. In Texas, a former prosecutor from World War II and the future Watergate special prosecutor, Leon Jaworski, thought he was viewing a newsreel from Nazi Germany.[2]

"Everybody in the world was angry," recalled Lano, who never believed he or the FBI should have been ordered to stop the independent investigation of a president.[3]

—

The impeachment of Richard Nixon doesn't begin with a break-in; it begins with a reckless and very public abuse of executive power on a Saturday night in October 1973. Since May 1973, Archibald Cox and the Watergate Special Prosecution Force had been investigating illegal activity by the Nixon administration, most notably links between the president's reelection campaign and the Watergate break-in in June 1972. In July 1973, Cox learned that Nixon had been secretly recording conversations in the White House since 1971. He sought the tapes for the evidence they might hold, and in doing so he posed a mortal threat to the Nixon presidency. The president knew better than almost anyone in his White House that his political future depended on no law enforcement official getting access to his White House recordings.

As Cox waged an increasingly successful court battle over access to ten recorded conversations, Nixon began scheming how to get rid of him before the issue reached the U.S. Supreme Court, where Nixon thought he might lose. "I'm going to clear the decks," an enraged president vowed to his top aides.[4] These aides, especially his chief of staff, Alexander M. Haig, Jr., had repeatedly talked Nixon off this political ledge. By October 20, after the White House floated a "compromise" that would involve giving the special prosecutor edited transcripts to be verified by an elderly Southern Democratic senator, John Stennis, which Cox refused, even Haig believed there was enough political cover to proceed—Cox's firing would now be a consequence of his own intransigence rather than Nixon's obstinacy and obstruction. Nixon ordered Attorney General Elliot Richardson to fire Cox and close the Watergate probe.[5]

The drama of what ensued—a series of events that became known as the Saturday Night Massacre—magnified Nixon's political miscalculation. Neither the attorney general nor the deputy attorney general, William Ruckelshaus, would fire Cox. Instead each resigned, arguing the special prosecutor had done nothing to warrant his removal. The third man in the hierarchy at Justice, Solicitor General Robert Bork, who was now acting attorney general, agreed to fire Cox. Then Nixon poured more fuel on the fire. Through Haig he ordered Bork to send the FBI to seal the offices of Cox's team and of Richardson and Ruckelshaus.

With that, Nixon pushed America across a psychological line. Until the night of October 20, the American political class and the country's media elite, let alone most Americans, were not seriously considering impeachment, despite living for more than sixteen months with the Watergate scandal. Since the summer of 1972 the public had learned about corrupt activities on the part of Nixon's lieutenants—a dirty tricks campaign involving a young Roger Stone, the hiring of private detectives to dig up dirt on Senator Edward Kennedy, a program of wiretapping White House aides and newsmen, an "Enemies List" of political adversaries to be targeted by the Internal Revenue Service, and a domestic covert operations team ("the Plumbers") that had broken into the office of the psychiatrist of Daniel Ellsberg, the country's most celebrated whistle-blower. All of this was dismaying, but with the exception of testimony by one White House insider—former White House counsel John W. Dean—there was no publicly available evidence linking Richard Nixon himself to what former attorney general John Mitchell called "the White House Horrors."

With the lone exception of liberal congressman Rev. Robert Drinan, a Jesuit priest from Massachusetts, Democrats had stayed away from advocating the impeachment of Nixon for the scandals swirling around his administration, despite controlling both houses of Congress and generally detesting the man. Senator Kennedy reflected the thinking of many in the congressional leadership when he told his sister privately that "a known quantity was better than an unknown." Even with the changed political climate, Kennedy was "a bit skeptical of the will of some of his colleagues."[6] Nearly twenty years earlier another Massachusetts senator, his brother and future president, John F. Kennedy, had described the impeachment of Andrew Johnson as "a reckless abuse of legislative power."[7] That impeachment was a discredited constitutional remedy had remained the prevailing view ever since.

The Saturday Night Massacre, which was inescapably Nixon's doing, awoke presidential impeachment from a century-long slumber. In the week following the firing of Cox, twenty impeachment resolutions were introduced in Congress.[8] For the first time, the Nixon administration requested a congressional head count of those for and against impeachment.[9]

Nevertheless, despite the bombshells of October 1973, the impeachment of Richard Nixon was anything but inevitable. There was no one alive who had witnessed its use against an American president. There were few experts in academia, and there wasn't a single federal legislator who had a clue how to go about it. The public had its own deep doubts. Although support for Nixon's removal from office had doubled from 19 to 38 percent in the wake of Cox's firing, a 51 percent majority simply opposed impeachment.[10] It was little known and, in some cases, feared by Americans. Some Alabamans, for example, were convinced that the process meant the loser of the previous election, Senator George McGovern of South Dakota, would become president.[11] To understand how a forgotten and suspect constitutional remedy ultimately beat the odds, we must start by looking at how Richard Nixon unintentionally revived the beast.

—

Why did President Nixon risk so much to keep his tapes hidden? Because he was part of a conspiracy he needed to hide. Nixon was in Key Biscayne, Florida, when he learned that five men working for his reelection committee had been caught early on the morning of Saturday, June 17, 1972, fixing listening devices they had already planted in the headquarters of the Democratic National Committee at the Watergate. At that moment the president had a historic decision to make: He could turn in his men for breaking the law, or he could obstruct justice by trying to cover it up.

When Nixon returned to Washington, D.C., on

Tuesday, June 20, he discussed the Watergate business with his chief of staff, H. Robbins "Bob" Haldeman. Haldeman and Nixon had weathered many political storms together. Back in 1971, Nixon had made plain to Haldeman his desire for both wiretapping for domestic political intelligence and a dirty tricks campaign linked to his reelection bid in 1972.[12]

The polls at the time showed the president barely more popular than his likely Democratic challenger, Senator Edmund Muskie of Maine. Later that year Haldeman had conferred with the president's designated reelection campaign manager, Attorney General John Mitchell, on selecting G. Gordon Liddy to run the espionage operation. Haldeman and Nixon knew Liddy and his operations chief, E. Howard Hunt, from the activities of the Plumbers in 1971. Haldeman was informed when Mitchell approved Liddy's program of spying and bugging but left the operational details to the Committee to Re-Elect the President, officially abbreviated as CRP but known by some as CREEP. Haldeman did insist in April 1972, however, that the program shift its focus from Muskie to the more likely Democratic nominee, George McGovern.[13]

At their first meeting on June 20, Nixon and Haldeman spent roughly eighteen and a half minutes discussing Watergate. Nixon did not order an investigation of how Mitchell, his former law partner, had messed up. Instead he went straight into damage control. Three days later, on June 23, the cover-up met its first challenge. The FBI, which had jurisdiction over investigating the Watergate break-in because it involved wiretapping, a federal crime, had found uncashed checks in the burglars' hotel room, and these would connect the crime to the Committee to Re-Elect the President. In a conversation that day which would later be known as "the smoking gun," Nixon ordered Haldeman to get the CIA to lie to the FBI, saying this was some kind of hush-hush national security matter, with the goal of getting the FBI to stop this politically dangerous avenue of investigation.[14]

The challenges of containing the damage quickly increased, ballooning into payments to the burglars' families to stay quiet—payments made by Nixon's personal lawyer, Herbert Kalmbach—and coaching administration members in lying to FBI investigators.

On September 15, 1972, a grand jury returned indictments against the five burglars as well as Hunt and Liddy for "conspiracy, burglary and violation of the federal laws against electronic interception of oral communications." Since no one in the reelection committee or the White House was also indicted, Nixon's cover-up seemed to be airtight.[15]

Meanwhile, the president, who believed that the best defense was offense, went on the offensive. A year earlier, on June 23, 1971, Nixon had ordered Haldeman to create a "tax list" of his political enemies for harassment by the IRS. When the DNC had launched a civil suit against the Committee to Re-Elect the President, Nixon wanted to go after the chairman of the DNC,

Lawrence F. O'Brien, whom he suspected of underre-porting lobbying income. As Nixon reminded Dean and Haldeman in a conversation on September 15, 1972, following the indictments—a recording that would later loom large in the impeachment in-quiry—he expected the IRS to be used as a weapon against his political enemies.[16]

Throughout the fall of 1972, as Nixon continued to maintain a huge lead in polls over Democratic nomi-nee George McGovern, two young reporters at **The Washington Post,** Bob Woodward and Carl Bern-stein, pushed hard to investigate possible links be-tween CRP, the White House, and the Liddy-Hunt operation. The Nixon White House denied all of it.

The Watergate scandal had no perceptible effect on the presidential election, which Nixon won in a land-slide. The cover-up, however, soon came under severe strain. As the trial of the seven indicted for involve-ment in the Watergate bugging operation began in January 1973, Judge John Sirica, a lifelong Republi-can who had been appointed to the D.C. bench by Dwight D. Eisenhower, smelled something foul. "Somebody's lying in my courtroom," he bellowed at his clerk D. Todd Christofferson.[17] Christofferson agreed, but neither could determine who from the CRP was the liar.

Even after the seven men were found guilty, Sirica refused to give up on the case. At the end of January, he handed down long sentences, hoping the men might talk. Nixon reacted by signaling through aides that there would be pardons in the future for the loyal. Meanwhile, Haldeman made leftover campaign funds available to feed the ever-greedier cover-up machine. In March, the first major crack appeared when one of the burglars, a CIA veteran, sent a letter to Sirica admitting that "there was political pressure applied to the defendants to plead guilty and remain silent."[18]

As the burglars' demands for cash and clemency grew, the president's point person for containment, White House counsel John Dean, approached Nixon on March 21, 1973, to warn that the cover-up was metastasizing as "a cancer on the presidency." Keeping Hunt and the burglars quiet was going to cost even more money, maybe as much as $1 million. To Dean's surprise,, the president didn't flinch at the number. Instead, he discussed how to raise the cash with his secretary, Rose Mary Woods. The next day, at a meeting with Dean, Haldeman, and Mitchell, he assured Mitchell that the goal was still "containment" and that he wanted everyone to "stonewall" the investigators.

On April 30, Nixon forced his chief of staff Haldeman and his domestic affairs adviser John Ehrlichman to resign, and he fired Dean over the Watergate scandal. With federal prosecutors getting closer to learning his role in the cover-up, John Dean sought immunity. In May, the Senate Watergate Committee began hearings, and Dean was granted immunity to testify. His highly detailed testimony riveted the nation. For the first time, one of the president's men placed him in the cover-up.

Had the major revelations stopped there, the story of Watergate would have been Nixon's word against Dean's, with the Nixon presidency likely surviving because enough Americans would have given their president the benefit of the doubt. Up to this point, Nixon's participation in "containment" payments and ties to the break-in in the first place remained behind closed White House doors. But there was another bombshell about to drop. White House staff secretary Alexander Butterfield revealed to the Senate in July that Nixon had a taping system. Apparently the president had recorded the key conversations that Dean had testified about. Indeed, he'd had a White House recording system installed in February 1971 and had been taping most of his conversations ever since.

Richard Nixon was not the first president to bug his own White House. John F. Kennedy and Lyndon Johnson had installed machines in some of the same places, but theirs had on/off switches, whereas Nixon's system was sound activated due to his inability to operate equipment. It had picked up almost everything he and his inner circle had said to one another in the White House—the good, the bad, and the ugly. And the ugly was criminal. It would be up to Archibald Cox, the recently appointed Watergate special prosecutor, to get those tapes.

Nixon never liked Cox, who had worked for

John F. Kennedy and attended Harvard, two of Nixon's top triggers. He also knew that Cox was a threat
to the cover-up. Cox would head the third investigation of the Watergate scandal, joining those conducted by the Senate and the assistant U.S. attorney
in D.C. working with the FBI. Of the three, Nixon
feared Cox' s investigation the most because of its
independence. For months the president fumed over
Cox's appointment, looking for the right moment to
get rid of him. In his obsession with Cox, Nixon never
imagined that removing him would prompt the
one major player in Washington not already investigating Watergate—the House of Representatives—
to take a serious interest.

—

In the wake of the Saturday Night Massacre, Democratic leaders in the House made two important decisions. The first was to pursue impeachment hearings,
which only now in retrospect seems inevitable. For
months, even before Cox's firing, pressure had been
building on the Speaker of the House Carl Albert and
House Majority Leader Thomas P. "Tip" O'Neill to
gear up for impeachment proceedings. For a number
of liberal Democrats, the Senate Watergate hearings
had produced more than enough evidence of a sleazy
administration to warrant impeachment. Albert and
O'Neill apparently disagreed, and until October 23,
1973, had found ways to keep the dogs of impeachment well leashed. But now that the public had so
decidedly turned against Nixon that even Republicans

were calling for a constitutional inquiry, Albert and O'Neill decided to start the process. The second decision involved giving the House Judiciary Committee, made up of twenty-one Democrats and seventeen Republicans, the responsibility for leading this effort, by shaping any articles of impeachment and deciding whether to bring them to the floor of the full House.

The House Judiciary Committee had initially served this function in 1868, so there was an argument to follow precedent.[19] But due to a shocking primary upset in Brooklyn in 1972 (won by the thirty-one-year-old Elizabeth Holtzman) that knocked out the venerable Judiciary Committee chair Emanuel Celler, the new chairman was an untested and undistinguished machine politician from Newark named Peter Rodino. Fellow Democrats had so little regard for Rodino that several lobbied to form a special committee to manage impeachment and put it all under someone else.[20]

It was easy to underestimate this man. In the words of Francis O'Brien, his chief of staff from August 1973 through the impeachment summer, the soft-spoken, bantam-sized Rodino "was not a forceful figure." Yet, he was territorial and insisted that impeachment go through the Judiciary Committee. For all his quiet resolve, Rodino would not have gotten the historic role that allowed him to transform his reputation had it not been for a strong, forceful patron: Tip O'Neill told everyone, "Peter is the perfect man for the job."[21]

Once Rodino had O'Neill's blessing to start the inquiry, he decided to pull an end run around the hardcore pro-impeachment faction of liberal Democrats on the Judiciary Committee. From the start, Rodino had a clear view of how to pull off a successful impeachment. The ghost of Andrew Johnson weighed heavily on him and the other Democratic leaders: Impeachment had a reputation as a tool of the disreputable partisan. Rodino saw the liberal impeachers as likely to drive Congress into a partisan prosecution of the president that would not only divide the nation but likely fail, as in 1868, to persuade two-thirds of the Senate, thanks to Nixon's support among Southern Democrats.

The end run involved displacing the committee's partisan majority counsel Jerome Zeifman, a favorite of the hard-line impeachers. Rodino told his young chief of staff Francis O'Brien that he wanted instead to hire a general counsel specifically for the inquiry that the Judiciary Committee would oversee. "This person should not be partisan. This person should be of high intellectual standing and should be honorable." Rodino said finding a registered Republican "would be the best of all worlds."[22]

O'Brien called law school deans from Harvard to Ohio State to Berkeley, looking for a choice everyone could support. "There were a lot of names, but there was no consensus," he found.[23] In a world before the Web, research was a time-consuming undertaking. In early November, Rodino's best friend reached out to

Albert Jenner, Jr., a fabled Chicago trial lawyer who had served in the staff of the Warren Commission in 1964, but Jenner did not want to leave his law practice. When he fell through, O'Brien was out of leads.[24]

Meanwhile, the pro-impeachment group, led by Texas Democrat Jack Brooks, operated as though they were in charge, even hiring Richard Cates, a Democratic state legislator in Wisconsin, to begin the inquiry, a move that infuriated Rodino. Rodino knew little about what Cates was doing, but he knew about Cates's supporters on his committee. "For them the case was closed," O'Brien recalled, "and that was a real problem."

As Rodino was wresting control of his own impeachment inquiry from the radical impeachers on the Judiciary Committee, the White House was struggling to avoid impeachment altogether. Dismayed by the national reaction to the Saturday Night Massacre, Haig asked for a quick sounding of congressional opinion from William Timmons, the president's assistant for legislative affairs. Timmons reported on Monday, October 22, 1973, that "loyal friends are still with the president, opponents are for impeachment, and the 'swing' voters are undecided at this point trying to feel the public pulse and anticipate the next action."[25] Although he assured Haig that "there is not sufficient support in the House to impeach the President or in the Senate to convict him," he said the margin for survival was narrow in the Senate, where at best Nixon could count on the support of only forty senators, mainly Republicans with some Southern Democrats. The House was Nixon's better bet. Best of all would be to stop the process in the House Judiciary Committee.

In the immediate aftermath of Cox's firing, Nixon and his team decided not to risk more erosion of public and congressional support. Haig had Bork remove all of the FBI agents guarding the offices of the special prosecutor, the attorney general, and the deputy attorney general. Bork himself went before Cox's former team and promised that they would all keep their jobs. The bigger surprises came when the White House announced that it would be hiring a replacement for Cox (ultimately it would be Texas Democrat Leon Jaworski), and that meanwhile it would hand over tapes of conversations that Cox had subpoenaed to the Sirica court, which was weighing indicting White House officials for obstruction of justice, perjury, and conspiracy, the two issues that had led to the Saturday Night Massacre.

This effort at transparency produced a new fiasco for the White House. Nixon's lawyers revealed to the court that on one of the tapes—of a conversation from June 20, 1972—there was an eighteen-and-a-half-minute gap; they claimed that two of the other subpoenaed conversations didn't exist at all. Even Bork, who had not heard any of these recordings, began to wonder whether Nixon was, indeed, guilty of something.[26]

Back in the House Judiciary Committee, as O'Brien

searched for a general counsel, Rodino found that he had enemies looking to break him before he could even start the impeachment inquiry. In late October or early November, journalist Jerry Landauer of **The Wall Street Journal** came to him with rumors that Rodino was under investigation by the Justice Department for being part of the Jersey mob.[27] Tip O'Neill suspected he knew who was to blame: the White House.[28] Though the rumors ultimately came to nothing, they worried Rodino and signaled to him and O'Brien just how aggressively the Nixon White House intended to fight impeachment.

O'Brien finally found Rodino's man in John Doar, a registered Republican who had been hired by Dwight Eisenhower to work in the Justice Department and stayed on to work for the Kennedys.[29] As a member of the civil rights division of the Justice Department, Doar had been a quiet, diligent, and courageous force for change in the South throughout the 1960s. His method was to amass oceans of data to force reluctant judges and juries to help the federal government dismantle the South's racial caste system. In 1967, he had successfully overseen the trial of the Klansmen accused of killing three civil rights workers in Philadelphia, Mississippi, in 1964.[30]

Rodino envisioned a process that would be as nonpartisan as possible, and told Doar he would have free rein to hire an impeachment inquiry staff. "We're going to be different," he explained. "We're not going to have a counsel to the Republicans.

We're not going to have a counsel to the Democrats. We're not going to have two different staffs working. We're going to have one staff and it's going to be integrated by everybody."[31]

Rodino announced his choice on December 21, 1973, and a few days later, at the urging of two Republican congressmen on the committee, Thomas Railsback and Wiley Mayne, Albert Jenner agreed to join Doar as his associate general counsel. In the spirit of Rodino's nonpartisan inquiry, Doar and Jenner jointly agreed that their staff would be hired as "a single law office with no real minority." All did not go perfectly for Doar, however. Just as he accepted the post, he learned about Dick Cates, who had already been hired for the impeachment probe. Since he hadn't recruited Cates, Doar wanted him fired. Rodino and O'Brien managed to persuade Doar to let him stay. They had to give a crumb to the hardcore pro-impeachment Democrats.[32]

Doar wasted little time in hiring his staff. Briefing the entire committee for the first time in early January 1974, he said he was hiring "some new lawyers." He would ultimately hire one hundred people, many of whom were lawyers.[33] He also wasted no time in trying to assemble the materials that his team would need. He went to the Senate Watergate Committee, which gave him full cooperation and eighteen boxes of materials.[34] Watergate special prosecutor Leon Jaworski, however, turned out to be less helpful, at least in the beginning.

—

The Constitution does not set out how the House is supposed to investigate a president at risk of impeachment, nor what power it has to get whatever information it feels necessary for the task. As Doar assembled his team to start the inquiry, two powerful men in Washington, from the other two branches of government, believed they already possessed sufficient information to impeach the president, but the question was, what could they—or must they—share with the branch that actually had the power to impeach?

In the second week of December 1973, Judge Sirica, who was presiding over the Watergate grand jury, and his law clerk D. Todd Christofferson, donned headphones for the first time and started listening to the White House tapes that Cox had subpoenaed and then lost his job over. On Monday, December 10, they reached the recording of the March 21, 1973, conversation between the president and John Dean, where Dean discussed the continuing cover-up as "a cancer on the presidency." It shocked them. Here was Nixon hearing about the cover-up and being told that for it to continue a million dollars in additional hush money needed to be found. Instead of throwing Dean out of the office, Nixon calmly discussed how to get it.

"Todd and I left the courthouse that evening tired and dispirited," Sirica later wrote. "I remembered Nixon saying earlier in the fall, 'I am not a crook.' Well, I felt we did have a dishonest man in the White

House, a president who had violated the law, who had conspired to obstruct the very laws he was sworn to uphold. It was a frightening thing to know."[35] After hearing the tape, the judge and his clerk concluded impeachment was "very possible."[36]

A few days later, after Sirica had deemed the conversation relevant to the Watergate investigation, the March 21 conversation was sent over to the Watergate Special Prosecution Force. Leon Jaworski reached the same conclusion as Sirica. Richard Nixon had engaged in obstruction of justice. "I had not come to Washington expecting this," Jaworski later wrote.[37]

Were Nixon an ordinary citizen, he would not only be indicted but likely convicted of a felony. But Jaworski—unlike his staff—did not believe that a sitting president, however guilty, could be indicted for obstruction of justice.[38] That the House had already started an impeachment inquiry made indicting the president even less justifiable to Jaworski. A president under these circumstances either resigned or was impeached and removed after a trial in the Senate. Jaworski, who wanted to get back to Texas as soon as he could, hoped Nixon would resign.[39] On December 21, he went to visit Haig to let him know about the tape. "I'm afraid the President engaged in criminal conduct," he told Haig. Haig brushed him off, saying that the White House had its own transcript of that conversation, and Nixon's White House lawyers were sure that it did not incriminate him. Jaworski suggested Nixon hire the best criminal lawyer in the country.[40]

Jaworski thought resignation would be a neater solution to the problem of a criminal president, because he was convinced that the Federal Rules of Criminal Procedure prevented him from formally sharing with Congress what he knew from the grand jury. Judge Sirica observed the absurdity of the situation: "As far as I could see, Jaworski had the evidence, but not the power to do much about the president. The [Judiciary] committee, and Congress, did have ultimate power, but in early 1974, they lacked the evidence."[41] Within the Watergate Special Prosecution Force, a debate arose over how to give Doar, for the sake of Congress, the March 21 tape. Jaworski's deputy, Henry Ruth, who had worked with Doar in the Justice Department, believed that the tape alone could impeach Nixon, forestalling an expensive and divisive inquiry.

In January 1974, Jaworski and Ruth informally briefed Doar as much as they felt they could. Ruth apparently went further, giving Doar details of the Nixon-Dean conversation without actually showing him a transcript. The Watergate prosecutors were energetically and creatively pushing Doar to use Rodino's authority to force Sirica and the grand jury to hand over the transcript. One of the younger committee staff who baby-sat Doar's son made use of the opportunity to urge the adolescent, "Tell your father to subpoena the March 21 tape."[42]

Doar resented the pressure and disagreed with how Ruth and the younger prosecutors understood the impeachment process. After dinner at Ruth's home one night in January, Doar outlined their disagreement.

> There are really two theories of this case. The first . . . the young, Harvard law school eastern liberal theory is that in order to impeach a President, you have to show that he is guilty of criminal conduct (Watergate). . . . The other theory . . . is that you first look at the totality of the President's conduct over an extended period of time to see whether or not there has been a pattern of improper conduct by key Presidential appointees acting for the Presidency. And second, that in some instances, the standard of Presidential responsibility depends on the seriousness or enormity of the threat to our institutions.[43]

Doar, who had fought the caste system in the South by looking for a pattern of institutional racism, was more at ease with the second theory. "I thought that the country shouldn't be left with making a decision about impeaching a president on the conduct of the president on one day. I thought that was . . . not going to help the country get over this, and so we tried to pull everything together of the president's conduct over a period of time."[44]

—

Doar likened the House inquiry to a grand jury in that it would take its information in secret and then decide whether or not to indict Richard Nixon.

Under the Constitution, the Senate would be the place for the trial. Doar believed the Judiciary Committee's fact-finding mission should not be adversarial and sold Rodino on the concept that the inquiry would be driven by the committee staff, which would then provide the members with all of the data. Neither Doar nor the committee staff would make any recommendations, leaving the decision of whether to impeach to the members themselves. Keeping with this approach, Rodino and Doar decided that what the staff collected would be described as "information," not evidence.

Behind this vision was some hard political strategy. Regardless of what the evidence showed, neither Rodino nor Doar wanted the process to fail as in 1868. This was not to be a partisan impeachment. If the members approved an article of impeachment, it needed to have a chance of being accepted by the entire House and then the Senate. This could happen only with broad bipartisan support, starting in the Judiciary Committee, itself. Effective bipartisanship would require sensitivity by Rodino and Doar to the concerns of Republican members and to those Democrats in very pro-Nixon districts.[45]

—

By late January 1974, Bryce Harlow, a White House counselor who had been advising Republican presidents since 1953 and was widely respected on both sides of the aisle, thought that the Nixon presidency was an impending train wreck. Harlow did not believe that impeachment was inevitable—Nixon had just hired the celebrated trial lawyer James St. Clair of Boston to lead his defense—but for the presidency to survive, there had to be an immediate course correction.

The biggest problem was that the president himself was disengaged. "Nixon was almost incommunicado," Harlow later recalled.[46] The second serious problem was that what little direction Nixon had given his lieutenants was wrongheaded. "Our present stance," Harlow noted, "is to 'stonewall' the Committee, giving nothing whatever." Harlow felt that Nixon was in a funk and did not fully appreciate that with the start of impeachment proceedings the game had changed.

Harlow recommended enlightened and deceptive cooperation. The president's defense team believed that whatever the special prosecutor had, Jaworski would make available to the Judiciary Committee "either voluntarily or through legislation." So it was better public relations to announce now that the White House wanted Jaworski to share his materials. What Harlow wanted to avoid was frustrating the committee so much that they issued a subpoena. "We must realize that a stonewalling of the Committee will arm the Committee with a devastating article of impeachment—one likely to sail through the House," Harlow wrote to Haig.[47]

The White House had already picked up that Rodino and Doar intended to make the impeachment inquiry as bipartisan as possible. Like an intelligence officer analyzing the weaknesses of an adversary, Harlow explained that they could use this noble effort against the House committee.

The goal of the White House should be to turn Rodino and Doar's apparent caution into a liability. The White House should pretend cooperation, accentuate public impatience, and force a vote by the committee and the House months before Doar and Rodino figured out they needed more taped conversations from the summer of 1972, which might include the June 23 moment when Nixon decided to use the CIA to obstruct the FBI's investigation, or Nixon's suggestions to Ehrlichman in July as to how CREEP aides could perjure themselves in interviews with the FBI. Nixon conversed about many subjects, foreign and domestic, on the tapes but most of the time when he mentioned Watergate to his closest advisers, he was actively committing a crime.

The counter-impeachment strategy required that intense pressure be put on Rodino, Doar, and the committee to wrap up their inquiry fast. The problem was that House Republicans, in general, did not want the White House to exert any direct pressure on members of the committee.

"This situation is intolerable," Harlow complained to Haig. As a result, Nixon's team suggested setting up a fake "national organization . . . to bring counterpressures to bear on the Committee and the House." While a fake lobby pushed in Washington, the White

House hoped to manipulate public pressure on Rodino and the Democrats by artificially inflating the economy to make Nixon look indispensable to the country's well-being.

—

At his very first meeting with committee members in January 1974, John Doar explained that he had no position on the definition of "high crimes and misdemeanors." The first task of his new team was to define the meaning of that phrase.[48] By February, the House Judiciary Committee staff had concluded that presidential impeachment was more than an extension of law enforcement. It was a device linked to the founders' basic desire for a Goldilocks executive: one not too weak but one not too strong. The staff reported that impeachment "was an integral element in a system of checks and balances which maintains an equilibrium among the separate powers of the government." In other words, a president could be impeached without having committed a crime.[49]

Meanwhile, lawyers at the Department of Justice and the White House had also completed reports on how to define an impeachable offense. Also at issue for them, too, was whether the president had to commit a criminal offense to be impeached. After studying the Constitution, the records of the Constitutional Convention, subsequent statements by the founders, and later impeachment precedents, the Nixon Justice Department determined there were two views of the matter but refused to pick a side.

The "narrow view" was founded in the conclusion that the offense had to involve the breaking of a criminal law. The "broad view" accepted noncriminal "political crimes" as the basis for impeachment. There was evidence supporting both views. But there was nothing that suggested one view was more correct than the other.

Not surprisingly, the White House disagreed with the equanimity of its own Justice Department and the "broad view" of the House Judiciary Committee staff. It believed that the framers had intentionally excluded political impeachments and that, eighty years later, the Senate had rejected the "broad view" in the trial of Andrew Johnson. They believed the founders wanted the legislative branch to have power to ensure "the obedience of the executive to the criminal law." In sum, a president should be removed only for committing a crime.[50]

In late February, John Doar, on behalf of the committee, made his first formal request to James St. Clair for additional materials from the White House. His letter, dated February 25, asked for several White House recordings from February, March, and April 1973. In addition, to help with future requests, Doar wrote, "we believe the next logical step is for you to outline for us how the White House files are indexed, how Presidential Papers are indexed and how Presidential conversations and memoranda are indexed."[51] The White House ignored this request. Despite the advice from senior aide Bryce Harlow, at this point

Richard Nixon could see no reason to offer any cooperation to his would-be impeachers.

Nixon's stance did not last long, however. On March 1, 1974, the Watergate grand jury, on the recommendation of the special prosecutor, returned indictments of seven of Nixon's key lieutenants, including Haldeman, Ehrlichman, and Mitchell, and secretly named Nixon as an unindicted co-conspirator. The indictments—which signaled the end of the grand jury's activities—freed Jaworski from the legal constraints on sharing what the grand jury had received from the White House—including the tape of Nixon's March 21, 1973, conversation with Dean—with the House. Understanding this, the president realized that it was time to implement the strategy of deceptive cooperation that Harlow had suggested in late January.

At a press conference on March 6, Nixon announced not only that he hoped Jaworski would share what he had received from the White House with the House Judiciary Committee, but the president added he was prepared to answer "written interrogatories" from the committee and would even meet with Rodino and Hutchinson to answer their questions, under oath.

This was a clever attempt at misdirection. While offering cooperation, Nixon said nothing about the committee's February 25 requests. Instead, when asked about how he would handle additional requests from the committee, Nixon replied that he thought the House already had what it needed to complete the expeditious impeachment inquiry it had promised:

[I]f all that is really involved in this instance is to cart everything that is in the White House down to a committee and to have them paw through it on a fishing expedition, it will take them not a matter of months, so that they can complete their investigation and, we trust, their decision by the first of May—which I understand is Mr. Rodino's object— but it would take them months and perhaps even as long as a year.

Nixon's press conference comments launched the White House strategy of demeaning Doar's efforts to collect additional information for the committee as a "fishing expedition" and therefore unnecessary and unfair.[52] On March 15, in front of a group of business executives in Chicago, Nixon repeated this line:

[W]hy not just give the members of the Judiciary Committee the right to come in and have all the tapes of every Presidential conversation, a fishing license or a complete right to go in and go through all the Presidential files in order to find out whether or not there is a possibility that some action had been taken which might be and might result in an impeachable offense [?]

The reason why we cannot go that far . . . is very simply this: It isn't a question that the President has something to hide; it is the fact that every President— Democrat and Republican—from the founding of this Republic, has recognized the necessity of protect-

ing the confidentiality of Presidential conversations
with his associates . . . [I]f that confidentiality principle is completely destroyed, future Presidents will not
have the benefit of the kind of advice that an executive
needs to make the right decision. He will be sur-
rounded by a group of eunuchs . . .[53]

Although the fate of the committee's own request
for materials remained uncertain, the indictment
had the unmistakable effect of dramatically improv-
ing the quality of information available to its inquiry.
On March 26, Doar picked up a "bulging briefcase"
that held not only the tape of the notorious March 21
"cancer on the presidency" conversation, but six others as well. And Jaworski had something else for the
House inquiry. His staff had prepared a document—
called the "road map"—linking Nixon directly to
a criminal conspiracy to obstruct justice. This was a
"series of guideposts if the House Judiciary Committee wished to follow them," Jaworski noted.[54]

—

The success of Nixon's strategy of deceptive cooperation with the impeachment process depended on convincing most Americans and their members of Congress
that Richard Nixon was being more reasonable than
the Democrats. The White House, however, did not
grasp the significance of how Rodino and Doar conceived of the impeachment process. Investigating
Nixon entailed more for Rodino and Doar than just
acquiring relevant evidence; it also involved exorcising

the ghost of Andrew Johnson's partisan impeachment. In practice this meant creating trust among those who dismissed most liberal Democrats as mindless impeachers. From the beginning of the process, Rodino, his chief aide O'Brien, and Doar made personal calls on what Rodino referred to as "the middle."

The middle on the Judiciary Committee was not defined by ideology; it was defined by the dilemma of suspecting Nixon was impeachable when neither your political tribe nor your constituents wanted you to vote for impeachment. On the Democratic side it consisted of two Southern conservatives, Walter Flowers of Alabama and James Mann of South Carolina, and a moderate from a very pro-Nixon district in Arkansas, Raymond Thornton. On the Republican side, it included liberal and moderate Republicans such as William Cohen of Maine, Hamilton Fish of New York, and Thomas Railsback of Illinois, as well as the Southern conservative M. Caldwell Butler.[55] Rodino and Doar's encouragement of the middle not only made swaying the undecideds possible; it would complicate Nixon's efforts to justify his stonewalling as a response to partisanship.

By March 1974, Rodino's handling of the pro-impeachment Democrats—whom Caldwell Butler called the "Hanging Democrats"—had already impressed all of the Republicans on the committee. "He has done a magnificent job of keeping them in line," the forty-eight-year-old Butler confided to his diary.[56] Butler prided himself on having an open mind on impeachment. But even a staunch Nixon supporter on the committee like Carlos Moorhead of California was impressed with the Democrat's efforts at impartiality. Moorhead reported to the White House just after the president's March 6 news conference that all of the Republicans believed that Rodino had "bent over backwards to be fair," and he saw this as a problem for Richard Nixon.

"The President must convince the American people he is bending over backwards," Moorhead pleaded. "He appears to offer cooperation one week and then withdraws it the next."[57]

At the end of March 1974, House Minority Leader John Rhodes warned the White House that if the president did not offer more cooperation to the Judiciary Committee, its members would be forced to use a subpoena to request more materials.[58] In response to this criticism from Republicans, the White House doubled down. After Congressman Thomas Railsback, a forty-two-year-old Republican member of the Judiciary Committee from the corn belt, sent a letter to President Nixon urging more cooperation, the White House reached out to the chairman of John Deere, the largest employer in his district, to apply pressure to Railsback to keep in line.[59]

—

No House committee had ever served a subpoena on a president in an impeachment hearing. In February, the full House had overwhelmingly passed a resolution giving the Judiciary Committee the right to issue subpoenas. The Constitution was silent on what should happen if the president refused to cooperate. In January, Bryce Harlow had warned Nixon that he needed to avoid that kind of constitutional clash because, at the very least, the House could respond by passing an article of impeachment just for noncompliance. But Harlow's suggested solution was a dodge, pretending to cooperate long enough to discredit the impeachment process.

And Nixon liked the odds of being able to turn the American people against the impeachers. "The law case will be decided by the PR case," Nixon wrote to Haig in early March.

"St. Clair sees it too much as a trial," he added in mid-March, "not as a public relations exercise."[60] The goal was to strip off not only the Republicans on the committee, turning them against the use of a subpoena, but also Southern Democrats whose constituents associated partisanship by congressional Democrats with East Coast liberalism.

The White House's cynical stirring of the pot to avoid a subpoena did not go unnoticed by Nixon's target audience. Forty-five-year-old freshman Democratic congressman Raymond Thornton of Arkansas was someone that Richard Nixon counted on to hold on to power. The large, rural fourth congressional district along the Arkansas-Louisiana border he represented was Nixon country. Although Thornton was himself comparatively moderate, his base supported the president.

Thornton, however, "couldn't stomach" the White House strategy.[61] It reminded him of a political observation Abraham Lincoln once made. "If you want to stop a church from being built," Lincoln advised, "don't attack the religion, but start an argument where the best location would be."

"It appears to me," Thornton continued, "that the strategy of the White House is to insist on withholding evidence and start an argument about the procedural methods used by the Committee in an effort to divide the Committee and make it appear that it is being unfair procedurally."[62]

Thus did the White House's hardball impeachment strategy build momentum for not only the first presidential impeachment subpoena but one that was bipartisan. On April 4, the ever-cautious Rodino opened a Judiciary Committee meeting with "a slight tremor" in his voice. It was time, he argued, to put additional pressure on the White House to comply with the committee's requests. It had been six weeks since John Doar had sent his first major request to St. Clair, and there was still no answer. "The patience of this Committee is now wearing thin."

Sensitive to the White House's refrain of "fishing expedition," Rodino stressed that Doar had made "a specific request . . . for specific evidence of specific facts of specific relevance to our inquiry." The ranking Republican on the Judiciary Committee, J. Edward Hutchinson, who actually opposed a subpoena, nevertheless backed up Rodino's plea for more White

House cooperation. "I cannot understand why," Hutchinson explained, "there should be at this late date any doubt in anyone's mind as to what it is we are after."[63] He and Rodino decided to send St. Clair another letter, giving the White House until April 9 to supply the materials voluntarily. If possible, they wanted them sooner.

With the impending collapse of its anti-subpoena strategy—and the president still adamantly against compliance—the White House returned to an idea that it had considered in late 1973. After the first batch of tapes was handed over to Sirica, some of Nixon's aides debated releasing transcripts of the tapes, including the damaging March 21 tape. The theory was that the White House could get ahead of the bad news by confusing the public about the meaning of the tapes. Bryce Harlow had convinced Haig before Christmas that this was a stupid idea, and the transcripts remained in White House files.[64]

The debate in April, as in December, revolved around the question of whether the country, in words later made famous by Jack Nicholson in the film **A Few Good Men,** could "handle the truth." Harlow resisted releasing the transcripts because the public would learn that Nixon was cold, calculating, and amoral. He believed that the American people were naïve and would punish Nixon when they learned the truth of how Washington really worked.

In April, Haig and Special White House Counsel J. Fred Buzhardt disagreed. They believed that Nixon's supporters were loyalists who would follow wherever he led; but he had to lead. Nixon himself was paralyzed with indecision. Although he was in too much of a funk to recall precisely what he had said on tape, he knew himself well enough to know it would be harsh and politically, if not legally, damaging. The president's hapless personal lawyer, James St. Clair, remained blissfully ignorant of the content of the tapes and just asked to be able to give the House something, anything.

Over Harlow's misgivings, Nixon accepted that the House had to receive something, so he approved restarting the transcription process suspended in December. The Judiciary Committee would receive transcripts but not tapes.[65] White House staff would now transcribe the additional forty-two conversations from late March and April 1973 that the committee had identified as relevant in February. None of the staffers tasked to do the job was a trained transcriber, nor was there time to establish any quality control. To keep the crash program confidential, no audio technicians were contracted to improve the quality of the copies of the recordings the junior staffers were using. Moreover, Nixon insisted that he personally edit every page of transcript. This was not only a recipe for creating inaccurate transcripts, but if Nixon personally edited out incriminating sections or altered words in legally helpful ways, this was a recipe for a charge of obstruction of justice.

And this process would take some time. On April 9,

1974, St. Clair wrote to Doar for a delay until after Congress's Easter recess because the materials were "under review." Nixon did not allow St. Clair to reveal to the committee or to the Republican congressional leadership that what was on the table were transcripts and not actual tapes. With the White House taking this gamble, Bryce Harlow quietly resigned. Henceforth, the president would have no impeachment adviser who had the gravitas to tell him no.

The White House's vague play for more time, without any consultation with Capitol Hill, widened cracks in the GOP caucus in the committee. At a Republican meeting on April 10, Railsback, Cohen, Fish, and even Nixon supporter Charles Sandman of New Jersey told their colleagues that with no end of White House evasions in sight, they were now prepared to join the Democrats in issuing a subpoena. Although Hutchinson agreed that St. Clair's letter was "evasive and offensive," he just couldn't subpoena a Republican president. Nevertheless he made no serious effort to dissuade his colleagues from voting with the Democrats.[66]

The next day, Thursday, April 11, 1974, Rodino and Doar thought the time had finally arrived to consider the historic step of subpoenaing the president. Although it was likely the committee would support a subpoena, the majority had no idea how many Republican votes they would get.[67] Earlier that morning Doar engaged in some hand-holding with one possible Republican ally, M. Caldwell Butler of Virginia, who wanted to know as much as he could about the draft subpoena.[68]

Rodino started the April 11 meeting by outlining a list of new concessions to Republican members. James St. Clair would be allowed to represent the president once the inquiry staff began its presentation of subpoenaed evidence to the members, and he would be invited to call any witnesses he wished to testify. Although Rodino said nothing about cross-examination, a demand also made by committee Republicans, he promised the issue would be resolved after the recess.

Then he had Doar describe a call received from St. Clair earlier that morning. The White House was now offering an as-yet-undefined "partial compliance" to stave off a subpoena.[69] This last-minute and vague White House gambit deflated the Republicans on the committee. "This is beneath the dignity of the White House," thought Caldwell Butler, who was now resolved to support a subpoena. "That triggered it. . . . He was trifling with us."[70] Only a week earlier the Virginia Republican had thought there was not enough evidence of noncompliance to warrant seeking a subpoena.[71] But St. Clair's stalling changed his mind.

The subpoena resolution, including an amendment advanced by Republican Delbert Latta of Ohio that Rodino had allowed as a last show of compromise to committee Republicans, passed 33 to 3, with only Hutchinson, Trent Lott of Mississippi, and Charles

Wiggins, who represented Nixon's birthplace of Yorba Linda, California, voting against it. Butler was impressed with the show. "You have to give Rodino credit. He played it by ear this morning."[72] The president had until April 25 to comply.

"The battle lines are drawn," Thornton of Arkansas noted to himself.[73] If Nixon chose to ignore the subpoena, his noncompliance could itself constitute an article of impeachment.

The April 11 subpoena and its deadline would open the door to Nixon's greatest blunder since the firing of Cox. The near unanimity of the vote in the committee undermined the president's defense that the subpoena was a partisan attack. The White House would have to give the committee something.

—

At the end of April, St. Clair asked for, and received, yet another stay of execution from the House. By this point, Nixon had decided that in order to show his supporters that he was trying to cooperate with an unfriendly House, he would release the transcripts publicly at the same time he released them to the House.

The House Judiciary Committee had no idea of the madness that its bipartisan subpoena provoked in the Nixon White House. Desperate to cling to the presidency, the president was in the residence, inaccessible to most of his staff, reading over a thousand pages of transcripts, cutting this and cutting that. At the eleventh hour Nixon reluctantly accepted a staff recommendation to include the March 21, 1973, transcript, along with transcripts of all of the other conversations that Archibald Cox had subpoenaed in 1973.

But Nixon drew the line on allowing the Congress to read anything that was unequivocally impeachable. He did not want the House to know everything he had said to Dean and Haldeman on September 15, 1972. Sirica had ruled the last thirteen minutes of that conversation, in which Nixon abused his authority as president to sic the IRS on his political enemies, as irrelevant to the Watergate trial. Nixon knew that presidential abuses of power were relevant to an impeachment inquiry, but he cut that section of tape out anyway. Similarly, the White House transcript for a March 22, 1973, conversation did not include the section where Nixon told his top lieutenants "I want you to stonewall it, let them plead the Fifth Amendment, cover-up . . . ."[74]

These last-minute decisions meant that the transcripts were not ready when Nixon spoke to the nation on April 29, 1974. "As far as what the president personally knew and did with regard to Watergate and the coverup is concerned," Nixon explained, "these materials—together with those already made available—will tell it all."[75] On a table beside him were two mounds of black binders said to contain the transcripts. They were empty. Once again, Nixon offered a deal. He told the televised audience that he would allow Chairman Rodino and Edward Hutchinson not only to verify the transcripts but to have access to the original tapes to check his edits for relevancy. The committee as a whole, and its staff of trained lawyers, would not, however, be permitted to listen. In a transparent appeal for sympathy, Nixon closed his speech likening himself to Abraham Lincoln, "another president . . . subjected to unmerciful attack."

Richard Nixon hadn't a clue of the entirety of the risks implicit in gaming the subpoena with transcripts. Since late March, another secret transcription project had been under way in Washington, D.C., and nothing had leaked about it to the White House. The "bulging briefcase" the committee had received from the Watergate grand jury included seven White House tapes. As soon as those tapes entered the vault at the inquiry staff offices in the old Congressional Hotel, Doar set up a team to transcribe them, empowering the staff to explore equipment to improve the audio quality of the copies they had, while testing the aural skills of the staff to identify those best suited to this tough transcription work. The White House transcripts released at the end of April included conversations that the House Judiciary Committee could now check against their own transcripts. Without understanding his jeopardy, the president had just authorized an easily verifiable obstruction of justice.[76]

—

When the White House started calling around Congress on April 29 to prepare Republicans for the fact that Nixon would respond to the subpoena with transcripts and not tapes, Congressman Railsback informed Doar and asked for his thoughts. Doar and his staff believed the tapes were needed to clarify two issues: Did Nixon order the payment of hush money, and once he heard about the cover-up by Dean, did he undertake a serious effort to end it and bring the perpetrators to justice? Transcripts edited by Nixon were unlikely to hold the answers to those questions. "This would be unacceptable," Doar replied. "It would be an affront to the Judiciary Committee."[77]

The transcripts started arriving the next day, and Rodino had a huge decision to make. He knew where his special counsel Doar stood, but what about the members of the committee, especially the Republicans? Their reaction mattered. If Nixon were held in noncompliance, his transcription offer could itself constitute an article of impeachment, or lead to a motion of censure on the floor of the House. Rodino's goal throughout this process was to pass bipartisan articles of impeachment, if any. In that spirit, he called Virginian Caldwell Butler to gauge his reaction to Nixon's offer.

"What do you think of things?" he asked Butler. "I want your calm, sober and reasoned views [on the events of the past twenty-four hours]."[78]

Remarkably, Butler told Rodino not to accept the president's offer as it stood. He was not suggesting that the committee refuse the transcripts and find Nixon in contempt. But Butler had heard enough about the difficulties of understanding the tapes that he wanted Rodino and Hutchinson to insist that when they went to the White House to verify the transcripts and the edits they be allowed to bring counsel and staff.[79]

On May 1, 1974, Rodino convened an unusual evening meeting of the committee to decide what to do. Rodino was caught in the middle. He wasn't sure he wanted to find the president in noncompliance. But some hard-line Democrats wanted to censure Nixon, and the other Democrats wanted to declare him at least in complete noncompliance of the subpoena. Most Republicans preferred to negotiate some more with Nixon and planned to let the Democrats take the lead in pressing for compliance. Ultimately, when two pro-impeachment Democrats decided not to support Rodino on any compromise, Bill Cohen of Maine became the only Republican to vote in favor of sending a terse letter of noncompliance. Had he not backed Rodino, the tally would have been 19 to 19, and the committee would have been paralyzed.[80]

Feeling good about the politics of the moment— especially after an outpouring of support for the president's speech, which had promised honest cooperation, and had preceded anyone actually reading any transcripts—the White House jumped on the committee's letter of noncompliance and used it to assail the entire committee for partisanship. The arrogance of the reaction was not limited to public criticism of the impeachment process. Nixon briefly considered making a different deal with the special prosecutor, who was asking for another group of tapes that included the recording of a June 23, 1972, meeting in which Nixon had approved using the CIA against the FBI for political reasons. But Nixon quickly changed his mind when he listened to that conversation on May 6. "No more tapes," he told Haig afterward. "We've done enough."[81]

On May 7, James St. Clair announced that Nixon would not be providing any more tapes to the House Judiciary Committee or to the Special Prosecutor. Nixon was doubling down again. He no longer cared that his treatment of a subpoena could become an article of impeachment.

Unfortunately for the president, many people took the time to wade through the 1,200 pages of transcripts, especially Republican congressmen. Within a few days, the ugliness of Nixon's approach to power leapt from the transcript pages and offended many, just as Bryce Harlow had feared. Elite opinion in Washington turned hard against Nixon. Most Democrats and all of the mainstream media were already there. But in the wake of reading the transcripts, for a brief moment even the Republican congressional leadership tried to bring the Nixon presidency to a swift end. The crisis didn't last very long, but it revealed that the president's support among congressional Republican leaders was soft.

On May 9, John Anderson, the head of the House Republican Conference, called for Nixon's "voluntary resignation." House Majority Leader John Rhodes also said that Nixon should consider resigning.[82] As the Republicans attacked a president from their own party, Democrats stayed relatively silent. For a moment, it looked as if Republicans would solve the country's Watergate problem.

The crisis was heating up on the day that the impeachment inquiry was scheduled to have its first public session after more than sixteen weeks of closed sessions. Caldwell Butler and Bill Cohen, who sat next to each other, wondered as they entered the chamber whether the impeachment process was about to be overtaken by events.[83] But it turned out that as of May 1974 the Republican congressional leadership lacked the collective will to force a Republican president to resign, however much it disliked and mistrusted him. When the resignation trial balloons appeared to anger the Nixon base, public Republican criticism ended for the sake of the midterms in November.[84]

Privately, however, prominent Republicans continued to doubt Nixon's long-term political survival. On May 14, Senate Majority Leader Mike Mansfield and Senate Minority Leader Hugh Scott met with Gerald Ford. They wanted him to start thinking about his presidency. The transcription fiasco had left the Nixon presidency so badly damaged that Mansfield and Scott had started jointly planning for a televised trial in the Senate, should the House impeach Nixon. "Jerry," Scott explained, "there's a better than fifty-fifty chance that you will be President before long."[85]

—

As Nixon struggled with the loyalty of the congressional Republican leadership, John Doar and the impeachment staff readied the materials they had painstakingly prepared to present to the committee. Starting on May 9 and for the next six weeks, Doar read out loud in his upper-Midwest monotone 7,200 pages, grouped into 650 "statements of information" from thirty-six binders.[86] The material, which was read to all members of the House Judiciary Committee in closed sessions, covered all of the controversial activities of the Nixon administration regarding the Watergate break-in and the Plumbers operation. It also provided detailed chronologies linked to concerns that Nixon had accepted bribes from milk producers, had manipulated anti-trust enforcement for the sake of telecom giant ITT, and had cheated on his personal tax returns. Doar decided to read every word to create a common baseline of facts and to be sure no member of Congress could plausibly deny having had access to a key piece of information.

The effect was unintentionally mind-numbing. "It was rather like studying a course in college," Raymond Thornton of Arkansas noted. Indeed, but this was not a popular class. "The clock did seem to stand still," he added.

But besides the tone there was the challenge presented by the mode of presentation. Doar read document after document without giving any interpretation. The committee members could follow along in their own binder copies, but there was no narrative through line. Rodino, who was careful not to criticize Doar in front of the members, privately told his personal staff that the "statements of information" were "too dense" and the whole presentation was "not understandable."[87]

The staff presentation came close to splitting apart the Democratic caucus on the committee. The long-simmering dissatisfaction of Rodino's pro-impeachment subcommittee chairmen—Jack Brooks, Robert Kastenmeier, John Conyers, Jr., and Don Edwards—boiled over into open rebellion against the Doar-led effort. "They tell me Doar is an archivist, not a prosecutor," Tip O'Neill told journalist Jimmy Breslin.[88]

Behind closed doors the Democratic partisans plotted to take control of the inquiry. Conyers and Edwards approached Dick Cates to see if he would consider sidelining Doar by becoming majority counsel for the Democrats. The partisans feared that due to Doar's nonpartisan approach when it came time to vote, they would lack a strong case to justify impeaching Nixon. But Cates refused to participate in a palace coup. In the months since Doar had tried to fire him, the two men had developed a deep mutual respect and an understanding of the differences in each other's approaches.[89]

Committee Republicans were largely oblivious to these rifts. Doar had certainly bored them and they were equally exhausted by the weeks of presentation, but they were not near open revolt. Most of them still respected Rodino and Doar for "bending over backwards" to be fair-minded. Their problem was that they lacked any leadership—either of the steady, meandering Rodino sort or of the hell-raisin' Jack Brooks variety.

With Ed Hutchinson hobbled by health issues, the number-two Republican, Robert McClory of Illinois, warned his colleagues that "the Democrats' scenario [is] to show one massive Watergate cover-up." The more discerning Charles Wiggins understood that Doar's effort was designed to assemble a pattern of misconduct.[90] The Republican problem was they couldn't agree over what to do about it. With the White House keeping them at arm's length and their own House leadership unsure as to whether to save the unpopular Nixon, the committee Republicans were largely on their own.[91] Most of the Republicans at least agreed with the "narrow view" of impeachment. They were not impressed with Doar's presentation of a pattern of misconduct, they needed evidence of criminal presidential conduct to impeach.

There was plenty of evidence of criminal presidential activity on the tapes. Starting in mid-May, regular members of the committee were permitted to listen to the raw tapes that the grand jury had turned over on March 26, including the infamous March 21, 1973, "cancer on the presidency" conversation.

However, it turned out that the Republican partisan mind refused to absorb the incriminating nature of the tapes. The reaction of the GOP hard-liners validated Doar's position in his debate with Jaworski's team. They rationalized what they heard.[92] They did not react as Sirica and Jaworski had when they'd first heard Nixon and Dean discuss paying hush money on March 21, 1973. Politicians were not about to give up on a president of their own party for misbehaving on one day. Wiggins, Sandman, and Hutchinson heard only that Nixon had not apparently gone through with the hush-money payment. The fact that he mused about it was disappointing but not impeachable. This was not the smoking gun regarding criminal conduct that the GOP partisans demanded to see or hear before considering impeaching the president.

Open-minded Republicans, the ones who saw their responsibilities as constitutional and not political, refused to rationalize Nixon's behavior as the partisans did, but they still wanted more information than was on the tapes. For them, the chance to interview witnesses seemed a way "to resolve the ambiguities" of Doar's staff presentation and the tapes. The request to Rodino and Doar that the committee have the opportunity to hear witnesses before ending its inquiry was something that united both the partisan and open-minded Republicans. Hard-core Nixon defenders believed witnesses, under friendly questioning, would demonstrate that the president had not done what Democrats inferred, whereas open-minded Republicans hoped that more information from these witnesses would help them connect some of Doar's many, many dots.[93]

"It is my belief at this point," Thomas Railsback noted privately in mid-June, "that if the Democrats fail to call such people as John Dean, Bob Haldeman, John Ehrlichman, [Charles] Colson, Henry Petersen that they will be asking for trouble and it is not likely that the Republicans will support an impeachment vote."[94]

Outside the political limelight, the Doar approach was having some positive effects. Quietly, a new group was gradually emerging that bridged party lines and included members who were not looking for a so-called smoking gun. These members were embracing the broad view of impeachment for which evidence of the commission of a crime by the president himself was not a requirement. Caldwell Butler was now satisfied that Nixon had overseen an amoral administration. The issue for him was whether it was in the public interest to remove him. In many ways he felt he had been a "good president."[95]

In mid-June, thirty-eight-year-old Democrat Barbara Jordan of Texas was asking the same questions, which she shared with Butler. The liberal African American woman and the conservative white Southern man, though undecided, were thinking about impeachment in similar ways. "We see eye-to-eye on impeachment," Butler noted in his diary after a brief conversation on the floor of the House.[96]

It took Rodino and Doar a while to appreciate the

importance of giving undecided Republicans the opportunity to ask questions of John Dean and others.
But, by the end of June, this compromise seemed
necessary. To shore up support among Republicans,
Rodino announced that the committee would invite
witnesses to whom the members could ask questions,
just as they had wanted. Admiringly and with some
frustration, Nixon defender Trent Lott of Mississippi
said to Rodino's chief of staff: "It's very frustrating
because he gives us everything we want."[97]

Rodino, ironically, at that moment in the impeachment process had a better feel for what the Republicans needed than his own party. On the morning of
June 27, 1974, he breezily told two reporters, Jack
Nelson of the **Los Angeles Times** and Sam Donaldson of ABC News, who were hanging out in Francis O'Brien's office, that he thought all twenty-one
committee Democrats would vote for impeachment,
and he even mentioned five Republicans—including
Railsback, Butler, and Cohen—who were likely to
support them. This chat was on the record. "That was
a mistake," O'Brien realized immediately, not because Rodino might be wrong, but because this kind
of statement ran counter to his painstaking efforts to
build confidence in a nonjudgmental, nonpartisan
inquiry. The inquiry, after all, was not yet over and
the debates had yet to begin.[98]

The scale of the chairman's problems multiplied
when he met with his caucus later in the day. When
Rodino continued to exude confidence about the di-

rection the process was going, a clutch of key Democrats—the three Southerners, Thornton, Mann, and Flowers—told the chairman they were not there. Even more shocking was the skepticism expressed by Paul Sarbanes of Maryland and Barbara Jordan of Texas. These undecided Democrats believed that the staff presentations didn't lead anywhere. Bewildered, Rodino told the caucus that he could not "understand how anyone who had seen and heard what he had heard could continue to have doubts." The Democratic majority was in disarray.[99]

And it was about to get worse. Shortly after the Democratic caucus, the **Los Angeles Times** broke the story of what Rodino had told its reporter that morning. Rodino asked O'Brien what to do. "I told him to go to the floor and deny it," O'Brien recalled. O'Brien and Rodino knew this would be a bold-faced lie. "To this day I regret that I did." Rodino went to the well of the House and lied.

Richard Nixon, who was in Moscow and noticed the **Los Angeles Times** story somewhat later, took Rodino's reported statement at face value. He had always assumed that the Democrats would play the impeachment game as hard and as single-mindedly as he would in their place. "There was no question in my mind that the House Judiciary Committee was going to vote to impeach me," he wrote after learning about Rodino's statement. "It was the margin of that vote that would assume a vital importance."[100]

Nixon had no idea that there were still good odds

that the Judiciary Committee might not impeach him. In the crucial month to come, the members would have to work hard to make sense of what Doar and the staff had provided them. If they somehow found a way to connect the dots, however, the nation's first bipartisan impeachment of a president was likely.

—

As July began, Doar's assumption that open-minded elected representatives would accept the removal of a president for a pattern of action that threatened the very institutions that protected their liberty was under severe strain. He was right in believing that if you gave them a mosaic of information they would be able to pull together a story themselves. These were intelligent, hardworking, and responsible individuals. Doar's mistake was in forgetting that besides being lawyers, they were politicians.

These representatives needed more than the solution to an intellectual puzzle to be able to vote against a man supported by their party or, in the case of the Southern Democrats, by most of their constituents. Not being a politician, Doar did not understand that these individuals had to feel they could advocate impeachment, on their own, in their own words and in a way their supporters could understand. By making them passive recipients of information, Doar had not helped them become advocates.

This process of turning supporters into advocates of impeaching Richard Nixon would take place in

July. Decades later Americans would ask themselves whether members of Congress were capable only of bitter partisanship. For four weeks at a pivotal moment in American history in 1974, a handful of elected representatives found that something greater than partisanship could guide them when the fate of the country hung in the balance.

"I wanted to get it 'right,'" remembered Raymond Thornton of Arkansas. "This was most likely the most important task that I would ever have in government."[101] From the beginning, Thornton had concluded impeachment was "a safety valve for our system of government, not merely a punishment for crimes or misbehavior." On June 4, 1974, he dictated for his personal record that "such charges must not be brought lightly, but on substantial evidence; the actions complained of threaten the continued existence of our country as a constitutional government under which all men are held equally accountable under the law." Thornton believed that he had to forget about the fact that he was an elected official. "This decision is too vital and too important to be based upon partisan politics or newspaper headlines."[102]

Remarkably, six other members of Congress came to a similar understanding around the same time. For months they had been connecting the dots—Doar's dots—on their own. It was noteworthy that they accepted the information pulled together by the impeachment staff as their baseline of facts. There was no alternative timeline or fake news conspiracy to distract them from deciding if this pattern of conduct warranted removal of a president from office. However inconvenient they might be, facts were facts. Not one of them doubted that the Nixon White House had become a criminal enterprise. The question was whether a fairly elected president should lose his job, if his direct responsibility could arguably only be inferred.

The month of July brought the moment of decision for these undecided representatives because Rodino had scheduled publicly televised hearings and a vote for the last week of the month. With this deadline looming, these men decided to seek one another out and start talking through the correct course of action as jurors and as politicians.[103] The first move occurred among the Republicans on July 9. Caldwell Butler noticed Hamilton Fish of New York and Bill Cohen of Maine chatting by the House water cooler—sharing what the old-fashioned Butler called "the scuttlebutt."

Joining the conversation, "partly by invitation, partly by aggression," Butler said "those of us who [were] still on the fence got to visit a little bit." They all had "the same problems": They were considering impeachment but were worried about how to justify it to themselves and, more important, to their constituents. "The elderly, primitive Republicans [were] his [Nixon's] strongest defenders," recalled Butler. Middle-age voters were not as rigid, and young people didn't believe in defending at all costs.[104] Butler, who had made up his own mind about Nixon, was still hung up on the issue of whether the country could stand the trauma of an impeachment. Fish had an answer: "It's already a tragedy. It's a great American tragedy."

The men realized that the impeachment of the president was in their hands. If the committee vote was close, Nixon might survive the vote in the House and there would be no trial in the Senate, but if a Southern Democrat like Walter Flowers joined the pro-impeachment Republicans, the president would be impeached. Drawing from history, Butler thought of his fellow undecided Republicans as similar to the "Mugwumps," the nineteenth-century Republicans who left the party to support Democrat Grover Cleveland for president. The twentieth-century Mugwumps felt a kinship with Southern Democrats. At their impromptu July 9 chat, Fish, Cohen, and Butler resolved it was time to reach out to Walter Flowers of Alabama, "who was in the same boat."[105]

Over the next few days, these men learned things that made justifying impeachment easier. Rodino's concession of allowing the committee to interview witnesses following John Doar's presentation of the facts turned out to be an unintended stroke of genius. The hearings with the witnesses "breathed new life into the proceedings," Walter Flowers recalled. "They made everything more vivid."

Between July 2 and July 17, 1974, the committee interviewed ten witnesses, a process that had a profound effect on the Mugwumps and the Southern Democrats. Later each man would point to a different moment with a different witness as making the difference in their decision making.

For Tom Railsback it was former White House counsel John Dean's July 11 testimony that moved him closer to voting against the president. Railsback was much less convinced of the pattern of conduct theory than the other Mugwumps. He was still looking for some sort of smoking gun of presidential involvement in the misconduct. Dean's revelation of his conversation with Nixon on September 15, 1972, about using the IRS against political enemies, was the evidence Railsback felt he needed to justify holding Nixon guilty of abusing his executive powers.

"Dean knew that that thirteen-minute segment of tape was eventually going to come out, so his recollection of that conversation had a certain authenticity," said Railsback.[106] The next day, Railsback told the Republican caucus that he might just vote for impeachment. "I hope you will be a minority of a minority," said Hutchinson, adding "his great offense of anyone voting to impeach a Republican president."[107]

Conservative South Carolina Democrat James Mann wasn't looking for a smoking gun. He needed to convince himself by talking to Nixon's lieutenants that Richard Nixon was the source of the amorality and criminality of his administration. On July 17 Herbert Kalmbach, the president's personal lawyer

who facilitated hush payments to the Watergate burglars in the summer of 1972, left Mann with no doubt
that Nixon had approved the payments.

> MANN: You regarded Haldeman as the right arm
> and Ehrlichman as the left arm, a man who had the
> total confidence of the President?
> KALMBACH: Yes, sir.
> MANN: And you went to him on July 26, to Mr.
> Ehrlichman, and you looked him in the eye and got
> his assurance that in effect, what you were doing was
> authorized—is that correct?
> KALMBACH: Yes, sir.[108]

"This did more to jell the thinking of the undecided," Mann recalled a year later, "when we realized
the monstrosity of what Richard Nixon had done
to the lives of certain people with no remorse
shown."[109] Whatever one might have thought of
Kalmbach's ethical compass, the president had hung
his personal lawyer out to dry.

Besides the testimony, the committee received another influential source of new information in July.
On July 9, the committee staff issued a report showing the differences between Nixon's transcripts
and the transcripts drawn from the tapes received
from the grand jury. The White House had omitted,
for example, a whole section from a March 22 conversation where the president had said, "I don't give a
shit what happens. I want you all to stonewall it, let

them plead the Fifth Amendment, cover-up or any-thing else, if it'll save it—save the plan. That's the whole point."[110]

Each manipulation of the transcripts was additional proof that President Nixon's cover-up was ongoing. The House didn't know that Nixon had edited these transcripts himself, but the fact that he vouched for them was enough to make him responsible. The im-peachment process rests on the presumption that Congress can get what it needs to pass judgment on the chief executive. One of the discoveries of the Im-peachment Summer of 1974 was that this process gets very difficult if the president uses his staff and the resources of the executive branch to actively subvert the process. Upstairs in the White House, Nixon had desperately tried to edit out his crimes to stay in of-fice. He had forgotten that the House had access to a few of the original tapes, and could make its own truer transcripts, because he had handed these tapes over to Sirica and the special prosecutor in late 1973. As a result, the April 30, 1974, transcripts were addi-tional proof of obstruction of justice, an impeachable offense.

Nixon's time in office was running out. On July 17, 1974, Butler went to lunch with a Republican col-league in the House Virginia delegation. Congress-man Joel T. Broyhill told Butler that the smart play would be to support the president: "A vote for im-peachment will offend your diehards, and you won't get any votes from Democrats," he said. Butler knew that, politically, Broyhill was right, but he considered the partisan argument a crutch since his obligations on the committee were constitutional, not political.

"You better start educating your people that impeachment is not a conviction," Butler replied. "A vote for impeachment is a vote for a trial." He had all but made up his mind.[111]

On July 18, Nixon's lawyer James St. Clair gave an elegant and powerful rebuttal before the committee. The president could not be impeached by the actions of his own lieutenants, he argued. Pointing to the perceived weakness of the materials amassed by the committee, St. Clair insisted that only "clear and convincing evidence" of presidential authorization for the misdeeds of Haldeman, Ehrlichman, Mitchell, and Dean should lead to impeachment. And St. Clair did not see any.

Then St. Clair made a mistake. He used a dramatic gesture to show how little the committee knew about his client's true motivation. He introduced a transcript of three minutes of tape from a conversation with Haldeman on March 22, 1973, that purported to show Nixon's unwillingness to proceed with the demands for hush money outlined by John Dean on March 21. Where had this tape been? It had been subpoenaed by the Judiciary Committee, but until this moment Nixon had not thought to offer it. The White House's ploy was more than cynical; it was offensive and stupid. By dangling a helpful piece of tape, Nixon and St. Clair were reminding the entire committee that they really didn't know what Nixon didn't want them to know. "It was a low blow," recalled Walter Flowers.[112]

Following St. Clair's defense statement, the House Republican leadership held an afternoon caucus. Despite his doubts about Nixon, which he had expressed back in May, Minority Leader John Rhodes had decided that at this pivotal moment in history Republicans had an obligation to defend Richard Nixon. Unlike the Mugwumps, Rhodes, who was a pedestrian leader, lacked the imagination to think beyond tribal loyalty. Ed Hutchinson chimed in that he assumed that all seventeen committee Republicans would vote against impeachment. The president's most articulate defender on the committee, Charles Wiggins of California, responded that there wasn't "a scintilla of evidence" proving the president himself had committed a crime. Wiggins was going to defend Yorba Linda's favorite son unless someone showed him the kind of smoking gun that sent people to jail in mystery novels.

But unanimity was impossible for the Republicans in July 1974. John Anderson, the third ranking Republican in the House, took "violent exception" to Wiggins. Since the mini-crisis in May when Anderson had called on the president to resign, he hadn't changed his mind that Nixon had to go. Anderson believed that anything less than impeachment would send the signal that Congress condoned Nixon's obstructionism and abuses of power. Railsback also spoke up.

Caldwell Butler said nothing at the meeting, but Rhodes's call for tribal loyalty did not move him. "I think we as the Republican Party ought to be measured by how it responds to the problem," he recorded in his diary the next day. "If we respond by condoning or putting our feet in the ground we are really going to hurt the party."[113]

The partisanship of the GOP leadership on July 18, 1974, spurred the Mugwumps on the committee to action. In the days since the water cooler conversation, they hadn't reached out to any Democrats. That evening three of them approached two of the key Southern Democratic members, James Mann and Walter Flowers, who were happy to see them. "I want to be sure we are not going to lose this thing on the floor [of the House] if I vote for impeachment," Flowers told the Republicans. He knew his vote would be influential among Southern Democrats. Flowers and Mann both believed that if they and Raymond Thornton of Arkansas presented a unified front, between thirty and forty Southern Democrats in the House would follow their lead. But the articles they approved must be defensible to others like them.[114]

Bill Cohen stressed that there were only two reasons to impeach Nixon: agency abuse and obstruction of justice. Mann and Flowers agreed. They disliked the view of liberal Democrats that Nixon should be removed for offenses beyond the context of the Watergate break-in and cover-up, such as for attacking Cambodia, for impounding money appropriated by Congress, or for selling ambassadorships. However distasteful these actions were, they did not warrant impeachment.[115]

—

The testimony from the live witnesses was not the only source of glue allowing the members to pull Doar's material together. Rodino and Doar had taken the shock of the Democrats' pushback at the end of June to heart, too. They encouraged Dick Cates, who remained loyal to Doar, to begin holding voluntary seminars with interested committee members to demonstrate how the evidence could be assembled to make the case of impeachment. Initially these discussions were for Democrats only, but in mid-July Cohen and Fish asked to be included. Fish, who had found the live witnesses less impressive, credited Cates with "having such familiarity with it that he could . . . weave a plausible story."[116] Despite the fact that Cates was now doing unofficially and quietly what Jack Brooks and the hard-line Democratic impeachment crowd had wanted him to do publicly and officially, pressure was still mounting on Doar among the Democrats to be an advocate for impeachment.[117]

"John felt strongly that the committee did not want the staff or John or anyone reaching a conclusion for them," recalled staff member Evan Davis.[118] But in July, Rodino made the case to Doar that he had to.

Jack Brooks had already started distributing his own draft articles of impeachment, and it was unlikely that any Republican or Southern Democrat would support them.

On July 19, Doar passed around some draft articles of impeachment, largely written by Judiciary Committee staff with input from him and his former special assistant at the Justice Department, professor Owen Fiss of the University of Chicago Law School. The staff also produced a "summary of information," a condensed and pointed version of the thirty-six volumes of statements of information. Finally, also on July 19, Doar himself gave a presentation arguing for impeachment.

Although they appreciated Doar's presentation, the Mugwumps and Southern Democrats did not believe they could vote for any of his articles either. "Running through those articles were allegations that . . . were not supported by evidence," Railsback recalled. In some cases this involved "imputing misconduct by his subordinates to the President and holding him impeachable for those reasons."

"I do not know of a Republican," he concluded, "who could support any one of those articles."[119] Among the southern Democrats, Walter Flowers didn't even read them.

On July 21, Railsback, while studying the summary of information at his home in Western Springs, Illinois, concluded he was ready to vote to impeach the president for direct involvement in the cover-up. "I could see that the President had not, in fact, been telling the American people the truth and that this was direct involvement on his part." Railsback now knew that Nixon had lied when he told the nation that once he had heard about the cover-up from Dean in March 1973, he had acted to shut it down. On April 29, in his televised speech introducing the infamous transcript, Nixon had vowed, "[A]fter March 21 . . . my actions were directed toward finding the facts and seeing that justice was done, fairly and according to the law."[120]

"There were statements that he made that had been reliably contradicted," Railsback recalled in thinking back to all of the times that Nixon had lied to the American people about Watergate. Doing this review "all of [a] sudden gave me a sense of decision and conclusion and finality that I could vote for impeachment and have good evidence behind me," Railsback recalled.[121] Once he had made up his mind to vote for impeachment, he also decided he had to do something about the draft articles.

James Mann knew something about Doar that Railsback didn't: Doar wasn't committed to his own articles. He cared only about getting the votes of the undecided. "I saw my role," John Doar later recalled, "if there was to be a vote to impeach the president, to have the vote of the committee be at least two-thirds, and if you want to know what I thought about all that six or seven months, that's what I thought about.[122]

Doar had a partner in James Mann, who was by now convinced that Nixon was guilty of impeachable conduct. In recent weeks, Doar had been conferring a lot with Mann, meeting him at about 8:00 A.M. almost every morning. Around July 16, two or three days before Doar formally sent his articles to the entire committee, he showed them to Mann. By Monday, July 22, 1974, Doar and Mann were heading a small group of staffers and Democrats secretly reworking the articles.[123]

The Democratic caucus on July 22 was the last one before the committee was set to begin a televised debate. All three Southern Democrats were ready to impeach Nixon, but they had yet to start working together, even though they still shared a concern that their liberal colleagues would present them with unacceptable articles of impeachment. "There was still strong discussion by some Democrats about Cambodia and about taxes and everything," Thornton recalled. Unknown to Mann or Doar, Thornton had written up his own article of impeachment, which emphasized Nixon's role in obstructing justice as a participant in the cover-up.[124] Thornton read it to the caucus and from Mann's reaction realized that they were on the same page.

The focal point of the entire impeachment process now shifted to this handful of Southern Democrats and the Republican Mugwumps. "Rodino understood," Elizabeth Holtzman of Brooklyn later recalled, "and I think by that time most of us understood, that impeachment was never going to happen unless Republicans participated and Southern Democrats participated."[125] Since not a single Republican vote could be taken for granted, Rodino needed a majority of the Southern Democrats—Flowers, Mann, and Thornton—to pass any articles of impeachment.

Following the afternoon meeting of the entire committee, where members discussed the procedures for the forthcoming televised debate, Walter Flowers went over to Tom Railsback to suggest a meeting of the Southern Democrats with the Mugwumps "for the purpose of deciding what we wanted to do."[126] Railsback suggested meeting in his office at 8:00 A.M. the next morning. That night, Mann, Flowers, and Thornton got together for the first time that impeachment summer to discuss over bourbon a common strategy with their new Republican allies.

The next morning the Mugwumps met the Southern Democrats. The meeting began with Flowers, Mann, Thornton, Butler, and the minority counsel Thomas Mooney joining Railsback in his office. Fish and Cohen then walked in.

The sight of Caldwell Butler emboldened Railsback. The fact that a conservative Southern Republican "would have enough guts to adhere to his convictions" was an immense source of confidence for Railsback. They were all bucking the pressure from their own leaders and constituents.

Even though the meeting took place in his office

and over the weekend he thought he had found direct evidence of Nixon's participation in the cover-
up, Railsback was still open to finding a way to
penalize the president short of impeachment. He
opened the meeting asking whether the right punishment for Nixon was truly impeachment. For about
thirty minutes, the group wondered whether it was
right to tie up Congress for six months, which would
be the effect of choosing to impeach Nixon rather
than censure him. To a man, however, they rejected
censure. Once all had rejected the idea of anything
less than impeachment, Flowers set the tone for the
meeting: "Let's get all this evidence and shake it down
and see what are the areas we really agree on here."

Thornton shared his conviction that Richard Nixon
represented a threat to the U.S. Constitution. Mann's
view was that the American people needed to be educated about the extent to which Nixon's conduct
posed a threat to the country. He couldn't think of an
alternative to impeachment to deliver that message.
The group decided that Nixon should be impeached
for obstructing justice—the cover-up—and for abusing his presidential powers. Flowers and Fish both
believed that the press, which all agreed was biased
against Nixon, was missing the big picture of the
threat that his very conduct posed.

Besides agreeing that they would all work together
to impeach Nixon, the group decided to draft the
necessary articles. The bipartisan coalition—which
Flowers called an "unholy alliance" and Railsback

later dubbed "the fragile coalition"—asked Thomas Mooney to work up a new article on obstruction of justice with Railsback, and Cohen and Mann were to write an article on abuse of power. Mann would route these drafts through the drafting group that he and Doar had set up earlier so that the partisans would not know where they came from. At the end, the group also decided they would not tell the press about themselves.[127]

For months, Lou Cannon of **The Washington Post** had been covering the impeachment proceedings. A Californian who had started in journalism covering Californian politics, Cannon typically started his day by checking in on his current beat with three of the Judiciary Committee's Californian members, Democrat Don Edwards, and Republicans Carlos Moorhead and Charles Wiggins. Today he doesn't recall who told him about the extraordinary meeting that had just occurred. When Cannon called Railsback to confirm what he had picked up, the congressman panicked. He wanted Cannon to hold the story. The group had just gotten together, and he worried that the GOP leadership would come after them. Cannon felt he had to go with the story but promised not to use the name of minority staffer Tom Mooney, who was working on an article of impeachment, since Railsback convinced him Ed Hutchinson would fire Mooney.[128]

Whoever told Cannon told others. Journalist Elizabeth Drew, whom Railsback had met for lunch the day before, noted in her impeachment diary on July 23 that "at the moment, the meeting is still something of a secret."[129] By the afternoon, news of the first meeting of "the unholy alliance" that morning had spread to the White House.

Just before 4:00 P.M. Washington time (1:00 P.M. at Nixon's Western White House in San Clemente), Bill Timmons called Haig to say that it looked as if the wall of Southern Democrats—Flowers, Mann, and Thornton—that Nixon counted on was crumbling in the House Judiciary Committee. After a series of calls to politicians across the country, and especially the South, to gauge opinions, Haig felt he had no choice but to call Alabama governor George Wallace, a potential last-ditch ally for Nixon among influential Southern Democrats. Months earlier the governor's chief aide, Taylor Hardin, had told Haig "to call on Wallace if there was anything he could do to help."[130] With impeachment closing in, there was no better moment. Wallace could probably help with Walter Flowers, who had been his campaign manager in 1968.

Haig called the governor's office at 3:11 San Clemente time, 5:11 P.M. in Montgomery, Alabama. Shockingly, Wallace's assistant said that the governor would not speak to the White House chief of staff. He would speak only with Nixon himself. The news was just getting worse. This turn of events must have stunned Nixon, because he didn't call Wallace immediately.

Mann, Thornton, and Flowers were highly respected, and if they were gone, Nixon could not hope to get the more than thirty to thirty-five conservative Democrats in the wider House to support him. Assuming that all of the Republicans would support Nixon—which the White House already knew was unlikely—he still did not have enough votes to suppress an impeachment vote in the House. However humiliating it might be, Nixon had to make the call to Wallace. He hoped Wallace could influence fellow Alabaman Walter Flowers's vote, not because it alone was enough to alter the outcome in the Judiciary Committee but because it could influence other Southern conservatives not to abandon their president when the entire House voted on impeachment. Nixon had to grovel. At 3:52 P.M., Nixon was speaking to Wallace. The conversation would be a turning point for Nixon in his impeachment crisis.

"When I got Wallace on the phone he played it cozy," Nixon later dictated to his diary. "He said he couldn't quite hear me at first, and then said that he hadn't expected the call, that nobody had told him about it."

Nixon must have said something about the weakness of the evidence that his enemies in the House had arrayed against him because, as Nixon noted, Wallace said "he hadn't examined the evidence" and added "that he prayed for me."

Nixon felt he still had to make his political request. He needed Wallace to call Flowers and ask him to support his president. Wallace told Nixon "he didn't think it proper for him to call Flowers, that he thought Flowers might resent it and that if he changed his mind he would let me know."

Nixon understood he was being brushed off. "I knew when I hung up the phone that he would not change his mind."

After the call with Wallace ended, Nixon turned to Haig and said, "Well, Al, there goes the presidency."[131]

—

Less than twenty-four hours later, Nixon's presidency suffered yet another blow. Outside the House, the special prosecutor Leon Jaworski had continued his fight for the Nixon tapes on a parallel track to the impeachment proceedings. After the White House refused to comply with an April 18, 1974, subpoena from the Watergate grand jury, Judge Sirica ruled against the president. Jaworski with St. Clair's agreement then opted to fast-track the issue to the Supreme Court.

At 11:05 A.M., July 24, 1974, the clerk announced the Supreme Court decision in **United States v. Nixon**. It was unanimous.

The court recognized the concept of executive privilege but said that it could not prevent the sharing of presidential materials—the tapes—with the investigation of a criminal matter. The court was not intervening in the impeachment proceedings, as this case had to do with materials subpoenaed by the special prosecutor in April 1974. But the decision would ultimately have the effect of cutting both the impeachment process and Nixon's second term short.

White House counsel Fred Buzhardt was the first high-level Nixon official to read the decision. The game was over for Nixon. For just over a year, Buzhardt had known that Nixon would be found guilty of obstruction of justice if the tapes from the summer of 1972 were ever released. Sometime in mid-1973, in an effort to be able to defend the president, Buzhardt had listened to those tapes. For a year, Buzhardt had apparently justified his role in preventing disclosure of evidence of the president's complicity in a crime as a lawyer would in defending a guilty client. But the Supreme Court decision had altered circumstances irrevocably. If the investigations continued and Nixon did not hand over the tapes, Buzhardt himself might be guilty of obstruction of justice.[132]

He called Alexander Haig in California. It was just after 8:00 A.M. at the Western White House. We will likely never know exactly what Buzhardt said, because he and Haig would later spin a web of deceit about the events of this day. "If you only knew what happened," Haig teasingly told Bob Woodward months after the Nixon presidency had ended.[133] But there is enough to sketch out the likely timetable of events. There can be no doubt that the country danced on the knife-edge of a constitutional crisis without most anybody outside San Clemente knowing it.

At some point that day—likely in the morning—Buzhardt laid out for Haig his recommendation for the president. Buzhardt believed Nixon should resign without complying with the order so that the tapes, especially the June 23, 1972, tape, never saw the light of day. Buzhardt also suggested "mooting" any future criminal case against Nixon by having him pardon all of the convicted and indicted men, and perhaps Buzhardt as well, just in case. Haig agreed to let Buzhardt begin drafting a list of people to be pardoned.[134]

Buzhardt also called Nixon's impeachment lawyer, James St. Clair, who was in San Clemente, to let him know. St. Clair dismissed Buzhardt's concerns. He did not believe any tape could be that damning. His advice to the president would be to comply with the court order and hand over the tapes.

Nixon was beside himself when he learned of the Supreme Court's decision from Haig.

"There's no air in it at all," said Haig.

"None at all?" Nixon asked incredulously.[135]

Nixon was determined never to let any judge, prosecutor, or member of Congress hear the June 23, 1972, tape in which he directed the CIA to quash the FBI investigation. His great hope had been that the Supreme Court would recognize a national security exemption—i.e., give him some "air"—that would allow him to declare the June 23 tape out of bounds because it involved the CIA. Richard Nixon still believed he deserved to be president of the United States whatever his conduct.

It was at this moment that General Alexander Haig defected to the Union. With the exception of the eight days that he had delayed the firing of Archibald

Cox in October 1973, Haig had actively enabled the darkest of Nixon's intentions since becoming chief of staff the previous May. He had actively avoided knowing what Buzhardt could have told him—he refused to listen to a single tape—with the effect that he could single-mindedly engage in thwarting the courts, the Congress, and the public from learning about Nixon's actual conduct—1972–73.

Now the U.S. Supreme Court had weighed in, the truth would come out, and Haig was not about to go down with the Nixon ship. Haig and Nixon spent the next four hours, largely alone but sometimes with St. Clair, discussing what to do. St. Clair counseled compliance, but he had no juice with the president. It was Haig who managed to wear Nixon down. Had Nixon followed his instincts that day, the United States would have plunged into a constitutional crisis.

In the end, Nixon accepted a middling position. He would not pardon anyone. He would respect the court order, but he would drag out compliance—holding on to the June 23 tape as long as possible, certainly past the vote the Judiciary Committee expected in a few days. At 7:00 P.M., eight hours after the court had issued its decision, St. Clair announced that Nixon would comply, as if there had never been a doubt.

—

The members of the emerging bipartisan block on the Judiciary Committee knew nothing about these events in California. They were caucusing again in

Railsback's office when the news broke of the 8–0 decision in **United States v. Nixon.** Their concern was still how to draft articles of impeachment that they could support. When they later heard that Nixon would comply with the court's decision, it was decided that they would leave it up to the full House to assess the import of the new tapes. The coalition felt they had enough to support impeachment for obstruction of justice and doubted Nixon would have fought so hard to prevent the release of tapes that would exonerate him. Railsback, at least, hoped there could be more evidence—directly implicating Nixon and not just his lieutenants—to justify the abuse of powers article.

A few hours later, likely in response to the Supreme Court decision, someone leaked that direct evidence to the media. At the tail end of the September 15, 1972, conversation with Dean after the first indictments, Nixon had complained about the lack of progress in siccing the IRS on his enemies. Initially Judge Sirica had ruled that portion of the conversation—lasting about seventeen minutes—irrelevant to the special prosecutor, and it neither went to Jaworski, nor later to the Judiciary Committee.[136] The leak was a transcript of those seventeen minutes, and the leaker was likely someone in the White House. Was it Haig? We may never know, but it was likely a Republican who wanted to give Nixon a final push out. No one in either the House of Representatives or on the Watergate Special Prosecution Force had that transcript, and the Sirica court did not make transcripts.

When a friendly journalist made sure Railsback saw this information even before it was published, the congressman immediately grasped that this was the hoped-for smoking gun to prove presidential abuse of powers.[137] The quotes from the tape confirmed John Dean's testimony to the Judiciary Committee. Railsback lost no time in telling Caldwell Butler and letting him take a look at it. Until that moment, Butler had believed there was only a "thin reed" linking Nixon to misuse of the IRS.[138] Railsback then arranged a secret meeting with three Nixon diehards—Wiggins, Wiley Mayne of Iowa, and David Dennis of Indiana—in a staffer's office.

"Look, men, here's what I've got. I wonder whether this will make a difference to you," Railsback explained. Wiggins shrugged it off. It was too late. The others agreed with Wiggins. They would vote no on any article of impeachment, and this piece of purloined evidence was not enough to change their minds.[139]

—

As the bipartisan group worked behind the scenes with the blessing of Rodino and Doar to develop articles that would be broadly supported, the public witnessed the first televised debate on presidential impeachment. Over the course of July 25 and July 26, 1974, each of the thirty-eight members of the Judiciary Committee would share their view of impeaching Richard Nixon with the American people.

All the Mugwumps and the Southern Democrats revealed that they intended to vote for impeachment, surprising and, in many cases, disappointing their constituents. Although ultimately not a member of the bipartisan group, Barbara Jordan had decided to support impeachment. In fact, Jordan would electrify the nation with her eloquence and become a household name.

There was an ugly side to this public disclosure. Overnight, Thomas Railsback began receiving death threats, and his family was given FBI protection. Caldwell Butler's wife was getting crank calls, and another caller told a member of his staff, "Your life isn't worth a nickel."[140] Similarly, Bill Cohen's wife received alarming calls, and anti-Semitic letters showed up at his office.[141]

Even before the start of the Judiciary Committee's public hearings, President Nixon's approval rating had dropped to 24 percent, the lowest of his presidency, with 53 percent of Americans supporting impeachment.[142] At the same time, Nixon's base seemed to be getting angrier and was lashing out in response to the growing calls for his removal.

Meanwhile, the bipartisan effort on the Judiciary Committee annoyed both Democratic and Republican partisans, and Friday, July 26, 1974, brought their last offensive. The Democratic partisans decided to force the Mugwumps to vote on every article of impeachment separately, thus drawing out the political pain for them, since each vote would be televised to their constituents. For some time the Southern Democrats and the Mugwumps had been telling Rodino it would make their task easier if they could vote on all of the articles of impeachment at once, rather than having the committee take up each article individually. Rodino tried to help them but lost this battle.

Later that day, the Republican partisans led their own attempt to get revenge. Charles Sandman and Charles Wiggins attacked the article on obstruction of justice for lacking specificity. At Doar's insistence, and with the acquiescence of the bipartisan group, the article alleged that Nixon had adopted "a policy" of covering up. In front of a national audience, Wiggins very effectively pressed the supporters of impeachment to prove that such a policy existed, and they couldn't.[143]

"By the time 6 P.M. rolled around . . . after constant requests for specificity, we, the coalition, felt like a battered boxer waiting for the bell to ring in order to retreat to a quiet corner," recalled Butler.[144] The bipartisan group gathered during the dinner break to figure out what to do. Bill Cohen believed the impeachment process was "in danger at that point."

"Damn it," he told the others, "I'll draft article one myself if I have to stay up all night to do it."[145]

None of them was considering throwing in the towel. It was too late for that. Walter Flowers believed they had a special moral obligation to respond directly to the challenge made by Nixon's defenders on the committee. "The American people identified with those of us in the middle," he recalled. Only this bipartisan coalition could effectively explain to most Americans why Nixon had to go. "If we are going to impeach the president of the United States," Flowers said to the group that evening, "we are going to have to do a good, clean job of it, and it's time we took over." Resolved to proceed, the men calmed one another down and decided against adding more specifics to the article—it would then be sixty pages long—but to find another way to include more details in the debate. They needed the impeachment inquiry staff's help.

Overnight, Doar's staff went into overdrive producing a document linking evidence to every part of the article. And Flowers used parliamentary procedure during the morning session to introduce specifics related to every count into the public record. Then Railsback proposed an amendment, which passed, that removed the reference to an explicit presidential policy. The article now very clearly stated that Nixon was being impeached for obstruction of justice because of demonstrable presidential actions and not because of a theory that the sum total of the actions of his subordinates suggested an explicit presidential policy.

At 7:00 P.M. on July 27, 1974, the committee finally voted on the first article of impeachment. Butler, Cohen, Fish, Flowers, Mann, Railsback, and Thornton supported article one, ensuring for the first time in U.S. history that the impeachment of a president could reflect a bipartisan will. With Republicans Lawrence Hogan of Maryland and Harold Froehlich of Wisconsin also supporting the article, the vote was a lopsided 27 to 11.

The abuse of powers article sailed through 28 to 10 on July 29, and a third article, dinging Nixon for refusing to comply with the committee's subpoenas, also passed. The third article, however, received fewer Mugwump votes, and Mann and Flowers opposed it. Articles regarding the secret bombing of Cambodia and Nixon's tax evasion did not pass, failing even to get enough Democratic votes.

At this point, Nixon's removal from office became highly likely. As the members of the bipartisan coalition understood, the fact that Southern Democrats and so many Republicans supported the first two articles of impeachment ensured that the president would be impeached by the House. And as he had been warned in the wake of the Saturday Night Massacre, his support was even weaker in the Senate.

Nixon made a last lonely, futile effort to cheat the odds. Buzhardt and Haig had transcripts made of the June 23, 1972, tape, in which Nixon ordered the CIA to obstruct the FBI Watergate investigation, and decided to test the waters with Nixon's diehards on the committee.

There is no one who had worked harder and more intelligently on the committee for Nixon than Charles Wiggins of California. Wiggins, who had voted against all of the articles, was invited to the White House on August 2 to read the transcript. Wiggins was devastated. It was one thing to receive a purloined tape transcript from a journalist, which was the case when Railsback had shown him the IRS conversation transcript on July 25. But this was the White House's official transcript. The president had committed a crime.

It takes great courage for a politician to change his mind after he has taken a public position on a matter of consequence. And there was nothing for that generation of elected officials of greater importance than the impeachment of Richard Nixon. "Holy smoke! It's all over," Wiggins told Haig, before bitterly criticizing the White House. He felt personally betrayed by Nixon.[146] Wiggins did not consider himself some mindless partisan who defended a president of his own party because that is what was expected. Rather, he had a narrow view of impeachment and had voted accordingly.

As journalist Lou Cannon, who knew Wiggins, later noted, "It was one of those rare cases in political history, when people change their position 180 degrees by the facts."[147] Wiggins issued a public statement saying he would vote for impeachment when the matter came before the whole House. So, too, did Trent Lott, who was also privately shown a transcript by the White House.[148]

The walls closed in on Nixon. When the White

House publicly released a transcript of the June 23
conversation, on Monday, August 5, 1974, Republican senators had the same reaction as Wiggins. Nixon
was a liar and a criminal. That night Bill Timmons
reported to Haig that the number of senators Nixon
could count on had dropped to seven. Nixon learned
the news while cruising on the presidential yacht **Se-
quoia.**[149]

The next morning Barber Conable of New York, an
influential Republican congressman, called the June
23 transcript "the smoking gun" and approached the
Democratic leadership to recommend fast-tracking
impeachment by the full House. Rodino contacted
Sarbanes of Maryland, Don Edwards of California,
Mann, and Railsback, who were likely to be the
House managers when the issue reached the Senate.[150]
The Democrats and the Republicans thought that
there was so little opposition they could get the
whole thing over with in the House in two days.

The president perceived that his remaining support
in the Congress had collapsed. That same day, August 6, Nixon tasked his best speechwriter, Raymond
Price, to write a resignation speech. After a choreo-
graphed dance that included a visit from Republican
congressional leaders on August 7, Nixon told the
nation of his decision to resign on August 8, effective
the next day.

On Friday, August 9, 1974, Nixon chose to give a
eulogy at his own political funeral. After leaving the

East Room and flying from the South Lawn on Marine One, Nixon left the capital before Congress could formally impeach him.

Barbara Bush, who witnessed the president and the First Lady's departure alongside her husband, chairman of the Republican National Committee George H. W. Bush, remembered that "by the time we reentered the White House all of the pictures [of Nixon] had been changed."[151] Gerald Ford's face now smiled from the official presidential portrait. The U.S. government hadn't missed a beat.

Another photograph was emblematic of this extraordinary historical moment. The day after the House Judiciary Committee had ended its impeachment hearings in July, Caldwell Butler and his wife, Virginia, visited with Peter Rodino in his office. Rodino was on the cover of the current issue of **Time,** and the Butlers wanted their copy of the magazine signed. Butler was as much of a conservative Republican as ever, but he was proud of his work with his liberal Democratic chairman. The signed photograph became a keepsake of an unusual bipartisan moment in American history.[152]

Had Richard Nixon not resigned, he would certainly have been impeached by the House and most likely convicted by the Senate. Peter Rodino and John Doar had been essentially right about the preconditions for a successful presidential impeachment: There had to be a commonly accepted baseline of facts, an atmosphere of trust among the members of the House Judiciary Committee, and a disciplined commitment by the committee chair and the inquiry staff to bipartisanship.

But those were only the preconditions.

Even still, Richard Nixon very nearly finished his second term. His impeachment holds worrisome lessons for future Congresses. Law enforcement and the judiciary had evidence of Nixon's criminal behavior eight months before he left office, and yet there was no predictable way to ensure his removal. Impeachment is a political process, not a legal one, and by hampering access to information while encouraging his defenders to demand a very high level of proof of direct presidential misconduct, Nixon almost stymied that process. But Nixon had made tapes, and the public and Congress learned about those tapes before he could destroy them. Fortunately for the nation, Richard Nixon could never figure out how to untangle himself from those tapes. Equally fortunate for the nation was the fact that in 1974 a group of elected officials, from both parties, were prepared to take political, and even personal, risks to follow that evidence wherever it led for the sake of a Constitution they all revered.

BILL CLINTON
Peter Baker

On the day in January 1998 when news broke that President Bill Clinton was under investigation for lying under oath and witness tampering to cover up a sexual affair with a former White House intern, the beleaguered commander in chief called his on-again, off-again political consultant Dick Morris for advice.

"With this girl, I just slipped up," Clinton told Morris. He did not elaborate, but Morris got the picture. What the president wanted to know was how the American people would react if he admitted it.[1]

Morris agreed to take an overnight poll to find out. Calling back with the results, he told Clinton that Americans would forgive adultery but not perjury or obstruction of justice.

"They're just not ready for it," Morris said.

"Well," Clinton replied, according to Morris, "we just have to win then."

With that, Clinton set the stage for the third presidential impeachment battle in American history, once again drawing in all three branches of government in a momentous struggle that would reframe the parameters of the constitutional order. If Andrew Johnson's impeachment had its origins in the profound debate over how the country should handle the racially charged aftermath of the Civil War and Richard Nixon's resignation stemmed from a massive abuse of power that diminished public faith in America's leadership, Clinton's impeachment and trial at first seemed to prove the old nostrum that history repeats itself, first as tragedy, then as farce. It seemed more fodder for tabloid headlines than for constitutional law books, a scandal rooted in sex rather than separation of powers.

But for all of the car-wreck captivation with the story of thongs and cigars and a stained blue dress, for all of the unseemly details of a tawdry sexual affair gone wrong, the battle between the White House and Congress over the fate of the Clinton presidency carried great import for the country. It exposed and deepened the corrosive, media-saturated partisanship of a new era. It challenged the country's views of public and private morality. And it defined, at least for the moment, the limits of accountability for the most powerful office on the planet. Just as the players in the Clinton drama headed to the library shelves to consult the precedents set during the Johnson and Nixon episodes, today's political strategists and constitutional experts are already looking back to the dramatic events of 1998 and 1999 in search of their own useful lessons.

James Madison and the other framers had always imagined that impeachment would be a political process, but Clinton's trial took it to new levels, posing the question of whether a president's private indiscretions, or even illegal activity to cover up those indiscretions, presented the sort of threat to the republic imagined during those sweltering days in Philadelphia.

For both Clinton and his foes, the impeachment battle was not so much a search for facts or even a debate about what this generation of Americans believed constituted high crimes and misdemeanors than it was another political contest to be won or lost. Indeed, Tom DeLay, the hard-charging House Republican majority whip from Texas, even dubbed his push for impeachment "The Campaign."[2] Clinton, as he confided to Morris, viewed it the same way. Each side sought to shape the public narrative to convince Americans that the other side was violating the norms of America's constitutional democracy—depending on who was doing the talking, this was either a violation of the law by a rogue president who did not believe the rules applied to him or an out-of-control coup d'état by prurient Republicans who sought to exploit personal failings for partisan gain.

Whether he deserved to be removed from office or not, Clinton brought the threat on himself with a breathtaking recklessness that stunned and disheartened even his own staff. Even though his West Wing romps with Monica Lewinsky, a woman barely older than his daughter, were consensual, that did not relieve him of his legal obligation to answer truthfully when asked about them under oath in a sexual harassment lawsuit brought by Paula Jones, a former Arkansas government employee who had accused Clinton of pressing her for sex when he was the state's governor. To prosecutors, Clinton not only committed perjury by denying "sexual relations" with Lewinsky, he also committed obstruction of justice by helping her find a job following their fling, find a false affidavit in the Jones case, and hide gifts that he had given her rather than complying with a subpoena from the Jones lawyers seeking evidence to prove the existence of the relationship.

The fight over impeachment took place against the backdrop of a changing political and media culture. This was the first major Washington scandal of the Internet era and the first since the advent of three twenty-four-hour cable news networks. Initial hints of the scandal had appeared on the Drudge Report, a conservative online tip sheet that was a must-read for Washington journalists and political operatives. The drumbeat of nonstop cable coverage by the recently launched Fox News Channel and other outlets pushed the Clinton scandal to the top of the national agenda for thirteen months. While social media had yet to emerge, the echo chamber amplified every charge and provided an outlet for even the most thinly sourced allegations. No longer did the barons of the old-line media at the major networks and newspapers control what got reported to the public; for the first time, they found themselves chasing a major story that slipped past the traditional mainstream media filter in a way that would have stunned the authors of the impeachment clause of the Constitution, some of them guilty of their own extramarital escapades.

To win The Campaign in this atmosphere, Clinton first had to assuage angry Democrats. His biggest fear was a Democratic repeat of the moment when Barry Goldwater, Hugh Scott, and John Rhodes marched down to the White House to tell Richard Nixon that his time was up. In hindsight, it may seem like Clinton was always destined to hang on, but there were moments when it appeared that Democrats might abandon him and force him out of office. Clinton prevented that from happening by successfully baiting all-too-willing Republicans into making the impeachment drive look partisan and by convincing the public that his indiscretions were a private matter rather than a criminal conspiracy. While only a third of Americans surveyed by pollsters considered him honest and trustworthy, as many as two-thirds approved of the job he was doing.[3] Indeed, his job ratings went up during the scandal rather than the other way around. The public delivered its own verdict.

—

Richard Nixon never knew Andrew Johnson. By the time Nixon faced impeachment, the only president to have undergone it was long since dead and his case more than a hundred years old. But for Bill Clinton, the Nixon impeachment crisis was a very real moment that had shaped his early life in politics.

Indeed, the Watergate era was a formative period for the young aspiring politician from Arkansas. He and his Yale Law School girlfriend, Hillary Rodham, worked on Democrat George McGovern's campaign in 1972, only to be crushed when he lost in a landslide to Nixon just months after the break-in at Democratic National Committee headquarters in the Watergate complex. Following graduation from Yale the next spring, Clinton was offered a position as a staff attorney at the House Judiciary Committee during its Watergate investigation, but turned it down to return to his home state as a law professor with an eye on his own political career. Hillary Rodham, however, accepted the same offer when it came to her.

Working in what she later described as "a mildewed office overlooking an alley," the future Hillary Clinton helped compose a memo exploring the constitutional grounds for impeaching a president and wrote a brief arguing that the committee could deny Nixon the right to counsel during its investigation.[4] She was mesmerized listening in a windowless room to one of the secret Nixon tapes as the embattled president outlined to himself justifications for his actions. "It was extraordinary to listen to Nixon's rehearsal for his own cover-up," she recalled.[5]

Her job ended with Nixon's resignation in August 1974, and she packed her car and drove thirty hours to Arkansas, where the twenty-eight-year-old Clinton, in his debut on the campaign trail, was running for Congress against Representative John Paul Hammerschmidt, a four-term Republican. The Nixon scandal had lifted the boats of Democrats across the country, and Clinton, armed at first with borrowed money and a fat Rolodex, hoped to launch his political career by riding the Watergate wave to Washington. But while Democrats picked up dozens of congressional seats across the country that November, Clinton fell short by 6,000 votes out of 190,000 cast.[6] He later went on to marry Hillary and to win elections as state attorney general and governor, but the seeds of their future troubles were planted during that early campaign when he carried on with another woman behind her back.[7]

Like many in their generation, the Clintons considered Nixon the great villain of their era. But by the time they reached the White House, their views had softened, or at least his had. Nixon, the disgraced former president in a perpetual quest for rehabilitation, advised Bill Clinton on foreign policy, particularly about Russia. Clinton treated him with the respect traditionally afforded an elder statesman. When Nixon died in 1994, the Democratic president gave a gracious eulogy at the funeral that essentially offered forgiveness on behalf of the nation. "May the day of judging President Nixon on anything less than his entire life and career come to a close," Clinton said.[8] Little might he have realized at the time that in less than four years, the two commanders in chief would share something else in common.

While Watergate started with a "third-rate burglary," the Clinton case started with the flash of a thong. Clinton had been dogged by scandal and investigations since the early days of his presidency, but they had never really posed a serious threat. The inquiry into irregularities in the Whitewater real estate deal—a venture in which the Clintons actually lost money—never developed the sort of evidence or stirred the sort of popular outrage necessary to sustain an impeachment effort. Neither did scandals involving Hillary Clinton's questionable profiteering through cattle futures, the Clinton team's rummaging through FBI files of aides to former president George H. W. Bush, the politically charged firing of the White House travel office staff, or the seedy campaign finance efforts that rewarded campaign donors with sleepovers in the Lincoln Bedroom. But Clinton's unquenchable appetite for women would come back to haunt him.

The vehicle was the sexual harassment civil lawsuit filed by Paula Jones. Clinton tried to avoid the case altogether by arguing that a sitting president should not be subject to such proceedings while in office, a question never directly addressed by the constitutional framers. But the Supreme Court was not buying it. Just as it had rejected Richard Nixon's assertion of executive privilege in **United States v. Nixon** more than two decades earlier, it unanimously rebuffed

Clinton's claim for temporary immunity from civil action, with even the two justices he appointed, Ruth Bader Ginsburg and Stephen Breyer, ruling against him. The decision in **Clinton v. Jones** set a powerful precedent that would affect subsequent presidents as well.

With Jones allowed to proceed, a federal judge agreed to let her lawyers search for a pattern of inappropriate behavior by Clinton with other subordinates in government positions. When the lawyers sat down for a deposition to interview Clinton under oath in January 1998, they were ready with the names of a half dozen women who had been linked to Clinton. One of them was Lewinsky, the onetime intern who had flirted with Clinton during a government shutdown by pulling her string underwear out of her waistband and soon was engaged in a sexual relationship with the president.

The Jones lawyers had been tipped off to Lewinsky's affair with Clinton, and they were armed with more information than the president expected them to have. Caught off guard by the specificity of their questions, he sought to mislead his way through the deposition. Along the way, he denied not only having sexual relations with Lewinsky but ever being alone with her. He was so troubled by the knowing questions that when he returned to the White House afterward, he canceled plans to have dinner with his chief of staff. He called his personal secretary, Betty Currie, to summon her to the office the next day to go over his story with her, asking a series of leading questions that seemed clearly intended to rehearse a false version of events in case anyone ever asked her about what happened.

"You were always there when she was there, right? We were never really alone."
"You could see and hear everything."
"Monica came on to me and I never touched her, right?"
"She wanted to have sex with me and I can't do that."[9]

Enter Kenneth Starr, the independent counsel who for years had been investigating the Whitewater land deal and other lesser scandals without finding a smoking gun involving the president. A former appeals court judge appointed by President Ronald Reagan and solicitor general appointed by Bush, Starr had been tapped to serve as independent counsel by a three-member panel of judges chosen by Chief Justice William Rehnquist to select special prosecutors. Starr derived his power from a law passed in its original form in 1978 after Watergate in an effort to insulate prosecutors investigating presidents, a law upheld by the Supreme Court in 1988 by an 8 to 1 decision in **Morrison v. Olson.**

Starr's pursuit of Whitewater was winding down when his office learned about tape recordings that Lewinsky's faithless friend, Linda Tripp, had surreptitiously made of her talking about her relationship with Clinton and the pressure on her to hide it during the Jones lawsuit. Tripp had held an administrative job in the White House under Bush and stayed for a while under Clinton, only to be transferred to the Pentagon, where she later met Lewinsky, who was eventually exiled from the White House as well.

Armed with possible evidence that the president was trying to impede the Jones lawsuit, Starr went to Janet Reno, the attorney general, seeking to expand his investigative mandate to look into the matter. The nexus between his investigation and what seemed to be happening in the Jones case was Vernon Jordan, a powerhouse Washington lawyer and close friend of the president. Starr had already been exploring whether Clinton had used Jordan to buy the silence of former associate attorney general Webster Hubbell, a onetime law partner of Hillary Clinton convicted of stealing from their firm. Jordan had helped arrange lucrative consulting contracts for Hubbell in what Starr's team suspected might be an attempt to keep him from disclosing any damaging information he might know about the Clintons. Starr's team learned from Tripp that Jordan, at Clinton's behest, had been working to find Lewinsky a job, too.

The scandal involving Lewinsky soon found its way into the public eye. Editors at **Newsweek,** nervous about accusing the president of the United States of cheating on his wife with a former White House intern based on secondhand sourcing, held off publishing a blockbuster article by its star investigative reporter, Michael Isikoff. But Matt Drudge, the conservative Internet pamphleteer, posted an item about the story being killed. **The Washington Post** then broke the story of Starr's investigation into a Clinton cover-up of the Lewinsky affair on January 21, 1998, setting off a political earthquake in Washington that would not subside for more than a year.[10] Unlike previous Clinton scandals, this one riveted the country with its tale of illicit sex, secret tapes, and brazen lies. By its end, Americans would witness their third president fighting for his political life against impeachment.

—

It took only hours from the time the first newspapers landed on doorsteps around the capital with news of Clinton's alleged affair for the I-word to be broached— and not just by Clinton's enemies. One of the first to raise the prospect was none other than George Stephanopoulos, one of the original campaign aides celebrated in the documentary **The War Room** for helping elect Clinton in 1992. Having since become a journalist with ABC News, Stephanopoulos said the morning of the **Post** story that if the allegations of lying under oath were true, "I think that would either lead towards the impeachment proceedings or resignation."[11]

That may have been premature, but it was also a bit prescient. The investigation that followed echoed the Watergate probe, exploring many of the same thorny political and legal issues, particularly the limits of a president's executive privilege. Relying on **United States v. Nixon,** Starr successfully forced White House aides, government lawyers, and even Secret Service agents to testify about what they had seen and heard involving the forty-second president. In the process, the battle between Clinton and Starr further narrowed the scope of the president's privilege and established precedents that would affect future holders of the office, with court rulings that no attorney–client privilege exists between a president and a government-paid lawyer and that there is no right to confidentiality involving Secret Service agents, despite their commitment to the privacy of the executives they guard.

Starr eventually issued a subpoena to compel Clinton himself to testify before a grand jury, an order that the president's lawyers concluded they likely could not overturn in court due to the Supreme Court rulings in the Nixon tapes case and the Jones lawsuit. To avoid the indignity of the president being marched down to the courthouse like a common defendant, Clinton's lawyers negotiated a deal with Starr to withdraw the subpoena in exchange for the president agreeing to testify voluntarily under more favorable conditions. The interrogation would take place at the White House rather than the courthouse, with grand jurors watching via closed-circuit television. The questioning would be limited to four hours, and the president's lawyers could be in the room.

Under any circumstances, it would be a moment of reckoning. By the time his date with the grand jury arrived on August 17, 1998, Clinton had been lying to his family, friends, aides, and the American public for seven months.

"There is not a sexual relationship," he said the day the first story ran, his use of the present tense immediately noticed by those accustomed to Clinton's history of word parsing.[12]

When that did not quell the storm, he tried again a few days later. "I did not have sex with that woman, Miss Lewinsky," a red-faced, finger-wagging president scolded reporters.[13]

His aides and supporters engaged in a whispering campaign, painting Lewinsky as a stalker and a fabulist, and they attacked Starr relentlessly as a sex-obsessed Inspector Javert consumed with taking down Clinton. But Lewinsky was, in fact, not only a truth teller; she had a remarkable memory for dates and events—and she had a navy blue dress from the Gap that was stained with semen, forensic evidence that would remove any doubt that she had had intimate relations with the president.

Once Starr obtained the dress and sealed an immunity deal with Lewinsky securing her testimony in exchange for guaranteeing that she would face no charges for her false affidavit in the Jones case, Clinton knew he was cornered. He resolved to make a confession, of sorts, in his grand jury appearance and then later in a nationally televised speech. He sent one of his lawyers to break the news to Hillary Clinton.

On the day of the grand jury appearance, David Kendall, the president's top personal attorney, took Starr aside for a private talk first. He told Starr that Clinton would make a difficult statement at the beginning of his testimony and warned the prosecutor not to push it with overly intrusive questions. "If you get into detail, I will fight you to the knife, both here and publicly," Kendall said.[14]

Starr then huddled privately with his prosecutors in the China Room of the White House and told them what Kendall had just said. "He was visibly shaken," recalled one of his deputies, Jay Apperson.[15]

Clinton was tense as he sat down with the prosecutors in the Map Room of the White House, where Franklin D. Roosevelt had tracked the movement of armies and fleets during World War II. Clinton pulled out a piece of paper from his pocket, put on his reading glasses, and conceded what by then had become obvious.

"When I was alone with Ms. Lewinsky on certain occasions in early 1996 and once in early 1997, I engaged in conduct that was wrong," he said, reading slowly from the paper. "These encounters did not consist of sexual intercourse. They did not constitute sexual relations as I understood that term to be defined at my January 17, 1998, deposition. But they did involve inappropriate intimate contact."[16]

Even now, as he was finally admitting to the relationship with Lewinsky, Clinton was engaging in linguistic gymnastics in hopes of avoiding legal jeopardy. Although he never explicitly described what he did with Lewinsky, he essentially was arguing that since the two engaged only in oral sex, not intercourse, it did not constitute sexual relations and therefore he did not lie under oath in the Paula Jones deposition. The absurdity of the assertion was highlighted when one of the prosecutors, Solomon Wisenberg, noted that the president had allowed his attorney to assert during the Jones deposition that there "is absolutely no sex of any kind in any manner, shape or form" between Clinton and Lewinsky.

That "was an utterly false statement. Is that correct?" Wisenberg asked.

"It depends on what the meaning of the word 'is' is," Clinton replied.[17]

In other words, he seemed to be arguing that because he was not at that very moment having sex with Lewinsky, the statement was literally accurate. The exchange would become infamous, for many encapsulating in one moment Clinton's habit of slicing the meaning of words in such a narrow way as to allow him to maintain that he was being technically truthful even though the intent was to deceive.

After four hours of testimony, Clinton emerged from the session steaming mad at the prosecutors. While he had been behind closed doors, his political advisers had been heatedly debating what he should say to the public, shouting and cursing at one another and storming out of rooms. Now Clinton joined the fray and made clear that while he would admit his misconduct and express regret, he also wanted to use the speech to assail the puritan prosecutors for what he considered their McCarthy-like witch hunt. Someone, he said, had to make clear how unfair this all was. Aides tried to talk him out of it, warning that it would dilute his appeal for forgiveness. But Clinton seemed determined to speak his mind. The last word came from Hillary Clinton, deeply wounded and red-eyed from crying, angry both at her husband for humiliating her before the world and at Starr for exposing their marital troubles. "Well, it's your speech," she told Clinton curtly. "You should say what you want to say."[18]

And so he did. After a shower and a change into a fresh dark suit with a sharp blue tie that he had worn at his first inauguration in 1993, Clinton returned to the Map Room to face the camera. "Indeed, I did have a relationship with Miss Lewinsky that was not appropriate," he told the American people in a speech without precedent in the nation's history. "In fact, it was wrong. It constituted a critical lapse in judgment and a personal failure on my part for which I am solely and completely responsible."[19] But he denied telling anyone to lie or violating the law himself.

Then his face turned dark and his eyes narrowed in that way they did when he let anger overcome his political judgment. While he may have been wrong, Clinton said, Starr had no right to dig into his life this way. "This has gone on too long, cost too much, and hurt too many innocent people," the president declared, bristling with grievance and resentment. He would "put it right" with his wife and daughter, he said. However, he added, "It's nobody's business but ours. Even presidents have private lives. It is time to stop the pursuit of personal destruction and the prying into private lives and get on with our national life."[20]

Clinton's televised speech lasted just four minutes, but they were four minutes that would change his presidency. He had just admitted that he had misled the country for seven months, dragged it through scandal and controversy, all because he could not control his sexual appetites. He had a point about presidents and private lives. Other occupants of the White House had indulged in affairs without being forced to prostrate themselves before the public, much less a grand jury.

But Clinton could not pretend that he did not have fair warning. Standards had changed since the days of Grover Cleveland, Warren Harding, Franklin Roosevelt, and John F. Kennedy—and Clinton certainly knew it. He had experienced it himself during his 1992 campaign when he was forced to confront charges by Gennifer Flowers that he had had an affair with her behind his wife's back. The public forgave him and elected him anyway, but with that came an implicit warning: Don't embarrass us while in office. Clinton understood the unspoken bargain, and yet he could not help himself when he spied that thong.

He was fortunate that while most Americans did not approve of his flagrant trysts, they did not particularly like the idea of prosecutors prying into his sexual exploits, either. Voters made a distinction between his job performance and his personal morality. Polls showed they thought he was a bad husband but a good president. In the days after his testimony and speech, a survey by CNN, **USA Today,** and Gallup found that the vast majority of Americans believed that Clinton had lied under oath, that he was not an honest person, and that he did not exercise good judgment. And yet only a quarter of respondents thought he should be impeached while 57 percent said his personal life did not matter to them, and roughly the same number said that in an era of economic prosperity at home and peace abroad they were glad he was president. In a hypothetical rematch of his 1996 reelection campaign against Republican Bob Dole, the poll found that Clinton would still win by ten percentage points.[21]

But in the hothouse environment of Washington, where Republicans were eager to take down a popular president of the other party and Democrats felt betrayed by their catastrophically undisciplined leader, Clinton's speech was seen as a disaster. In the Solarium of the White House, where his aides watched, there was a sinking feeling. To many of his advisers, the speech hit the wrong notes. He did not sound like a man apologizing and asking forgiveness. He sounded angry and entitled. Rather than seeking to end the ordeal through confession and redemption, he cast himself as a victim and attacked those who had forced him to tell the truth against his will.

The instant reaction on television was harsh and unrelentingly negative. "What do they expect me to do?" Clinton fumed at aides. "Roll over and let Starr do this and just take it?"[22]

Among his most partisan Republican enemies, the speech only fueled their animus and strengthened their resolve to hold Clinton to account. In the war room of Tom DeLay's Campaign, they were suiting up for battle.

"He looked into americas eyes and lied," one DeLay aide emailed another that night.

The other aide agreed. "This whole thing about not kicking someone when they are down is BS," he replied. "Not only do you kick him—you kick him until he passes out—then beat him over the head with a baseball bat—then roll him up in an old rug—and throw him off a cliff into the pound surf below!!!!!"[23]

—

While Starr was operating under the independent counsel law giving him greater autonomy and protection than the special prosecutors had during Watergate, he was exploring some of the same tricky constitutional issues his predecessors had. Just as Leon Jaworski's staff drafted a memo in 1974 arguing that he had the power to indict a sitting president, so, too, did Starr's team in the spring of 1998, a legal conclusion that has never been definitively established, then or now. The fifty-six-page legal analysis was kept secret for nearly two decades until the National Archives released it to **The New York Times** in 2017 in response to a request under the Freedom of Information Act. "In this country, no one, even President Clinton, is above the law," the memo said, adding new insight into an old argument and offering additional context to the decisions that Starr would make.[24]

Much like Jaworski, who considered impeachment a more appropriate remedy, Starr opted against testing the thesis in court, and instead of indicting Clinton decided to refer the matter to the House of Representatives for possible impeachment. His was an easier choice than Jaworski had. The post-Watergate law that had created Starr's office specifically contained a provision obliging an independent counsel to provide Congress with "any substantial and credible information" that "may constitute grounds for impeachment."[25] So on September 9, 1998, with just ten minutes' warning, two vans carrying thirty-six boxes of evidence rolled from the independent counsel's office to the U.S. Capitol. Television cameras followed the vans as if they were monitoring O. J. Simpson's white Bronco in the slow-motion police chase that captivated the country four years earlier. The public braced for another impeachment drama just twenty-four years after Nixon left office.

In his referral, Starr charged Clinton with eleven impeachable offenses—four alleging perjury in his deposition in the Paula Jones lawsuit, one alleging perjury in his grand jury appearance, five alleging obstruction of justice, and one alleging abuse of office. According to Starr, Clinton lied during the deposition when he said he had no specific recollection of being alone with Lewinsky or of any gifts he had given her and denied that he had had "sexual relations" with her. He impeded the lawsuit, according to Starr, by encouraging Lewinsky to lie, by helping to arrange a job for her to encourage her silence, by helping her hide the gifts he had given her, by coaching Betty Currie with a false version of events, and by lying to other aides who would ultimately be called before a grand jury to repeat those lies. And Starr accused Clinton of abusing his power by making frivolous claims of executive privilege to prevent the truth from being discovered. "When such acts are committed by the President of the United States, we believe those acts 'may constitute grounds for an impeachment,'" Starr wrote in the 453-page report.[26]

In form, if not in substance, the charges mirrored those in Watergate. Precedent, however, did not give the House leaders any guidance on what to do with the report once they received it. Starr had not told the lawmakers what was in it, and neither Republicans nor Democrats were sure whether to make it public or not. They opted not to look at it themselves first for fear that the minute they did, one side or the other would selectively leak parts of the report seen as most advantageous to their point of view. So the House voted to release it sight unseen, giving everyone a first look at it simultaneously and leading to the extraordinary spectacle of news anchors reading its most salacious details on live television.

Not expecting lawmakers to make it public without reviewing it first, Starr and his team had laced the report with an explicit account of the ten sexual encounters between Clinton and Lewinsky, helpfully letting lawmakers know that the two had twice "engaged in oral-anal contact" and that on another occasion they had used a cigar as a sexual stimulant. Prosecutors reasoned that they needed that level of detail to make abundantly clear that Clinton had lied when he testified in both the Paula Jones deposition and the grand jury appearance that he had not had "sexual relations" with Lewinsky as he understood the term. It was Clinton himself who forced the Starr team to be so specific, went the argument.

But the almost pornographic precision backfired on Starr and the Republicans, making them look as voyeuristic and intrusive as Clinton had charged and raising the question of what that had to do with his performance as president. For Clinton, the release of the report was a public humiliation but a political boon. It did not stop the House Republicans from proceeding with an impeachment inquiry, but it helped Clinton portray it as an illegitimate and offensive exercise.

In the search for precedent, neither side paid much heed to the Andrew Johnson impeachment. It was too old, too different. To the partisan warriors of 1998, it did not seem to offer many lessons about the contours of impeachment or the definition of high crimes and misdemeanors. The resolution passed by the House impeaching Johnson contained just a single sentence without any specificity, only to be replaced by eleven articles after the fact. To the extent that it came up at all, the Clinton camp used the Johnson case as a cautionary tale to warn against political impeachments.

But as the Clinton impeachment process got under way that fall, both sides turned to the Nixon case repeatedly in seeking historical justification, albeit with each side engaged in a little political role reversal—the Republicans in this case on the attack and the Democrats on the defense. Advised by Tom Mooney, the aide who helped pro-impeachment Republicans during Watergate, Representative Henry Hyde of Illinois, the Republican chairman of the House Judiciary Committee that would first consider Starr's charges, crafted the structure of his impeachment inquiry based on the one run by Peter Rodino, adapting it nearly word for word from the 1974 variant. But even though Clinton's White House and its Democratic allies in Congress had demanded "Rodino-style rules," reasoning that they would be fairer to the president, they quickly denounced the Hyde plan as a wide-open fishing expedition.

Whatever the substantive objections, Democrats resolved to oppose the Republicans every step of the way as a matter of strategy. They concluded that they could not let the Republicans win, even though a successful impeachment conviction would still leave Vice President Al Gore in the Oval Office, because it would weaken their party and reward what they considered an unfair crusade by the other side. And so they decided to turn every issue into a party-line struggle, regardless of the merits. The more partisan the impeachment effort looked, the less legitimate it would seem in the eyes of the public. While they decried partisanship, the Democrats intentionally tried to promote it—and they had willing if unwitting allies in this among the Republicans who were perfectly inclined to operate on the basis of party all on their own.

As the Judiciary Committee voted on redactions to the evidence that would be released to the public after the original Starr report, for instance, Democrats panicked when they realized that Republicans were going along with most of their motions, producing unanimous, bipartisan votes. They needed party-line votes to argue to the public that the whole venture was just a partisan exercise, so they quickly came up with more provocative motions that they assumed Republicans would oppose so that they could produce the split votes they needed. The Republicans obliged. "Win by losing," the Democrats privately called their strategy.[27]

Clinton's supporters also had a field day unearthing the sexual misadventures of his pursuers to cast them as hypocrites, further framing the context of the impeachment in terms of a sexual liaison rather than perjury or obstruction of justice. Larry Flynt, publisher of **Hustler** magazine, even offered $1 million to anyone who would bring him "documentary evidence of illicit sexual relations" with a member of Congress or high-ranking government official.[28] Through the fall, one Republican after another suddenly found himself—or herself—on the receiving end of the scrutiny that had scorched Clinton for much of the year. Henry Hyde's affair with a hairdresser in the 1960s was exposed, for example. He defended himself by saying it was a "youthful indiscretion"—never mind that he had been in his forties at the time of the affair.[29] He offered to resign, but Speaker Newt Gingrich refused to accept.

Embarrassing revelations were aired about several other Republican members of Congress, including Representatives Bob Barr of Georgia, Helen Chenoweth of Idaho, and Dan Burton of Indiana. Others spent the fall worried that they, too, would be exposed. Representative Asa Hutchinson of Arkansas, a member of the Judiciary Committee from the president's home state, was warned that he was the "next target." Representative Lindsey Graham of South Carolina, another committee member, received phone calls threatening to reveal that he was, alternately, gay or sleeping with various women. Another committee member, Representative Steve Buyer of Indiana, was so anxious that he preemptively confessed his own indiscretions to his wife in case they got reported. (They never were.) And Gingrich himself, one of the driving forces behind The Campaign, was at that very time conducting an adulterous affair with a House clerk, perhaps explaining why he was not all that eager to accept Hyde's offer to step down and set a precedent for resignation that could trip him up if the truth were to come out, which it did not until after the impeachment drama was over. For Clinton's defenders, the point was to make the whole issue about sex rather than lying under oath.

The Republicans made the case that their own affairs were not the same thing—Clinton was the target of impeachment not because he violated his marital vows but because he violated the law. The president of the United States had given false testimony under oath and sought to impede a civil lawsuit, according to the evidence collected and analyzed by Starr. However aggrieved Clinton felt over the intrusion into his private life, he was not entitled to ignore the law or the orders of a judge who not only directed him to answer the questions posed by Paula Jones's lawyers but flew to Washington to personally oversee the deposition. Yet that argument, logical though it might have been, did not seem especially persuasive to many Americans who saw Republican two-timers trying to punish a Democratic philanderer.

The fact that the impeachment inquiry was playing out against the backdrop of a midterm congressional election would provide a real-time test of public attitudes about the case. Republicans were convinced that the scandal would weigh down Democrats, just as Watergate did to Republicans in 1974. Gingrich authorized campaign advertisements openly addressing the issue, including one with footage of Clinton's angry, finger-wagging denial of any sex with "that woman." While the ads were meant to be used only in strategically chosen races where they might be helpful, they were replayed on national television news and became the image for the race overall—driving Democrats out to the polls rather than Republicans.

Gingrich did not see what was coming. Indeed, even on Election Day, he boldly predicted to fellow House Republicans on a morning conference call that they would pick up some twenty seats by the end of the evening. Instead, Democrats were the winners, not only holding on to their share of the House but increasing it by five seats.[30] The balance shifted to 223 Republicans to 212 Democrats (counting Bernie Sanders, an independent and self-described socialist who caucused with the Democrats), meaning that on any given issue a defection of just six votes would cost the GOP control. The Democratic victory defied historical trends as well as contemporaneous expectations; the incumbent president's party usually lost seats in the sixth year of an administration. The last time it actually captured more seats in such an election was in 1822 when James Monroe was president during what was called the Era of Good Feelings.[31] This was definitely not that kind of era.

Clinton watched the results come in from his chief of staff's office. He was pumped up by the results. Not only had Democrats beaten history and Gingrich, Clinton assumed they had succeeded in ending the threat to his presidency. After such a reversal, he reasoned, the House Republicans would of course drop impeachment.

Clinton hugged a friend. "We made it through," he said.[32]

—

Many Republicans assumed the same thing. The election verdict was clearly a repudiation of the drive for impeachment. Gingrich had explicitly made the election about the scandal, and voters had not punished the president's party for his misconduct. So if the public did not see Clinton's transgressions as worthy of his removal, it seemed logical to conclude that the people's representatives would act accordingly.

In the days following the election the Republicans fell into a fratricidal civil war over the debacle. When Representative Bob Livingston of Louisiana, the Republican chairman of the powerful House Appropriations Committee, announced that he would challenge Gingrich for Speaker, it was clear that the restive majority would hold its leader accountable for his miscalculation. Bitter and resentful, Gingrich got the message and announced that he would step down rather than be voted out.

Now the putative Speaker, Livingston had less of the taste for the jugular when it came to impeaching

Clinton, but Tom DeLay, still the hard-charging House majority whip, had more than enough for both of them. Just because they lost the election did not mean they should surrender the Campaign. And so while the White House anticipated that the threat would go away, the Republican majority kept heading down the path it had been on. Just two days after the election, Henry Hyde sent the White House a series of eighty-one questions for Clinton to answer, and soon began scheduling hearings.

The star of the hearings would be Kenneth Starr. On November 19, 1998, the independent counsel appeared before the Judiciary Committee to explain his report—and himself. For months, he had remained publicly silent as he and his team's work were dissected and debated. He had become, to many, a cartoon figure, the embodiment of a system gone awry. He was seen as a fanatic, a right-winger. That was a far cry from the reserved, decent man that Starr's staff and admirers saw, but as a prosecutor, he had felt constrained about defending himself publicly. He did not make the rounds on the television talk shows or give public speeches, so the hearing would finally give him the opportunity to present his case and rebut the charges of overzealousness. In his opening statement, Starr insisted that he was concerned only with the law with a wry allusion to his dismal public image. "I am not a man of politics, of public relations, or of polls," he said, "which I suppose is patently obvious by now."[33]

He then spent a long day responding to questions from members of the committee and their top lawyers—hostile allegations from Democrats meant to discredit him, friendly softballs from Republicans meant to rehabilitate him. But the real fireworks did not come until the evening when Hyde gave David Kendall, the president's longtime personal attorney who had vowed to fight Starr "to the knife," a chance to question the independent counsel. The two had jousted for years without such a personal confrontation and so there was an almost cinematic quality to the long-anticipated showdown. It started off with faux familiarity, as they addressed each other as "David" and "Ken." But it quickly evolved into a razor-sharp exchange in which Kendall accused his adversary of abusing power and leaking information while Starr depicted himself as an aboveboard investigator pursuing the facts wherever they took him, however sordid and unpleasant that might be.

It was fascinating theater, but it also served to embolden the Judiciary Committee Republicans, who found Starr impressive, and it reinforced their conviction that they had to press forward despite the election results. They were further stirred by the answers Clinton gave to the eighty-one written questions they had submitted, which in their view were full of legalistic arguments rather than any genuine admission or sense of regret.

The White House did not waken to the reality of what was happening until Thanksgiving weekend

when Clinton's White House chief of staff, John Podesta, went for a brisk run in the capital city's bucolic
Rock Creek Park. Suddenly all the pieces came together in his mind. This was a runaway train, and it
was not going to stop despite the midterm elections.

The following Monday, Podesta strode into the
morning staff meeting at the White House and announced his conclusion. "This thing is rigged," he told
stunned colleagues. "We are going to lose."[34]

—

The Judiciary Committee inquiry involved little original investigation of its own but instead relied largely
on the evidence gathered by Starr and the rebuttals
presented by Clinton's lawyers. But the Republican
counsel, David Schippers, and several of the Republican members also explored whether to expand the
case beyond the Monica Lewinsky affair.

In particular, the Republicans looked at allegations
lodged against Clinton by other women, in theory, at
least, seeking a pattern of lies, obstruction, and in-
timidation of accusers. Among them was Kathleen
Willey, a former White House volunteer who accused
the president of kissing and groping her in the Oval
Office in 1993. Willey had suggested that Nathan
Landow, a Democratic fundraiser from Maryland,
had tried to discourage her from testifying about her
interactions with Clinton. Robert Bennett, a lawyer
for Clinton, had tried to convince Daniel Gecker,
Willey's attorney, to hire a friend of his to represent
her with the idea that they could share information

in a joint defense agreement, in effect putting them on the same team against the Paula Jones lawyers and making it easier to coordinate their stories. Republicans wondered whether this amounted to another example of obstruction of justice by the president.

Another woman whose story caught their attention was Juanita Broaddrick, who owned a nursing home in Arkansas and had privately alleged that Clinton, while serving as state attorney general and running for governor in 1978, had raped her in a hotel room. Unlike Willey, who went on **60 Minutes** to publicly air her charges, Broaddrick had avoided the spotlight and, indeed, when initially approached by investigators working for Paula Jones's lawyers, signed an affidavit denying that anything had happened with Clinton. But she had since changed her mind, recanted her denial, and told Starr's investigators her story.

The examination of the women's stories put both parties in awkward positions, reinforcing their situational—and opportunistic—ethics. Republicans who had sought to undercut Anita Hill's charges of sexual harassment against Clarence Thomas during his confirmation hearings for the Supreme Court just seven years earlier were now championing women who had been victimized by a president of the other party. Democrats who considered themselves feminists were questioning the credibility of women making accusations against a president they counted as an ally on issues like abortion rights.

Starr had not included the Willey or Broaddrick ac-

cusations in his charges to the House because in neither case did he conclude that there was enough
evidence of an impeachable offense such as perjury or
obstruction of justice. The Republicans, however,
wanted to see for themselves. Schippers, the Republican counsel, went to interview Willey and deemed
her a powerful witness. At the same time, Asa Hutchinson, the committee member from Arkansas, drove to
the small town of Greenwood to meet with Broaddrick and found her story disturbing. But Broaddrick
said no one connected to the president had tried to
pressure her to remain silent, so Hutchinson concluded her case did not fit a pattern. And while Schippers was impressed by Willey, Henry Hyde did not
consider her case strong enough to prove obstruction.

The lawmakers then were left to decide the questions underlying every case of impeachment: What
had the founders truly meant by the term "high
crimes and misdemeanors"? And what did those
words mean for their own day? Could they include
actions in a private civil lawsuit unrelated to the presidency? Even if the president were proven to have
violated the law, did his lies and efforts to impede the
lawsuit constitute such a threat to the health of
the republic that they merited his impeachment and
removal from office?

Andrew Johnson and Richard Nixon were both accused of abusing the power of their office. While Starr
had contended that Clinton had, too, by making patently unmerited and self-serving executive privilege

claims, the essence of the case against him was the cover-up of the affair, which did not involve the use of presidential authority. Still, even after Johnson and Nixon, no one could say for sure what an impeachable offense really was any more than Gerald Ford's famous nostrum about it being whatever a majority of the House said it was. "It's like pornography," Hyde said, in an unfortunate analogy for this particular scandal. "You know it when you see it, but you have trouble defining it."[35]

Still, the Republicans wanted to move forward. When it came time to draft articles of impeachment, Hyde turned again to the Nixon model. The young lawyer he put in charge of writing the articles even used "Rodino" as the password on the computer. Hyde's team adopted the same three-paragraph introduction that Peter Rodino's committee had used during Watergate at the start of each of its articles, accusing Clinton of violating his oath "to faithfully execute the office of President of the United States." And it used the same two paragraphs at the end of each article, asserting that his misconduct "warrants impeachment and trial, and removal from office." The specifics from the Clinton situation were then inserted in between.

Hyde and his team were struck by the surface similarity between the Nixon charges and the ones they developed against Clinton—false statements and obstruction of justice. But by so consciously emulating the Watergate case, they unintentionally suggested that Clinton's crimes were as serious as Nixon's, handing an argument to the other side, which maintained that lying about sex hardly seemed as significant as spying on the opposition party, paying hush money to burglars, and sponsoring a wide-ranging campaign of harassment against critics of the sitting president in advance of an election.

Still, the committee Republicans decided Clinton's actions did meet the uncertain criteria for impeachment and sent the question to the House floor. They approved four articles of impeachment, alleging perjury before the grand jury, perjury in the Paula Jones lawsuit, obstruction of justice, and abuse of power. Three of the four passed on strictly party line votes, while one Republican, Lindsey Graham, balked on the article accusing Clinton of lying in the Jones case because it came during a civil lawsuit that had since been dismissed. John Podesta was right—despite the midterm election results, Republicans had not backed off and planned to pursue the case as far as they could.

—

For some Republicans, including Asa Hutchinson, there was still a desire to find some sort of middle ground, such as a resolution that would formally censure the president while not impeaching him. There was a precedent: The Senate had censured Andrew Jackson in 1834 in a dispute over documents related to the Bank of the United States that he had refused to turn over to lawmakers.[36]

Various back-channel discussions sought to craft such

a formulation to resolve the Clinton case; some Democrats saw it as a reasonable way out just as some Republicans did. Neither side wanted to let Clinton off the hook entirely, though they did not want to set a precedent by removing him from office over a tawdry affair and an effort to cover it up.

But Tom DeLay resolved to kill the idea by preventing any vote on censure and forcing members into a yes-or-no decision on impeachment. He did so behind the scenes, his orchestration carefully hidden. He had his staff draft three letters. The first was to be sent by Henry Hyde to Bob Livingston and Newt Gingrich, expressing opposition to allowing a censure vote on the floor. Since Hyde had allowed such a vote in his committee, it was critical that he make the argument that a repeat by the full House was not appropriate. The second letter would be a response from Livingston to Hyde agreeing that such a vote should be barred. And the third letter would be sent to Hyde by Gingrich, who was serving his last days as Speaker before Livingston's ascension, announcing that he would summon the House back into a lame-duck session to take up impeachment without allowing censure to be considered.

DeLay's staff then took the letters around Capitol Hill to get them signed by the three leaders. Hyde signed the letter in his name, but when the DeLay aides could not find Livingston, they simply had the incoming Speaker's chief of staff sign his boss's name for him. Gingrich could not be found either, so a

DeLay aide who had previously worked for the Speaker signed it herself, tracing his signature from a sample of stationery. Neither Livingston nor Gingrich objected. The one name not signed to any of the three letters was that of DeLay, their real author, but when they were publicly released, it put an end to the movement for censure in the House.

Given no choice but to support or oppose impeachment in the absence of any middle-ground option, most House members lined up with their party. But as the floor debate approached, enough Republicans seemed up in the air that Clinton still harbored hopes of defeating the impeachment articles. Worried about being accused of improperly pressuring Republicans, Clinton reached out mainly to those few he knew were his allies and counted on them to help. But DeLay was a formidable adversary and knew his caucus better than Clinton did. Like the president, he did not want to be seen directly lobbying colleagues for their vote as if it were just another spending bill, so instead he quietly enlisted fund-raisers, party officials, and even local luminaries back in home districts to lean on fence straddlers.

In case that was not enough, undecided Republicans were encouraged to head down to the locked office in the Ford House Office Building where Starr's secret evidence was stored, specifically to look at the files on Jane Doe No. 5, the designation given to Juanita Broaddrick. Overall, forty-five Republicans checked out the unreleased evidence personally.

While Broaddrick's chilling tale of rape was not included in the four articles of impeachment, many of those who learned about it in the Ford office found it too troubling to ignore.

Formally, at least, they were to vote only on the evidence officially presented to them, but some at least were also forming their decisions on their general sense of Clinton's character. James Madison did not want "maladministration" to be an impeachable offense because he did not think the ultimate constitutional tool should be used to resolve partisan differences. But nothing in the document that he and his colleagues finally signed explicitly forbade lawmakers from bringing their own wider judgments to bear, and it could be argued that the character of the nation's chief magistrate was, in fact, central to the integrity of the union.

—

The impeachment battle was heading toward a dramatic climax even as other momentous events were playing out half a world away. In Iraq, the dictator Saddam Hussein was refusing to cooperate with international weapons inspections in defiance of a United Nations Security Council resolution from the days of the Gulf War of 1991. Clinton was preparing to launch air strikes in retaliation.

The timing seemed suspicious even to Iraq hawks, too much like **Wag the Dog**, a recent Robert De Niro–Dustin Hoffman movie in which a president waged a fake war to distract attention from his own scandal. Clinton was helped by the fact that his defense secretary, William Cohen, was a former Republican senator who told his onetime colleagues on Capitol Hill that the decision to take action had nothing to do with the brewing impeachment debate.

Among the skeptics, however, was Bob Livingston. As American warships moved into position, he agreed to postpone the start of the impeachment debate for one day—but just one day. At the same time, he was facing an ordeal of his own. He confessed to fellow House Republican leaders that he, too, had had relationships outside of his marriage and informed them that one past paramour was about to go public with **Hustler** magazine. "I've been Larry Flynted," he told them.[37] Within minutes, the story leaked to the media.

The impeachment debate opened on the House floor on December 18, 1998, as American warplanes and cruise missiles rained destruction down on Baghdad thousands of miles away. The mood on the floor was raw and combustible. Democrats were outraged that the Republicans were moving to impeach the commander in chief with troops in the field. Republicans were still reeling from the revelations about Livingston on the eve of his ascension to the speakership and in some cases were convinced that Democratic dirty tricksters must have had something to do with the disclosure. Members of both parties toggled back and forth between uncertainty and indignation.

Henry Hyde led the charge against Clinton, trying

to elevate a case rooted in sexual misconduct to loftier heights as he invoked the spirit of the Ten Commandments, Mosaic law, Roman law, the Magna Carta, Bunker Hill, Concord and Lexington, Abraham Lincoln, and the soldiers of World War II. "The president is our flag bearer," he declared. "He stands out in front of our people, and the flag is falling. Catch the falling flag as we keep our appointment with history."[38]

Democrats bridled at what they saw as high-handed rhetoric and complained that rather than an act of patriotism, the House was engaged in a Republican putsch. Representative Dick Gephardt of Missouri, the Democratic minority leader, led the defense. "We are now at the height of a cycle of the politics of negative attacks, character assassination, personal smears of good people, decent people, worthy people," he said, in an implicit nod to Livingston's case. He added, "The politics of smear and slash and burn must end."[39]

Emotions spilled out of the chamber and into the hallways and side rooms. After Bob Barr, one of the Republicans advocating impeachment, quoted John Kennedy, saying that "Americans are free to disagree with the law but not to disobey it," the late president's nephew, Representative Patrick J. Kennedy of Rhode Island, accosted him in the Speaker's Lobby.

"Anybody who has been to a racist group has no right invoking my uncle's memory!" Kennedy shouted.

Barr had spoken earlier in the year to a group that

was an outgrowth of old white councils that had fought integration in the South, explaining when confronted afterward that he did not know its history.

"Young man, you are showing a lack of decorum," Barr, who was fifty, scolded the thirty-one-year-old Democrat.[40]

The conflict in the Capitol had grown so caustic, so corrosive, that Bob Livingston began entertaining second thoughts. "We've got to stop this," he told an aide. "This is crazy. We're about to impeach the president of the United States."[41]

Livingston was contemplating shutting down The Campaign at the eleventh hour, a reflection of his own ambivalence over the magnitude of the events transpiring. Instead, he would allow the House to vote on censure.

The aide pushed back, insisting that Livingston had to go to the Ford office building to look at the secret evidence himself. The aide, Marc Curallo, pushed back. "Boss," Curallo said, "we have a **rapist** in the White House."

Livingston backed down and decided against pulling the plug on the impeachment. Instead, he headed home to write a speech of his own. The next morning, he got up on the floor as the second day of debate opened and castigated Clinton for doing "great damage to this nation" through his lies. "I say that you have the power to terminate that damage and heal the wounds that you have created," Livingston declared, addressing the president directly. "You, sir, may resign your post."[42]

Democrats on the other side of the chamber erupted in anger.

"You resign!" Representative Maxine Waters of California shouted. "You resign! You resign!"[43]

Others took up the chant but Representative John Conyers of Michigan, the Nixon foe who now served as top Democrat on the Judiciary Committee, flapped his arms to silence his fellow party members, sensing that there was more to come.

Indeed, Livingston continued, saying that because of his own circumstances he had realized that he could not be the kind of leader that he wanted to be. "So I must set the example that I hope President Clinton will follow," he said. "I will not stand for Speaker of the House on January sixth."[44]

Shock swept through the chamber. Almost no one had seen that coming. Just like that, the impeachment fight had claimed a second House Speaker, another casualty to the politics of the moment. Republicans were dazed to see their leadership once again collapse. Democrats regretted looking like they had egged Livingston on. And Clinton's aides watching on television as the White House instantly feared that Livingston's sacrifice for his sins would produce pressure on the president to do the same.

With Livingston's fate decided, the House began voting on Clinton's. The tally fell largely along party lines. The first article, on grand jury perjury, was approved

228 to 206, with five members of each party breaking ranks to vote the other way.[45] The House went on to approve a second article on obstruction of justice but rejected the articles charging perjury in the Paula Jones case and abuse of power. Dozens of Republicans concluded that lying in a civil lawsuit was not as serious as lying to a grand jury, and they likewise rejected the abuse of power article as overreaching.

With that, Clinton became the first president impeached since Andrew Johnson and the first elected president ever sent to trial in the Senate. The Campaign kicked off by Tom DeLay had succeeded, at least to this point. In an era of presidential supremacy, Congress had reasserted its powerful place in the American system of government, albeit in a partisan clash that would forever flavor its legacy. As for Clinton, history would record this distinction no matter what happened from here on.

But the immediate danger to his presidency, he recognized, was the possibility that pressure would build on him to follow Livingston's example. To forestall that, dozens of House Democrats piled into buses after the vote for the short ride down Pennsylvania Avenue to the White House, where they stood by their president's side in the Rose Garden as he defiantly vowed to keep fighting. Some Democrats had initially balked at what amounted to a pep rally in the midst of such serious proceedings, but with Livingston's resignation it now served to show that Clinton's party had not abandoned him. Al Gore set the tone by declaring that by voting for impeachment, the House had done "a great disservice to a man I believe will be regarded in the history books as one of our greatest presidents."[46]

In his own short speech, Clinton asserted that he had spent six years working to build consensus across party lines. "It's what I intend to do for two more," he declared, "until the last hour of the last day of my term."[47] In other words, whatever Livingston had done, whatever many members of Congress might wish him to do, Clinton did not plan on going anywhere.

—

That, of course, would be up to the Senate. On paper, Clinton had every reason for confidence. While Republicans controlled the upper chamber with fifty-five out of the hundred seats, conviction required a two-thirds vote, or sixty-seven senators. That meant that Clinton could count on acquittal as long as he did not lose twelve Democrats.

While his survival seemed likely, it did not always feel that way at the time. More independent minded and less partisan than their House colleagues, senators were not always predictable. After the House vote, Senator Tom Daschle of South Dakota, the Democratic minority leader, contacted every member of his caucus and concluded that he would likely lose just five or six Democrats if things did not change—but in a worst-case scenario, if momentum turned on the president, he counted up to twenty

Democrats who could potentially vote to remove Clinton from office.

That seemed improbable but not impossible, making it all the more important how the trial would play out. Since no president had been put on trial in more than a century, there was little to go by. Richard Nixon had resigned long before the matter made it to the Senate, leaving only the Andrew Johnson trial for a precedent. Given how dated that was, and how discredited that prosecution would later be viewed by history, Daschle and Senator Trent Lott, the onetime Nixon defender who was now serving as Republican majority leader, in effect had to make it all up as they went along with little guidance.

Unlike their House counterparts, Lott and Daschle were determined to work together to ensure a smoother, less polarized process. They had both been turned off by the ugly House proceedings and wanted to avoid letting the Senate tear itself apart in the same way. In a telephone conversation shortly after the House vote, they were both relieved to find each other of similar minds about how to proceed, if not the final outcome. Daschle agreed to help "co-pilot the plane" to a safe landing.[48]

The general outlines of a trial were established by the Johnson episode. Just as Chief Justice Salmon Chase presided over that tribunal, Chief Justice Rehnquist would officiate this time around. Just as senators Charles Sumner, Benjamin Wade, and Edward Ross did in 1868, modern-day senators would remain mute at their desks, silent witnesses rather than the drivers of the process they were used to being. Just as Representative Thaddeus Stevens did before them, Henry Hyde and a team of "managers" from the House would come over from the other side of the Capitol to prosecute the case. And just as Johnson dispatched attorneys to defend him, so would Clinton. As it happened, the players this time would have at least one expert in that case in their midst—Rehnquist had published a book six years earlier on the Johnson trial called **Grand Inquests,** conveniently rereleased in paperback just in time for the Clinton trial.

But beyond the emulation of form, there really was no road map. Would the president testify in his own defense? Could he be compelled to if he did not want to? Would the managers present other witnesses on the floor of the Senate? How much time would each side have to describe its case? Could they interrupt each other? Could senators interject?

Few scenarios unnerved senators of both parties more than the prospect of Monica Lewinsky being called to the Senate floor to testify about the president touching her private parts and leaving a stain on her blue dress. Lott tried to restrain Hyde and the managers, arguing that they did not need witnesses anyway because the facts had been established. The managers pushed back, complaining that the senators—**Republican** senators— were trying to hamstring them from doing their duty in the most important issue to confront the Congress

in years. They had become so invested in their impeachment drive, so convinced that they had to hold a
wayward president to account, that they were consumed with making their case even if they had no real
hope of winning a conviction.

But in approving a set of rules for the trial, it was
more important to Lott to secure bipartisan consensus, and if that meant alienating his House colleagues,
so be it. He and Daschle agreed on a process for the
trial that would postpone the question of witnesses
until after both sides presented their cases and senators had a chance to ask questions. At that point, the
managers could make a motion to call witnesses and
the Senate would vote whether to grant it. Having
punted the hardest question, the Senate then approved the trial procedure 100 to 0, a sharp contrast
from the partisanship of the other chamber across the
Capitol. Lott and Daschle were relieved, but Clinton
and his team were not. Consensus was their enemy;
partisanship was the key to acquittal.

Opening arguments began on January 14, 1999,
and no one was entirely sure what would happen. As
David Kendall told associates, it was as if all of them
were in parachutes plunging through the night sky
into the murky darkness below. Rehnquist's only in-
struction to the managers and the president's lawyers
evoked the tone of a referee at a boxing match. "Fight
fair," he told them before they headed out onto the
floor.[49] No one really thought it had been a fair fight

up until that point, but both sides had different perspectives on who had been hitting below the belt.

Hyde and the rest of his thirteen-member team of managers sat at a table on the left side of the chamber as they faced the rostrum, which happened to be where the Democrats' desks were arranged, while Kendall and the rest of the seven-member team of presidential attorneys sat on the other side, where the Republicans were located. Both teams had separately asked if they could switch sides to sit near the senators closer to them politically, but the sergeant at arms refused, saying this was the way it was done in Andrew Johnson's day.

Not there in Johnson's day were the four large, flat-screen, high-definition television screens now set up on the floor, two on each side of Rehnquist. This was a radical breach of protocol, never before seen on the Senate floor, and traditionalists complained, but they were deemed necessary to show videotape of the president's grand jury testimony.

Hyde opened the prosecution case with typically grandiloquent oratory about the meaning of the oath and justice, then left it to the other managers to outline the specific charges and evidence. Thirteen managers were too many, of course, and senators quickly grew tired of hearing the same arguments laid out again and again.

But the real stars quickly emerged—three young Republican lawyers, Asa Hutchinson, Lindsey Graham, and James Rogan of California. Methodically and powerfully, using charts and the television screens, they recounted a story of deceit and cover-up, knitting together meetings, phone calls, and court actions to assemble a narrative that proved more powerful than some Democrats had expected. Senators who had never really immersed themselves in the details before left the chamber thinking there might actually be a case for conviction. Some were particularly struck when Graham described Clinton as a champion of civil rights who had failed to uphold the right of a woman to lodge her own civil rights claim; others thought a comparison with judges who had been impeached and removed from office for perjury made it harder to dismiss the importance of the allegations against the president.

Clinton had been anxiously watching and concluded that he needed help. His lawyers were fine, but the managers were on a roll and the president wanted someone who could speak directly to the senators as a peer. The White House had reached out before to big-name defenders without luck, but now Senator Tom Harkin of Iowa, an ally, contacted three former Democratic senators on the president's behalf: George Mitchell of Maine, John Glenn of Ohio, and Dale Bumpers of Arkansas. The first two begged off. Bumpers tried to as well, but Clinton called personally to implore him, and the former senator accepted.

David Kendall was joined by Charles Ruff, the White House counsel, and a team of other lawyers who opened their presentation with their own rendition of the facts and timetable intended to poke holes in the managers' case. Unlike the others, Ruff brought the experience of having been the fourth and final Watergate special prosecutor, and thus was acutely aware of what impeachment meant. Without saying it quite so bluntly, Ruff made the point that Clinton was no Nixon. "You are free to criticize him, to find his personal conduct distasteful," Ruff told the senators. "But ask whether this is the moment when, for the first time in our history, the actions of a president have so put at risk the government the framers created that there is only one solution."[50]

It fell to Bumpers to connect with senators on their level. The silver-haired, silver-tongued lawyer from Clinton's home state spoke from handwritten notes on a legal pad without addressing any of the particulars of the legal case. Instead, he boiled the issue down to its essence, a story about politicians as human beings, flawed and weak and ultimately redeemable. "When you hear somebody say, 'This is not about sex,' it's about sex," Bumpers told his former colleagues with his Ozark drawl. Clinton deserved reproach, he agreed. "You pick your own adjective to describe the president's conduct. Here are some that I would use: indefensible, outrageous, unforgiveable, shameless." But he said, "We are, none of us, perfect."[51]

When the time came for witnesses, a compromise was reached. The managers would be allowed to take testimony from three players in the long-running drama but not on the Senate floor. Instead, they would be deposed on videotape in another location and the two sides could then show the senators excerpts from the interviews to make their arguments. Monica Lewinsky would, of course, be the star witness. The other two would be Vernon Jordan, the president's friend who had helped Lewinsky get a job in what prosecutors called an attempt to influence her testimony in the Paula Jones case, and Sidney Blumenthal, a White House official and leading Clinton defender who was suspected of orchestrating the whisper campaign impugning Lewinsky as a stalker.

Hyde tapped Representative Ed Bryant of Tennessee, a genial, low-key former prosecutor, to interview Lewinsky. The session was held in the $5,000-a-night presidential suite of the city's landmark Mayflower Hotel, complete with a backlit presidential seal etched in aqua glass inset in the floor. By the time she arrived, Lewinsky had already been through two dozen depositions, FBI interviews, and grand jury appearances. She had become a professional testifier. And she ran rings around Bryant. She referred him back to her grand jury testimony. She adopted Clinton's semantic defense by contending that her affidavit denying their relationship could be both "misleading" and "literally true." She maintained that it was in her own interest to file a false affidavit, rather than the president's, meaning that he did not need to influence her testimony. By the end of the interview, Clinton's lawyers did not bother to ask her any questions since she had only helped their case. "She's the best witness I ever saw," Tom Griffith, the chief Senate lawyer, who served as an adviser to the senators, told one of Lewinsky's attorneys afterward.[52]

The subsequent interviews with Jordan and Blumenthal yielded nothing more significant, leaving the managers to work with the same case they had had when they started the trial. The witnesses who were not called, though, still had their say, at least as shadows of the trial. Kathleen Willey met privately with at least one Republican senator to explain what Clinton did to her, the sort of contact that would be deemed improper in a normal criminal court but was not subject to the same rules in the political process of an impeachment proceeding. And Juanita Broaddrick gave an interview to Lisa Myers of NBC News detailing her allegations publicly for the first time. Executives at NBC held the interview, unsure whether to air a sensational and impossible-to-prove charge that the president of the United States had raped a woman two decades earlier, especially given that it was not officially part of the trial. But word about the unaired interview got out, and it became a minor cause célèbre among conservatives. One Republican senator even wore a "Free Lisa Myers" button on the Senate floor during the trial.[53]

Even so, the worst-case scenario that Tom Daschle had feared did not materialize. There were clearly not enough votes for conviction, so senators began looking for a way to finally bring the case to an end without giving Clinton a pure victory. They explored alternative ideas such as approving a censure resolution or adjourning without taking a final up-or-down vote on the articles of impeachment. One option never contemplated by James Madison or Alexander Hamilton would be a "finding of facts" that would conclude that Clinton had committed some of the acts he was accused of, even if they did not rise to the constitutional level of justifying his removal from office.

But no matter how creative the senators were, it came down to the same yes-or-no choice that Tom DeLay had forced the House to make. The Campaign demanded a straightforward verdict.

So, it seemed, did the public. "Good God Almighty!" a man with a graying beard shouted from the gallery at one point. "Take the vote and get it over with!"[54]

They did on February 12, 1999. One by one, a clerk called out the names of the senators, who stood at their desks and called out "Guilty" or "Not guilty"— with the exception of Senator Arlen Specter, a Republican from Pennsylvania, who offered his own variant: "Not proved, therefore not guilty."

Within a few minutes, the tally was taken. On article one, charging perjury before the grand jury, only forty-five senators voted guilty, fully twenty-two short of the two-thirds necessary for conviction. Fifty-five senators voted not guilty, including every Democrat and ten Republicans.[55]

After another roll call, article two, charging obstruction, was rejected as well, this time on a 50 to 50 tie vote, with five Republicans joining the unanimous Democrats.[56] The managers had failed to win even a simple majority. Clinton had been acquitted. He would serve out his final 708 days in office. And the Senate had come through the ordeal without the meltdown that Trent Lott and Tom Daschle had feared.

"We did it," Daschle said.

"We sure did," Lott replied.[57]

Informed by his Watergate experience, Lott's determination to work across the aisle for a calm, orderly, and dignified outcome rather than simply play to the partisan passions of the moment would stand out as Washington grew increasingly polarized in the years that followed. A generation later, his example seems especially striking as politicians on both sides appear more committed to party than to any larger sense of duty.

At the White House, Clinton emerged one more time in the Rose Garden, this time all by himself without the pep rally. He sought to avoid looking like he was gloating and repeated that he was "profoundly sorry" for "what I said and did to trigger these events and the great burden they have imposed on the Congress and on the American people."[58]

He then turned to head back into the West Wing, only to hear the ABC journalist Sam Donaldson call after him. "In your heart, sir, can you forgive and forget?"

Clinton pivoted back to the podium. "I believe any person who asks for forgiveness has to be prepared to give it," he said.[59]

—

In the end, the stonewalling strategy Clinton adopted after Dick Morris's poll actually worked. By denying for seven months that he had had "sexual relations with that woman, Miss Lewinsky," he effectively diminished the shock when he finally confessed in August 1998. By that point, the public had already processed the situation, and the political momentum that might have gathered for his resignation in January never picked up enough steam in the fall. When the matter reached the House floor in December, Clinton and his allies made the question more about the Republicans' behavior than his own, rallying otherwise queasy Democrats back into his corner. Once the House vote fell along party lines, it set the paradigm for the trial that would follow in the Senate, where Republicans could not convince enough Democrats to join them to reach the two-thirds vote needed for conviction and removal from office.

When the dust settled, even some key Republicans concluded that they had gone too far. No impeachment will succeed, they learned, if it is not bipartisan. And while lying under oath is still illegal even if it is about sex, the remedy of removal from office struck most Americans as out of proportion to the crime. Still, Clinton paid a price. In a deal with Robert Ray, Kenneth Starr's successor as independent counsel, that was hammered out in his final days in office nearly two years after the Senate trial, the president finally admitted that he had not told the truth under oath and agreed to the suspension of his law license and a $25,000 fine. Clinton settled the Paula Jones lawsuit for $850,000—more than she had sought in her original complaint—but without admitting her allegations. Susan Webber Wright, the judge in the case, found him in contempt of court for giving "intentionally false" testimony in the deposition she had personally supervised and fined him $90,000, the first president ever so sanctioned while in office.

Newt Gingrich, who at one point led the impeachment drive, later suggested that the split decision of a House impeachment followed by a Senate acquittal was the appropriate end result. "It may have had the right outcome, frankly," he said. "We sent the signal— presidents, even when popular, can't break the law. But at the same time, I think the country didn't want an impeachment, a conviction in the Senate."[60]

Whatever George Washington and the other framers thought of the importance of reputation, Clinton refused to see the result as any kind of dishonor and instead held himself out as a hero for standing up to renegade Republicans. "I do not regard this impeachment vote as some great badge of shame," he told one interviewer before leaving office.[61] He later told a conference that when it came to impeachment, "I am proud of what we did there because I think we saved the Constitution of the United States."[62] Many Americans agreed with him, sensing like James Madison two centuries before that such a drastic measure as impeachment should not be taken for partisan purposes.

Twenty years later, though, the view of history has shifted a bit. Once dismissed as a national distraction while more serious issues such as international terrorism and Wall Street corruption went ignored, the Clinton scandal looks a little different in the age of the #MeToo moment. If Clinton's conduct was too easily forgiven at the time, did it then pave the way for another president who boasted of grabbing women's genitals, was accused of harassment by more than a dozen women, defended an accused child molester, and sought to buy the silence of a porn star who claimed an affair with $130,000 in hush money?

Today some of the key figures in the Clinton impeachment are reassessing. Monica Lewinsky, who always insisted that she was no victim since she was a willing sex partner with Clinton, has now come to believe that the power differential between a president and a former intern by itself made the relationship exploitive. Kathleen Willey and Juanita Broaddrick, who like Jones alleged forcible behavior against their will, are now being reevaluated through the lens of a movement that demands that accusers be believed.

Even some Democrats once close to the Clintons have changed their minds. After allegations against the Hollywood mogul Harvey Weinstein and other powerful figures were brought to light in 2017, Senator Kirsten Gillibrand of New York, who took Hillary Clinton's seat when she became U.S. secretary of state in 2009, now says Bill Clinton should have resigned.[63] Chris Hayes, the MSNBC host, said, "Democrats and the center left are overdue for a real reckoning with the allegations against him." Matthew Yglesias, a liberal blogger who once worked for a Clinton-allied research organization, declared that by defending him, "we got it wrong."[64]

If the Andrew Johnson impeachment was judged by history to be illegitimate because it essentially litigated a policy dispute rather than a high crime and if the Richard Nixon scandal was judged to be clear-cut in meeting the standard for removing a president from office, then the Clinton episode fell somewhere in the murky middle. It was neither a slam-dunk obvious case that compelled conviction nor was it easy to dismiss out of hand. A president should not be able to violate the law, and yet there was no consensus that this particular violation was so egregious as to trigger the ultimate constitutional sanction.

In the end, as the framers anticipated, impeachment is a political action, not a legal one. It is, in a sense, another campaign to be won. High crimes and misdemeanors remain undefined, and Gerald Ford's assessment seems as true today as it ever was. Clinton's experience, coming so soon after Watergate and driven by so many who had experienced and even come of age during that scandal, reset the rules first established by Johnson's trial.

Any impeachment, however legitimate or not, however wise or not, rewrites the rules for the presidents who follow—until the next one comes along and rewrites them all over again.

CONCLUSION
Jeffrey A. Engel

They are rare, but increasingly relevant. Congress impeached only one president in the country's first 184 years. The next two impeachment crises took a mere twenty-five more. Plotted on a timeline their pace thus appears to be quickening, but we need not employ so crude a measure as dots and graph paper to tell us that talk of impeachment swirls today as rarely before. The word echoed throughout the final days of the 2016 presidential election. "This is a cesspool . . . beyond Watergate," a campaign insider railed against their opponent and the prospect that "we are this close to having this criminal organization take over the White House." Should such a miscreant win office, he promised, impeachment would soon follow. "It's just going to happen. We're going to sort of vote for a Watergate."

"I guarantee you within one year she'll be impeached. One year," Rudy Giuliani said. "And indicted."[1]

Perhaps you were expecting a different pronoun or a partisan from the other side? Donald Trump's unconventional campaign pushed talk of impeachment to the fore well before election day, raising questions not only of his electability to high office but his durability once there. "Trump will eventually be impeached by a Republican Congress that would prefer a President Mike Pence," a leading electoral prognosticator offered in September 2016, arguing they'd choose the latter's seeming stability over Trump's crowd-enchanting spontaneity and simultaneous risk of spontaneous combustion.[2]

The candidate himself returned volley. Hillary Clinton's presidency would create "an unprecedented and protracted constitutional crisis," Trump told a campaign rally less than a week before voters went to the polls. A vote for her, he said, was a vote for endless investigations, mind-numbing hearings, and political gridlock. "Haven't we just been through a lot with the Clintons?" he asked. It was a question, and a threat. Given her vilification within the party likely to retain Congress, he may well have been right. "The work of government," Trump warned, "would grind to a halt if ever she were elected."[3]

Of course he won instead, refocusing investigative glare back upon himself. Washington pundits and politicians alike have waited breathlessly ever since for the next revelation, be it from a journalist or a special prosecutor, in what seems a tireless search to prove or exonerate Trump's culpability in something that might approach an impeachable offense. Voter attention, newspaper subscriptions, and television ratings have all soared accordingly, even as Americans simultaneously claim to tire of the Trump-induced intensity. The prize for winning the presidency used to be prestige, power, and a sure place in history. Added to that list now seems to be a hefty personal legal team. Bill Clinton infamously claimed to have left the White House in debt to his lawyers. Trump pays his personal defense counsel from campaign funds.

Impeachment's prominence should trouble citizens of every stripe. The process for legislatively removing a chief executive outlined in the Constitution was never designed as a partisan tool or campaign talking point. It was instead the framers' safeguard, a nuclear option provided to halt tyranny and corruption at the top, to employ a term they would neither have employed nor understood. That election of either candidate in 2016 generated talk of its use demonstrates the opposite. Rather than accept the will of their fellow voters, Americans on both sides of the aisle today are instead ready as never before to reject the legitimacy of an Election Day's verdict before their opponent even swears their oath of office. This is neither a recipe for political amity nor for efficiency in the halls of government. "They're already promising even more unprecedented dysfunction in Washington" and immediate impeachment hearings, outgoing president Barack Obama lamented to voters as the battle to succeed him stumbled to a close, at once rebuking Trump's charge against Clinton yet inadvertently previewing a fair portion of his party's response to the actual outcome. "How can our democracy function like that?"[4]

In truth, it cannot. At least not well. None of the three cases of presidential impeachment discussed in these pages offers any comparable example of a president threatened with losing his office so soon upon taking power. None offers a comparable case of voters and politicians seemingly so comfortable with invalidating elections. Andrew Johnson was not elected president in the traditional sense, but even he enjoyed a honeymoon of support from a nation shocked by the realization that their age of sorrow could indeed get worse. Richard Nixon and Bill Clinton did not hear cries for impeachment of the kind with which Trump began his presidency until their second terms, in each case after voters, unaware of the depth of their first-term misdeeds, renewed their leases on the Oval Office by landslide margins. Trump's investigations and talk of his impeachability while still a candidate, or the not unthinkable prospect of impeachment hearings begun by a Republican majority in the House of Representatives had November 2016 turned out the way most pollsters expected, thus offer an unprecedented escalation of this ultimate constitutional remedy for electoral failure. Judged on these terms alone, one might think more Americans than ever have become sore losers, willing to kick over the playing board rather than play out a poor hand.

Those are not the only terms to consider, however.

After twenty-plus years of concerted assault by Hillary Clinton's critics, a fair number of Americans wholeheartedly believed her a criminal by 2016. Chants of "lock her up" formed the background score of Trump rallies. She was not, in other words, a "normal" candidate in this sense. Of course, neither was he, and if the suspicions lodged against Trump in the wake of his surprising electoral upset prove in any way true, a constitutional crisis will no doubt ensue.

Please note the conditional tense of that phrase, but also the magnitude of the potential charges. Investigations were launched during Trump's first year in office to determine if his campaign colluded with a foreign power to sway his election; to discover if he was somehow financially or otherwise controlled by a foreign power when he ran for the Oval Office; and finally to determine if he in turn conspired to impede an investigation into either of the aforementioned claims, employing his constitutional powers to halt or undermine a lawful inquiry. Trump of course vigorously denies each of these charges, proclaiming himself victim of a "rabid witch hunt" coordinated by an intransigent deep state supported by a hostile liberal media, while repeatedly rejecting the unanimous judgment of the American intelligence and national security community that foreign foes indeed tried to manipulate the election to improve his electoral chances. These are serious charges indeed, or an insidious witch hunt of epic proportion. Time will tell.

Time has already told what the Constitution's framers would have made of someone in power who committed the type of crime of which Trump stands accused. They feared these very things. Someday a president "might pervert his administration into a scheme of peculation or oppression," James Madison warned his fellow delegates when explaining impeachment's necessity, or "might betray his trust to foreign powers." Gouverneur Morris added to the list. "He may be bribed by a greater interest to betray his trust," and no one would say that "we ought to expose ourselves to the danger of seeing the first magistrate in foreign pay." Neither, Morris added, would any reasonable person dispute that a president should not be "impeachable for treachery."[5]

Given the president's principal role in determining the nation's foreign and military policies, physically protecting the state and its citizenry in the most literal sense, the Constitution's architects specifically dreaded the prospect of a future officeholder controlled by a foreign land lowering the nation's defenses, or enabling an enemy threat to grow. "Guilt wherever found ought to be punished," Edmund Randolph proclaimed. "The executive will have great opportunities of abusing his power; particularly in time of war when the military force, and in some respects the public money will be in his hands." As noted earlier in this book, one should pause, and perhaps even reconsider, if about to begin a statement with "the founders believed." This sentiment, however, requires no such caution: The founders believed any president corrupted by foreign influence should be impeached. Period. They had just fought a war to liberate themselves from foreign rule, after all.[6]

Ultimately, when George Mason asked "Shall any man be above justice?" the phrase oft-quoted when discussion of presidential impeachments arise, he did not mean simply that powerful leaders should not be allowed to pervert fair and equitable application of the law. He meant something more profound: that those entrusted with great power—those atop the law, if you will—were not just subject to its reach but additionally responsible for maintaining the rule of law itself. Injustice in a single case is wrong, but injustice that undermines our ability to pursue fair and respectable justice weakens the very fabric of democracy. Those entrusted with the American people's fate, therefore, should never rank their personal well-being higher. No man was above justice, that is true, but for Mason and those around him, no leader was more important than those he led, and liberty would surely die if Americans ever forgot that point.[7]

This, too, we can confidently say the founders believed, and their inheritors understood that vigilance is indeed freedom's price. "Freedom is never more than one generation away from extinction," President Ronald Reagan reminded Americans in the 1980s. "We didn't pass it to our children in the bloodstream. It must be fought for, protected, and handed on for them to do the same." The sentiment, prevalent in every generation since the 1770s, transcends partisanship. "My faith in the Constitution is whole, it is complete, it is total," Texas Democrat Barbara Jordan told the House Judiciary Committee in 1974 as Watergate came to a head. Those are impeachable who behave amiss or betray the public's trust, she argued, citing the Constitution's authors. If those subsequently charged with securing democracy's survival would not act when confronted with evidence of that trust's abuse at the highest level, "then perhaps that eighteenth-century Constitution should be abandoned to a twentieth-century paper shredder." No one was above justice, Mason said in 1787, or could be so long as Americans hoped to retain their republic.

There have been more perilous moments in American history than our own. The years 1777, 1863, and 1932 immediately leap to mind. Each time the republic overcame daunting odds, albeit at great cost, though our track record does not guarantee survival against the next threat. This should ring true no matter one's political party, tribe, or opinion of the problems besetting the nation today or the accusations currently encircling Trump's presidency. The same logic applies to our three prior cases of presidential impeachment and the prospect of someday a fourth. Each of the former was a political crisis that threatened—and even damaged—but none destroyed our democracy. We survived. The Constitution's ability to withstand a fourth time is not guaranteed.

The history of impeachments teaches us not only to be wary of going down that perilous road again, but each case additionally provides a useful insight should a fourth impeachment case ever arise. Andrew Johnson went first, and his lesson is at once the broadest, revealing that impeachments built upon constitutional questions—that is, conflicts that arise from a president's deployment of the powers granted his office and governed by the separation of powers at the document's heart—prompt genuine constitutional reflection among those charged with rendering a verdict. These are issues of presidential power and prerogatives, requiring consideration of what the Constitution forbids, allows, or leaves to future generations to address. Questions of mere illegality need not apply to join this category. Rather, if the questions underlying an impeachment case are best judged not by a criminal defense lawyer or prosecutors but instead by constitutional scholars, forcing consideration of what the document's architects believed and wrote in 1787, the case is, simply put, constitutional in nature.

Johnson's was one such constitutional case. He was impeached in 1867 for, frankly, being a jerk, but that was not the question up for debate as senators pondered his fate. Racist even by the offensive standards of his own day, inflexible where his predecessor had been preternaturally nuanced, and ultimately unwilling to follow an overwhelming congressional majority even though he'd run on its national ticket, Johnson was a pain in Republican sides from the moment he showed up drunk to his vice-presidential swearing-in.

Americans had never to that point in their history impeached a president merely for being, as Benjamin Franklin put it, "obnoxious." Neither had they sought his removal merely for being controversial or even incompetent. British troops burned the White House on James Madison's watch. He remained through the end of his term. Andrew Jackson's critics feared his imperial aspirations and bemoaned his boorish style and consistent degradation of political decorum, the "norms" of the day if we employ a term from our own. He nonetheless served eight full years. James Polk launched a war of aggression on feeble pretexts, and James Buchanan's inertia and duplicity helped ensure an even greater national calamity. Both completed their terms without facing formal articles of impeachment.

What made Johnson different? It was not merely that he was obnoxious or inept, but rather that he directly contradicted congressional will, explicitly overstepping what the legislative branch desired to allow the executive. As Jon Meacham shows within these pages, Johnson was despised well before he violated the Tenure of Office Act, which legislators laid out in part as a constitutional trap, pitting their right to dictate a president's cabinet against the executive's. They'd not have laid that trap if he'd been adored. Yet the narrow issue upon which Johnson's fate was ultimately decided was not one of popularity or even politics, but instead of constitutional prerogative, decided by the handful of Republican senators who voted against their party and for Johnson's retention simply and profoundly because their reading of the Constitution rebutted the trumped-up charges against him.

Or for other reasons. Seven Republican senators voted to acquit, rejecting the omnibus charge that summarized the ten specific complaints lodged against him. Historian David Greenberg argues that an additional four likely would have voted to acquit if they believed their ballot the decisive one. None liked or agreed with Johnson. But in a narrative tinged with nostalgic glow these seven looked beyond party and instead toward a broader understanding of their responsibility to the republic, and to its long-term survival, by concluding that no matter how despised or despicable, Johnson had acted as the Constitution allowed. One, Kansas senator Edmund Ross, earned a place in John F. Kennedy's collection of essays on political heroism, **Profiles in Courage,** including the verdict that his vote "may well have preserved . . . constitutional government in the United States."[8]

Let us not get carried away: Some of those seven, Ross especially, looked to their own personal fortunes as well as to the republic's when deciding Johnson's fate, believing their prospects better with him in power than his likely successor. Some miscalculated, failing to gain the patronage or fame they hoped siding with Johnson might bring. Others considered their vote in light of their reading of the Constitution's intent.

None of those seven ever won election to public office again. Voting against one's party has consequences. Then again, senators from their same states who voted with the Republican majority and against Johnson also lost their ensuing reelection bids, as, like a shaken snow globe, the American electorate slowly settled into new positions following the disruptive war.

What, then, are we to draw from Johnson's case? That because the fundamental issues at hand in his trial transcended party loyalty, partisanship alone did not seal his fate. Several Republican senators voted their conscience; others their personal interest. Either way, their votes reveal that in impeachments centered on the separation of powers—in this case, the potential dominance of the legislature over the executive in contravention of the balance envisioned by the Constitution's architects—party allegiances proved less powerful than personal conviction, at least for a decisive portion of senators. Johnson's case thus teaches that should a future president be impeached and come to trial over an issue whose adjudication requires direct reading and interpretation of the Constitution itself, we should expect senators to at least consider voting across party lines. Some might even find the basic moral courage to cast their votes not only for the politics of today but for the sake of future generations.

Nixon's impeachment offers lessons as well, indeed several from which to choose. His deliberate undermining of his accusers' credibility scarred American politics for decades, and his prolonged defense demonstrated the lengths to which a guilty president might go to protest his innocence, and how long he might drag out a case against him before admitting defeat. Nixon may well have believed the actions he took that led to his impeachment were both just and legal. But he never considered them laudatory. Why else would he have worked so hard and so long to keep his real relationship to the Watergate burglars and the ensuing scandal secret, unless he knew most citizens would find grave fault in the revelation? He was, after all, in on the crime from the beginning.

In retirement he famously justified his behavior by explaining that "if a president does it, that means it's not illegal," but no matter how much he believed this in his heart, he knew full well the likelihood that prosecutors and a court—whether composed of senators weighing his political fate or a jury called to reach a verdict in a criminal matter—would likely see matters quite differently. Nixon's case demonstrates that a guilty president can long retain his office, and might even survive long enough to complete his elected term. As Tim Naftali demonstrates, but for a different legal strategy or series of events, Nixon might well never have been forced to leave office prematurely.[9]

These are not, however, the most important lessons to draw from Nixon's saga, and more specifically from his resignation offered in lieu of eventual impeachment and conviction. Rather, we should heed the speed by which he ultimately fell. Though he was able to defer and distract and plead his innocence for nearly all of his second term, once legislators reviewed undeniable proof of his systemic abuse of executive power, they swiftly pushed for his resignation before they would have been required to force him out.

Nixon's saga reveals that when support for an embattled presidency fades, it cascades.[10] In March 1974, little more than a third of Americans favored his removal from office despite nearly two years of Watergate-related revelations. By April, nearly half supported his dismissal. The number never dipped below 50 percent again, until it spiked higher in the final days before his resignation. By August he was gone.

Why did so many Americans change their minds so quickly? Because the facts changed. Nixon's "smoking gun" tape, released to the public in late July 1974, offered clear evidence of his complicity and guilt. Most Americans had accepted their president's word during the months and years he'd proclaimed his innocence. Then they heard his own words tell a different tale when he thought no one was listening. A who's who of White House and Republican officials in turn delicately but firmly advised their agitated leader that his time was up, including Chief of Staff Alexander Haig, Secretary of State Henry Kissinger, Chair of the Republican

National Committee George H. W. Bush, key senators and congressional leaders, and trusted West Wing advisers. Lawyers were no longer required. This was politics.

All believed resignation inevitable by August 1974. They might persuade 50 congressmen to vote against an impeachment resolution, senior House legislators privately confided to the president, but nowhere near the 218 votes he'd need to avoid that indignity. As for the Senate? There they might have 15 votes, one-time Republican standard-bearer Senator Barry Goldwater told a still-wavering Nixon on Wednesday, August 7. Another senator doubted they could get more than 12, either way far short of the 34 acquittal required. Goldwater called the situation "hopeless."[11]

Nixon knew they were right. He'd been in Washington long enough to count votes. "I just wanted to hear it from you," he told his fellow Republican leaders. The next day he informed Vice President Gerald Ford of his decision, then announced his resignation to the country. By noon Friday, he was gone.[12]

Richard Nixon's defense collapsed once enough solid evidence emerged to convince even staunch defenders that they'd been lied to by the White House, and worse yet, been made to lie for Nixon in front of the American people. "We had been betrayed," New York congressman Henry P. Smith exclaimed. Others had harsher words less suitable for publication.[13]

Nixon's case tells us, therefore, that proof matters. Should a future president find him- or herself confronted by hard evidence of impeachable offenses—be they documents, tapes, bank records, or something else the general public can easily understand—the longer their record of denial the faster it will drag them down. The president's legion of supporters, realizing they'd been lied to and made liars, will dissipate. One thing to note about "witch hunts," a phrase both Nixon and Trump have employed to protest their unfair persecution, is that no modern-day standard of evidence exists to convict a witch. The charge is itself ludicrous.[14] One cannot be proven to be something that does not exist. But if the charge is treason, bribery, or other high crimes and misdemeanors, for which clear and indisputable proof **can** be produced, a witch hunt quickly transforms into a real trial, overseen, in a president's case, by the chief justice of the Supreme Court.

That Nixonian lesson holds true, however, only if the evidence is indeed irrefutable, a level of proof more difficult to imagine the more tribal our politics becomes. Thus we must tweak this lesson of 1974 for our current circumstance. A guilty president's support will evaporate the moment his constituents accept his guilt. Imagining what piece of evidence could so overwhelmingly persuade any supermajority of Americans—and thus their senators—of guilt or innocence is today difficult indeed. Videos can be doctored and audio constructed anew from prior recordings; email and social media accounts are frequently hacked, and anyone with a printer and Photoshop can forge documents that might not withstand expert scrutiny but still sway public sentiment. There may indeed be proof enough for prosecutors of a future president's treason, bribery, or commission of a high crime or misdemeanor, but so long as more than a third of voters—or, rather, voters from a third of the states—tell their senators they remain unconvinced, conviction is hard to imagine.[15]

The number of Americans who distrust the president's veracity consequently matters less in our current age than how many trust him no matter what. President Trump has by some accounts lied or misled an average of six times a day during his first eighteen months in office. Ninety-four percent of registered Democrats recently polled agreed that he tells the truth only "some of the time, or less." Seventy-four percent of Republicans conversely consider Trump truthful "all or most of the time." So long as truth is subject to partisan interpretation, which ceased to be the case in Nixon's final days in office, his successors need have little fear of Senate conviction.[16] Trump's lawyers understood this. "Truth isn't truth," Giuliani explained. With reputations and an entire administration perhaps at stake, seemingly everyone had become a post-modernist less than two years into Trump's presidency.[17]

Bill Clinton was impeached on the narrowest grounds of all, on the charge that he'd committed perjury and abused the power of his office not so much to expand presidential power or malevolently harm the American people, but instead to conceal his private stupidity. He lied. Of that there is no doubt. He acted despicably. This, too, no reasonable person should dispute. Whether those lies warranted removal from office as "high" crimes or misdemeanors likely to materially damage the body politic was another matter, indeed it was the principal matter at hand when the Senate decided his fate.

They, of course, voted to keep him in office. Unlike in Johnson's case, not a single Democrat broke ranks to vote against their party leadership or, in this case, against their president. Upon reflection, Clinton was never truly in danger of losing the support of a supermajority of senators. He faced the more likely prospect of succumbing to overwhelming political pressure to resign during the first months after news of the scandal broke than of losing his impeachment trial once it ultimately began. Republicans held a relatively small majority in the Senate, a mere five seats, nowhere near the sixteen-seat majority required to convict a president along straight party lines. Indeed, as Peter Baker sagely notes, Senate leaders on both sides of the aisle worked from the trial's beginning to check the House of Representative's zeal for Clinton's removal.

Clinton's impeachment thus offered the least pressing constitutional crisis of our three cases, being not about the balance of power or even the abuse of presidential power for political purposes, but merely about misdeeds outside of his constitutional responsibilities. His case is thus—in retrospect though not at the time—the only difficult one of the three. Historians overwhelmingly condemn Johnson's leadership, yet by the same margin believe him innocent of treason, bribery, or the commission of any high crime or misdemeanor. The same overwhelming majority today judge Nixon guilty. No such consensus exists, however, when judging a president who clearly lied about matters far more personal than political, and far more petty than presidential.

Being the least engaged with the Constitution's separation of powers, Clinton's fate was decided not only in the Senate as the Constitution prescribed, but in broader tallies of his popularity, which rose considerably over the course of his trial. What Baker terms "The Campaign" to maximize public approval worked, leaving little room or reason for wavering senators to vote against a man whose favorability ratings likely outpaced their own. Once it became obvious that a supermajority would not be materializing against him, senators had no real reason to vote their conscience (or their prospects) as was the case with Andrew Johnson. They could vote with their party, or after listening to their pollsters. Clinton's lesson for today is therefore at once the most obvious yet also the most important: Popular presidents may get impeached in the House where majority rules, but are remarkably unlikely to find themselves convicted by the Senate's far higher standards. Recall Gerald Ford's famous quip—"an impeachable offense is whatever the majority of the House of Representatives thinks it is at the time"—just long enough to note its obvious irrelevance to a president's ultimate fate in Congress's other chamber.

Deployment of history to consider and predict the present and future is always more art than science, though just as each of our impeachment cases offers lessons for our own day, so, too, does their collective palette reveal the likely outcome of future House votes or Senate trials on the matter. Like Clinton, if a future president is accused of crimes that appear more personal than broadly political (say, malfeasance generated by greed or spite, or simply evidence of a badly flawed character, before taking office or after, rather than to directly violate the Constitution or his oath of office), he may well be impeached if his opposition holds the House. If accused only of personal transgressions he is unlikely, however, to face any real threat of conviction in the Senate. Party loyalty is more likely to prevail should such a case arise, and we are far from either party capturing a solid supermajority in the Senate.

Like Nixon, however, if evidence appears of treason or bribery tied to a president's execution of his authority, or he is shown to have committed a high crime designed to undermine the Constitution or its restraints on power, then there might be a real possibility of conviction and removal from office. Provided, of course, that evidence can be widely if not unanimously accepted—an unlikely hurdle for prosecutors and the president's opponents to clear in this day and age. Nixon's quick fall upon revelation of irrefutable evidence reminds us of how unlikely we are to witness similar consensus today.

Only if a future impeachment case plays out like Johnson's, in which senators are called to consider their consciences as well as their constituents, and at the same time like Nixon's with conclusive evidence strong enough to justify lawmakers' breaking party discipline, should a president truly fear impeachment. Such scenarios might involve a president demonstrated to be under the sway of a foreign power, or who profited from his office, or who consciously overstepped the Constitution's constraints on executive power. Here it would not matter if actual crimes were committed, or even if those crimes took place before a president took office. If any president is shown to have lied to win office in the first place, for example by not fully disclosing his inability or disinclination to faithfully preserve, protect, and defend the American people and the Constitution that binds them, he would undoubtedly be impeachable, and may well be convicted. As the constitutional debates of 1787 made plain, one need not act illegally in order to act treasonably.

It is hard to imagine this final scenario playing out in the foreseeable future absent some tectonic shift in our current political universe, not because senators lack conviction or devotion to democratic ideals, but rather because they answer to a higher authority: voters. Morality derives from a group's consensus of right and wrong, and nowhere more than in politics. Determinations of right and wrong require evaluation of circumstance, motive, and result. Given that we live in a tribal political environment unable to agree on basic facts, we are unlikely to generate the widespread moral outrage necessary to prompt senators to risk eviction by voting against their constituents or against their party. It would require a genuine constitutional crisis of the sort Johnson's opponents generated, coupled with a clear train of irrefutable evidence agreed upon by all sides such as sunk Nixon, and then frosted by a president's wild unpopularity, the very opposite of Clinton, for his judges in any impeachment trial to make their vote anything more than a referendum on the prior election's results.

This is a hypothetical scenario several steps too far removed from our current reality to expect its occurrence. As noted in the introduction, those who study history are destined to repeat it, though with less surprise. An addendum to that thought: Those who study history need not be surprised at all, even if frustration with the current centrality of talk of impeachment extends through 2018, 2020, 2024, and beyond. Frankly this is as the Constitution's framers would have wanted it: for impeachment to be such a high political bar that it exceeds mere partisan fury, but instead requires a president whose proof of malfeasance is unquestioned, lest the question itself split the nation further and perhaps beyond repair.

So long as there are doubts, there is always another election. And with the important caveat that so long as there remains no doubt that the next election will occur (and its results trusted), we would all be less frustrated if we focused on winning the next rather than litigating the last. This is truly what the study of history teaches: that the past cannot be changed, merely employed to bring about a better future.

—JEFFREY A. ENGEL

ACKNOWLEDGMENTS

This book began with an illuminating question posed and debated by the staff and fellows of Southern Methodist University's Center for Presidential History: What does the history of impeachment reveal about its potential? They deserve credit for the idea behind this project, and then for employing their expertise in answering the obvious ensuing question: Whom would you ask? This book is more proof that the creativity of the whole exceeds the sum of its individual parts, demonstrating anew the wisdom of the university's leadership in forging a center where the best young scholars of presidential history— American history on the largest scale—can gather and grow.

Jeffrey Engel thanks Peter Baker, Lindsey Chervinsky, Ben Engel, Elaine Carté Engel, Josh Engel, Marshall Carté Engel, Brian Franklin, Alan Lowe, Daniel Margolies, Molly Turpin, and Molly Wood for their assistance in honing the book's introduction, first chapter, and conclusion. Dan Orlovsky generously ensured time to write at an unexpected time. Too many ideas within belong to Kate Carté Engel to separate or identify, the result of her twenty years' effort to instruct a historian of the present about America's real past.

Jon Meacham is grateful to David O. Stewart, who generously read a draft of the chapter and offered excellent counsel, and to Lamar Alexander, who supplied a copy of Edmund Ross's memoir of the impeachment. Thanks as well to Annette Gordon-Reed, Evan Thomas, and Eric Foner.

From Timothy Naftali: The Nixon section of this book would not have been possible without the assistance of many people. I would like to thank archivist and librarian John Jacob of the Washington and Lee University School of Law for his tireless help with M. Caldwell Butler's materials, which provided me with digital access to the former congressman's invaluable audio diary from the impeachment process and digital copies of other key materials; archivists Desiree Butterfield-Nagy and Paige Lilly, who were superb guides to former congressman William S. Cohen's extensive impeachment-related collection at the University of Maine; former congressman Thomas F. Railsback and archivist Bill Cook, who gave critical assistance with the Railsback papers at Western Illinois University; archivist and former colleague David A. Olson at the Columbia Center for Oral History; archivist and former colleague Ira Pemstein at the Ronald Reagan Presidential Library and Museum, who processed the William Timmons collection at the federal Nixon Library; and archivists and former colleagues Carla Braswell, Meghan Lee-Parker, Ryan Pettigrew, and Jason Schultz at the Richard Nixon Presidential Library and Museum. I also benefited from Sarah Riva's superb research assistance with former congressman Raymond H. Thornton, Jr.'s, papers at the University of Arkansas and research assistance from Meghan Hooper at the Nixon Library. I am also grateful to Francis O'Brien, Lou Cannon, Elizabeth Drew, and Thomas Railsback for talking with me about this project; to Nixon Library director Mike Ellzey for his commitment to the library's Watergate gallery and to keeping the evidence that supports it on the library's website; to Gail Ross, for her help as agent and lawyer; to our editor, Molly Turpin, for her patience; to Juan Spade for kindly listening and making the opening better; to Jackie Applebaum and Stephen Sheanin for hosting us in the Hills; to Mindy Farmer for lending me a book and her wisdom; to Zachary Karabell and Nicole Alger for letting me write near a pool; and to my mum for wanting me to text her whenever I am on a research trip. Finally, I would like to thank those who did the most to introduce me and many others to the people behind the impeachment of Richard Nixon—former colleagues Paul Musgrave and Michael Koncewicz, who assisted with the Nixon Library's video oral history project; archivists and former colleagues John Powers, Sahr Conway-Lanz, and Cary McStay, who successively supervised the awesome team at the Nixon White House tapes project at the Nixon Presidential Materials Project and then at the federal Nixon Library; and Evan A. Davis, Michael Conway, and Maureen Barden, who led the push to record the recollections of John Doar and members of the House Judiciary Committee's impeachment staff for posterity.

From Peter Baker: Very few people emerge from an impeachment battle better off than when they went in, but count me among them. Susan Glasser and I were brought together covering the Bill Clinton scandal in 1998–99 at **The Washington Post**, where she was my remarkable editor, and we have since been joined by our fabulous son, Theo. They have been the best and most supportive family anyone could ask for, along with my parents, Ted and Martha Baker and Linda and Keith Sinrod; my sister and sister-in-law, Karin Baker and Kait Nolan; and the entire Glasser clan.

Thanks, too, to the rest of our impeachment corps at **The Post** from way back in the day, especially John Harris, Susan Schmidt, Juliet Eilperin, Karen De-Young, and Bill Hamilton. I'm lucky to still work with Bill, one of the absolute best in the business, at **The New York Times,** where we thrive under the leadership of A. G. Sulzberger, Dean Baquet, Joseph Kahn, Matt Purdy, and Elisabeth Bumiller. Many thanks to my amazingly talented partners on the White House beat for their forbearance and friendship: Michael Shear, Julie Hirschfeld Davis, Maggie Haberman, Mark Landler, and Katie Rogers. And as always to Raphael Sagalyn, agent, adviser, and friend.

Notes

Introduction

1. For "liberal pundits" and "ominous thing," see Nicole Hemmer, "A Forgotten Lesson of Watergate: Conservatives May Rally Around Trump," **Vox**, May 17, 2017.
2. Ben Stein, "The Truth About Nixon," CNN.com, June 16, 2015.
3. Lydia Saad, "Americans' Faith in Government Shaken But Not Shattered by Watergate," Gallup News Service, June 19, 1997, https://news.gallup.com/poll/4378/americans-faith-government-shaken-shattered-watergate.aspx. For more recent analysis and polling data, see Pew Research Center, "Beyond Distrust: How Americans View Their Government," November 23, 2015, http://www.people-press.org/2015/11/23/beyond-distrust-how-americans-view-their-government.
4. Pew Research Center, "Beyond Distrust."
5. Jessica Kwong, "Bill Clinton Is a Sexual Predator, Not a Victim, Most Americans Say in New Poll," **Newsweek**, June 11, 2018.

6. For "boring," see Nolan McCaskill, "Trump: Acting More Presidential Would Be 'Boring as Hell,'" **Politico,** April 4, 2016. For "Lincoln," see "Trump: 'I can be more presidential than all U.S. Presidents except Lincoln,'" **The Washington Post,** July 25, 2017.

7. Linda Qiu, "Did Trump Fire Comey over the Russian Investigation or Not?" **The New York Times,** May 31, 2018.

8. Mallory Shelbourne, "Support for Trump Impeachment Hearings at 41 Percent in New Poll," **The Hill,** December 20, 2017. See also Sam Schwarz, "Support for Donald Trump's Impeachment Is Higher Than His Re-Election Chances," **Newsweek,** December 20, 2017.

9. Michael S. Schmidt and Maggie Haberman, "Shifting Strategies, Trump's Lawyers Set New Conditions for Mueller Interview," **The New York Times,** July 6, 2018. For comparisons of public support, see Matt Ford, "How Not to Remove a President," **The New Republic,** April 16, 2018.

10. Cristiano Lima, "Pelosi: Impeaching Trump 'Not Someplace That I Think We Should Go,'" **Politico,** November 5, 2017.

11. For "up or down," see Elizabeth Brown-Kaiser and Will Parsons, "Midterm Elections Are an 'Up or Down Vote' on Impeaching Trump, Says Bannon," ABC News, June 17, 2018. For "keep the House," see Morgan Gstalter, "Trump: If Dems Win in 2018 Midterms, They Will Impeach Me," **The Hill,** April 28, 2018.

The Constitution by Jeffrey A. Engel

1. For "losing all confidence," see Henry D. Gilpin, ed., **The Papers of James Madison** (Washington: Library of Congress, 1841), 2:640. For Madison's critical role as our primary resource for the Constitutional Convention's debates, see Mary Sarah Bilder, **Madison's Hand: Revising the Constitutional Convention** (Cambridge, Mass.: Harvard University Press, 2015).

2. "Patrick Henry, Speech to the Virginia Ratification Convention, June 5, 1788," in **The Complete Anti-Federalist,** ed. Herbert J. Storing (Chicago: University of Chicago Press, 1981), 225.

3. "Notes on the Debates in the Federal Convention," June 2, 1787, Avalon Project, Yale Law School Lillian Goldman Law Library, http://avalon.law.yale.edu/18th_century/debates_602.asp. Hereafter "Madison's Notes."

4. For Kennedy, see "Excerpts from Supreme Court Decision Striking Down Sodomy Law," **The New York Times,** June 27, 2003. For Scalia, see Alan Dershowitz, "Scalia Speaks," **The New York Times,** October 30, 2017.

5. For useful discussions from our own age of "high crimes and misdemeanors," see Raoul Berger, **Impeachment: The Constitutional Problems** (Cambridge, Mass.: Harvard University Press, 1973); Michael Gerhardt, **The Federal Impeachment Process: A Constitutional and Historical Analysis** (Chicago: University of Chicago Press, 2000);

Cass R. Sunstein, **Impeachment: A Citizen's Guide** (Cambridge, Mass.: Harvard University Press, 2017); and Lawrence Tribe and Joshua Matz, **To End a Presidency: The Power of Impeachment** (New York: Basic Books, 2018).

6. The period's gendered presumptions offend twenty-first-century sensibilities, and I look forward to one day expanding the range of pronouns employed to discuss American presidents. Yet I have hereafter retained masculine pronouns whenever discussing the Constitution's framers' conception of a future president, whom they could no more imagine being a woman than an enslaved African American, the latter whose value for voting purposes they considered merely three-fifths of a citizen.

7. The literature on the Constitutional Convention is vast and ever growing. For useful overviews see Akhil Amar, **America's Constitution: A Biography** (New York: Random House, 2005); Richard Beeman, **Plain, Honest Men: The Making of the American Constitution** (New York: Random House, 2009); Carol Berkin, **A Brilliant Solution: Inventing the American Constitution** (New York: Harcourt, 2002); Michael J. Klarman, **The Framers' Coup: The Making of the United States Constitution** (New York: Oxford University Press, 2016); Pauline Maier, **Ratification: The People Debate the Constitution** (New York: Simon & Schuster, 2010); Forrest McDonald, **Novus Ordo Seclorum: The Intellectual Origins of the Constitution** (Lawrence: University of Kansas Press, 1985); Jack Rakove, **Original Mean-**

ings: Politics and Ideas in the Making of the Constitution (New York: A. A. Knopf, 1996); David O. Stewart, The Summer of 1787: The Men Who Invented the Constitution (New York: Simon & Schuster, 2007).

History likes winners, thus less has been written on the Articles of Confederation than the Constitution that took its place. For a recent study, see George Van Cleve, We Have Not a Government: The Articles of Confederation and the Road to the Constitution (Chicago: University of Chicago Press, 2017).

8. Works on George Washington outnumber even those on the Constitution. For biographical primers, see Ron Chernow, Washington: A Life (New York: Penguin Press, 2010); James Flexner, Washington: The Indispensable Man (Boston: Little, Brown, 1974); Joseph Ellis, His Excellency: George Washington (New York: Knopf, 2004); Don Higginbotham, George Washington: Uniting a Nation (Lanham, Md.: Rowman & Littlefield, 2002); and Edward J. Larson, The Return of George Washington: Uniting the States, 1783–1789 (New York: Harper Collins, 2015).

9. Klarman, Framers' Coup, 24.

10. Ibid., 37–38.

11. Ibid., 19.

12. Larson, Return of George Washington, 73.

13. For resolutions and revenue, see Klarman, Framers' Coup, 18–22, and Edward J. Larson, The Constitutional Convention: A Narrative History (New

York: Modern Library, 2005), 73. For "climax of popular absurdity," see National Archives and Records Administration (hereafter "NARA"), Founders Online, "From George Washington to John Jay, August 15, 1786," https://founders.archives.gov /GEWN-04-04-02-0199.

14. NARA, Founders online, "From James Madison to Edmund Pendleton, 24 February 1787," http:// founders.archives.gov/documents/Madison /01-09-02-0151. For "too good an opinion," see NARA, Founders Online, "From George Washington to John Jay, August, 15, 1786," https://founders.archives.gov /GEWN-04-04-02-0199.

15. Klarman, **Framers' Coup,** 67.

16. For state constitutions, see Paul Adams, **The First American Constitutions: Republican Ideology and the Making of the State Constitutions in the Revolutionary Era** (Chapel Hill: University of North Carolina Press, 1980). For "monarchical part," see Gordon S. Wood, **The Creation of the American Republic, 1776–1787** (Chapel Hill: University of North Carolina Press, 1969), 430.

17. For "mistaken," see Wood, **Creation of the American Republic,** 430. For "was supposed," and "mischief," see Thomas Paine, **Collected Writings,** ed. Eric Foner (New York: Library of America, 1995), 330 and 360. For Hamilton, see NARA, Founders Online, "From Alexander Hamilton to Robert Morris, August 13, 1782," https://founders.archives.gov /documents/Hamilton/01–03–02–0057–0001. For Jefferson, see "Notes on the State of Virginia, Query

13, 120–121," **The Founders Constitution,** University of Chicago Online Resource, http://press-pubs .uchicago.edu/founders/documents/v1ch10s9.html.

18. For "overtly monarchical," see Brendan McConville, **The King's Three Faces: The Rise and Fall of Royal America, 1688–1776** (Chapel Hill: Omohundro Institute and University of North Carolina Press, 2007), 138; for "ongoing struggle," 7; for "brightest gem," 254.

19. Bernard Bailyn, **Ideological Origins of the American Revolution** (Cambridge, Mass.: Harvard University Press, 2017), 124.

20. Edwin Wolf, "The Authorship of the 1774 Address to the King Restudied," **The William and Mary Quarterly** 22, no. 2 (April 1965): 189–224.

21. **The Works of Benjamin Franklin** (Boston: Hilliard, Gray, 1840), 10:436. See also Edmund Morgan, **Benjamin Franklin** (New Haven, Conn.: Yale University Press, 2002), 213.

22. Pauline Maier, **American Scripture: Making the Declaration of Independence** (New York: Vintage, 1998), 156.

23. For "depravity," see Bailyn, **Ideological Origins of the American Revolution,** 60. For "succession," see Richard J. Ellis, ed., **Founding the American Presidency** (Oxford: Rowman & Littlefield, 1999), 73. Bruce Springsteen sagely made the same point in his 1978 "Badlands": "Poor man wanna be rich, rich man wanna be king / And a king ain't satisfied till he rules everything."

24. Klarman, **Framers' Coup,** 88.

25. For discussion of the effect of Shays's rebellion on constitutional reform, see Melvin Yazawa, **Contested Conventions: The Struggle to Establish the Constitution and Save the Union** (Baltimore: Johns Hopkins University Press, 2016), 15. For "slaughtering," see Stewart, **Summer of 1787,** 15. For "lowest abyss," see Klarman, **Framers' Coup,** 99.

26. For a Hamiltonian reading of the ensuing constitutional debates, in which support for a strong state capable of imposing order predominated, see Max Edling, **A Revolution in Favor of Government: Origins of the U.S. Constitution and the Making of the American State** (New York: Oxford University Press, 2008). For "may pervade," see Klarman, **Framers' Coup,** 92.

27. NARA, Founders Online, "From Washington to Lafayette," February 1, 1784," https://founders.archives.gov/docu ments/Washington/04–01–02–0064.

28. "To George Washington from John Tucker, 16 July, 1785," **The Papers of George Washington,** Confederation Series, vol. 3, 19 May 1785–31 March 1786, ed. W. W. Abbot (Charlottesville: University Press of Virginia, 1994), 129–30. For Washington as a substitute for lost monarchy, see the insightful Kathleen Bartoloni-Tuazon, **For Fear of an Elective King: George Washington and the Presidential Title Controversy of 1789** (Ithaca, N.Y.: Cornell University Press, 2014). For "omnipotent," see Bartoloni-Tuazon, **For Fear of an Elective King,** 39.

29. For "principle conduct," see NARA, Founders Online, "George Washington to Thomas Jefferson, Feb-

ruary 25, 1785," https://founders.archives.gov/docu ments/Jefferson/01–08–02–0001. For Wood, see Don Higginbotham, **George Washington Reconsidered** (Charlottesville: University of Virginia Press, 2001), 317. For "bestowed," see Joanne B. Freeman, **Affairs of Honor: National Politics in the New Republic** (New Haven, Conn.: Yale University Press, 2002), xvi.

30. For "eye of the world," see NARA, Founders Online, "From George Washington to Benjamin Harrison, January 22, 1785," http://founders.archives .gov/documents/Washington/04–02–02–0202. For "radical cures," see ibid., "From George Washington to James Madison, March 31, 1787," http:// founders.archives.gov/docu ments/Washington/04 –05–02–0111.

31. Ibid., "From Henry Knox to George Washington, April 9, 1787," http://founders.archives.gov/docu ments/Washington/04–05–02–0129.

32. Klarman, **Framers' Coup,** 122.

33. NARA, Founders Online, "From Washington to Lafayette, May 5, 1787," http://founders.archives .gov/docu ments/Washington/04–05–02–0200l.

34. Chernow, **Washington,** 526. See also Ellis, **His Excellency,** 171.

35. Madison's Notes, June 1, 1787.

36. Gordon S. Wood, **The Radicalism of the American Revolution** (New York: Vintage Books, 2003), 206.

37. Madison's Notes, June 4.

38. For "following your plow," see NARA, Founders Online, "From Henry Knox to George Washington,"

March 24, 1785, http://founders.archives.gov/docu ments/Washington/04–02–02–0316. See also Gary Wills's appropriately titled **Cincinnatus: George Washington and the Enlightenment** (Garden City, N.Y.: Doubleday, 1984).

39. For "moving emblem," see Wills, **Cincinnatus,** 19. For "arresting the progress," see Chernow, **Washington,** 531.

40. For "Slushington," see Bartoloni-Tuazon, **For Fear of an Elective King,** 62. For "good one," see Madison's Notes, June 4.

41. Logan Beirne, **Blood of Tyrants: George Washington and the Forging of the Presidency** (New York: Encounter Books, 2013), 46.

42. Madison's Notes, June 4.

43. Ibid., June 2.

44. For the best single source on impeachment's trajectory from the fourteenth to the eighteenth centuries, see Berger, **Impeachment,** 7–54. For Williamson, see Madison's Notes, June 2.

45. Madison's Notes, July 20.

46. Ibid., July 19.

47. Ibid.

48. Ibid.

49. Ibid., July 20.

50. Ibid.

51. Ibid.

52. Ibid.

53. Ibid.

54. Ibid.

55. Madison's Notes, September 8.

56. Ibid.

57. John T. Noonan, Jr., **Bribes** (Berkeley: University of California Press, 1987), 43.

58. Madison's Notes, July 24.

59. Gary L. McDowell, **The Language of Law and the Foundations of American Constitutionalism** (Cambridge: Cambridge University Press, 2010), 225–26.

60. "At the very least," historian Jack Rakove concluded, "English history would suggest that 'high crimes and misdemeanors' were regarded as high and grave indeed—posing deep threats to the survival of the constitution and even the kingdom and the preservation of essential rights and liberties." Rakove, "Statement on the Background and History of Impeachment," **George Washington Law Review** 67 (1999): 684. For "very being," see Gary L. McDowell, " 'High Crimes and Misdemeanors': Recovering the Intentions of the Founders," **George Washington Law Review** 67 (1999): 641.

61. Madison's Notes, July 20. See also Sunstein, **Impeachment**, 43.

62. For "lying to the American people," see Mark Lander and Matt Apuzzo, "Brett Kavanaugh, Supreme Court Front-Runner, Once Argued Broad Grounds for Impeachment," **The New York Times**, July 5, 2018. For "public men," see Sunstein, **Impeachment**, 62. For Hamilton, see "The Federalist Papers: No. 65," Avalon Project, http://avalon.law.yale.edu/18th_century/fed65.asp.

63. For Randolph, see **Constitutional Grounds for**

Presidential Impeachment: Report by the Staff of the Impeachment Inquiry, Committee on the Judiciary, House of Representatives, 93rd Cong. (February 1974), https://archive.org/stream/constitutional_grounds_for_presidential_impeachment_-_house_judiciary_comm_staff_report_february_1974/constitutional_grounds_for_presidential_impeachment_-_house_judiciary_comm_staff_report_february_1974_djvu.txt. For "wicked motive," see Klarman, **Framers' Coup**, 366.

64. For "MAN OF THE PEOPLE," see Daniel T. McCarthy, "James Wilson and the Creation of the Presidency," **Presidential Studies Quarterly** 17, no. 4 (Spring 1987): 693, emphasis in original. For "personally responsible" and the Virginia ratification debates, see Jonathan Elliot, ed., **The Debates in the Several State Conventions on the Adoption of the Federal Constitution** (Washington, D.C., 1836), 4:74.

65. Klarman, **Framers' Coup**, 366.

66. For Madison, see ibid., 377. "The argument that only criminal offenses are impeachable is deeply and profoundly wrong," Tribe and Matz argue. "Even having died a thousand deaths, this theory staggers on like a vengeful zombie. Democrats and Republicans alike have invoked it when doing so suited their partisan needs—and then flipflopped when that seemed more expedient." Tribe and Matz, **To End a Presidency**, 45. Sunstein agrees: "Shoplifting isn't an impeachable offense, nor is jaywalking," he said, "nor is income tax fraud. For impeachment, we need

an abuse of presidential authority." Christina Pazzanese, "Sunstein on Impeachment," **The Harvard Gazette,** October 30, 2017.

67. For "chastisement," see "The Federalist Papers: No. 65," Avalon Project. "Nowhere does the Constitution state or otherwise imply that Congress must remove a president whenever that standard [impeachment] has been met," Tribe and Matz note. "Even when members of the House and Senate believe that the president has committed 'high crimes and misdemeanors,' they possess a legally unlimited prerogative not to end his term in office." Tribe and Matz, **To End a Presidency,** 70.

68. For "thousand voices," see John P. Kaminski and Jill Adair McCaughan, eds., **A Great and Good Man: George Washington in the Eyes of His Contemporaries** (Madison, Wis.: Madison House Publishers, 1989). For "too low," see Edward J. Larson, **George Washington: Nationalist** (Charlottesville: University of Virginia Press, 2016), 71.

69. For "dangerous one," see David O. Stewart, **Madison's Gift: Five Partnerships That Built America** (New York: Simon & Schuster, 2016), 75.

ANDREW JOHNSON BY JON MEACHAM

1. William A. Russ, Jr., "Was There Danger of a Second Civil War During Reconstruction?" **Mississippi Valley Historical Review** 25 (June 1938): 39.
2. Ibid., 41.
3. Ibid., 54.
4. Robert Penn Warren, **The Legacy of the Civil War:**

Meditations on the Centennial (New York: Random House, 1961), 15.

5. For my treatment of the Johnson impeachment, I am chiefly indebted to David M. DeWitt, **The Impeachment and Trial of Andrew Johnson** (New York: Macmillan, 1903); Annette Gordon-Reed, **Andrew Johnson** (New York: Times Books, 2011); Chester G. Hearn, **The Impeachment of Andrew Johnson** (Jefferson, N.C.: McFarland, 2000); John F. Kennedy, **Profiles in Courage** (New York: Harper, 1956); Michael Les Benedict, **The Impeachment and Trial of Andrew Johnson** (New York: Norton, 1973); Eric L. McKitrick, **Andrew Johnson and Reconstruction** (Chicago: University of Chicago Press, 1960); William H. Rehnquist, **Grand Inquests: The Historic Impeachments of Justice Samuel Chase and President Andrew Johnson** (New York: Morrow, 1992); Edmund G. Ross, **History of the Impeachment of Andrew Johnson, President of the United States, by the House of Representatives and His Trial by the Senate for High Crimes and Misdemeanors in Office** (Santa Fe, N.M.: 1896); Gene Smith, **High Crimes and Misdemeanors: The Impeachment and Trial of Andrew Johnson** (New York: Morrow, 1977); David O. Stewart, **Impeached: The Trial of Andrew Johnson and the Fight for Lincoln's Legacy** (New York: Simon & Schuster, 2009); Hans L. Trefousse, **Andrew Johnson: A Biography** (New York: Norton, 1989), and Trefousse, **Impeachment of a President: Andrew Johnson, the**

Blacks, and Reconstruction (New York: Fordham University Press, 1999).

6. On Reconstruction in general, see Eric Foner, **Reconstruction: America's Unfinished Revolution, 1863–1877** (New York: Harper Collins, 2014); Foner, **Forever Free: The Story of Emancipation and Reconstruction** (New York: Knopf, 2005); Douglas R. Egerton, **The Wars of Reconstruction: The Brief, Violent History of America's Most Progressive Era** (New York: Bloomsbury, 2014); David M. Blight, **Race and Reunion: The Civil War in American Memory** (Cambridge, Mass.: Belknap Press of Harvard University Press, 2002); Gregory Downs, **After Appomattox: Military Occupation and the Ends of War** (Cambridge, Mass.: Harvard University Press, 2015).

7. Foner, **Reconstruction,** 177.

8. Ibid., 178.

9. Ibid., 180.

10. Ibid.

11. Ibid.

12. Ibid., 189.

13. Ibid., 250.

14. For these points I drew on my treatment of the subject in my **The Soul of America: The Battle for Our Better Angels** (New York: Random House, 2018), 62–65.

15. Tenure of Office Act of 1867, 39th Cong. (1867), https://www.senate.gov/artandhistory/history/resources/pdf/Johnson_TenureofOfficeAct.pdf.

16. McKitrick, **Andrew Johnson and Reconstruction,** 491–509.
17. Smith, **High Crimes and Misdemeanors,** 56–57.
18. Edward Pessen, **Riches, Class, and Power Before the Civil War** (New Brunswick, N.J.: Transaction, 1990), 77.
19. Gordon-Reed, **Andrew Johnson,** 18–19.
20. Ibid., 22.
21. Ibid., 24.
22. Ibid., 61.
23. Smith, **High Crimes and Misdemeanors,** 51.
24. Stewart, **Impeached,** 14.
25. Smith, **High Crimes and Misdemeanors,** 51.
26. The Abraham Lincoln Association, **The Collected Works of Abraham Lincoln,** vol. 7, https://quod.lib.umich.edu/l/lincoln/lincoln7/1:1124?rgn=div1;view=fulltext.
27. Ibid.
28. Smith, **High Crimes and Misdemeanors,** 58.
29. Noah Brooks, **Lincoln Observed: Civil War Dispatches of Noah Brooks,** ed. Michael Burlingame (Baltimore: Johns Hopkins University Press, 1998), 166–67.
30. Stewart, **Impeached,** 11.
31. Gordon-Reed, **Andrew Johnson,** 85–86.
32. Ibid., 2.
33. Smith, **High Crimes and Misdemeanors,** 75.
34. Ibid., 82.
35. Stewart, **Impeached,** 17–18.
36. Eric Foner, **The Fiery Trial: Abraham Lincoln and American Slavery** (New York: W. W. Norton, 2010),

is the standard work on Lincoln, slavery, and emancipation.

37. Louis P. Masur, **Lincoln's Last Speech: Wartime Reconstruction and the Crisis of Reunion** (New York: Oxford University Press, 2015), 189.

38. Les Benedict, **Impeachment and Trial of Andrew Johnson**, 3.

39. Ibid.

40. Ibid., 11–12.

41. Rehnquist, **Grand Inquests**, 204.

42. Les Benedict, **Impeachment and Trial of Andrew Johnson**, 12.

43. Foner, **Reconstruction**, 249.

44. Ibid.

45. Edward Alfred Pollard, **The Lost Cause: A New Southern History of the War of the Confederates** (New York: E. B. Treat, 1866), 750.

46. Ibid., 752.

47. Meacham, **Soul of America**, 15.

48. Ibid., 16.

49. Ibid.

50. Les Benedict, **Impeachment and Trial of Andrew Johnson**, 187. This and the quotations below are from the tenth article of impeachment.

51. Ibid.

52. Ibid.

53. Ibid., 187–88.

54. Rehnquist, **Grand Inquests**, 209.

55. Ibid., 210.

56. Stewart, **Impeached**, 75.

57. Rehnquist, **Grand Inquests**, 209–10.

58. Ibid., 210.
59. Stewart, **Impeached**, 83.
60. Ibid., 75.
61. Ibid., 81–82.
62. Ibid., 83.
63. Ibid.
64. Ibid., 84.
65. Ibid.
66. Ibid., 84–85.
67. Les Benedict, **Impeachment and Trial of Andrew Johnson**, 46–53.
68. Stewart, **Impeached**, 81.
69. Ibid., 96.
70. Ibid.
71. Rehnquist, **Grand Inquests**, 214.
72. Ibid.
73. Ibid.
74. Stewart, **Impeached**, 102.
75. Ibid., 106.
76. Les Benedict, **Impeachment and Trial of Andrew Johnson**, 78.
77. Stewart, **Impeached**, 111.
78. Rehnquist, **Grand Inquests**, 215.
79. Stewart, **Impeached**, 111–12.
80. Andrew Johnson, "Third Annual Message," December 3, 1867, American Presidency Project, University of California, Santa Barbara, http://www.presidency.ucsb.edu/ws/?pid=29508.
81. Stewart, **Impeached**, 117.
82. Ibid., 118–23.
83. Ibid., 136–40.

84. Ibid., 148.

85. Ibid., 153.

86. Ibid.

87. Les Benedict, **Impeachment and Trial of Andrew Johnson,** 184–88.

88. Stewart, **Impeached,** 154–55.

89. Ross, **Johnson Impeachment,** 134.

90. Ibid., 98.

91. Smith, **High Crimes and Misdemeanors,** 246.

92. Ibid., 250.

93. For accounts of the wheeling and dealing, see, for instance, Stewart, **Impeached,** 181–92, 240–49, and 221–22.

94. Smith, **High Crimes and Misdemeanors,** 247.

95. Ibid., 249.

96. Ibid., 254.

97. McKitrick, **Andrew Johnson and Reconstruction,** 490.

98. Ibid.

99. Ibid., 507.

100. Smith, **High Crimes and Misdemeanors,** 282.

101. Ibid., 283.

102. Ibid.

103. Kennedy, **Profiles in Courage,** 122.

104. Ibid., 128–29.

105. Smith, **High Crimes and Misdemeanors,** 285–95; Stewart, **Impeached,** 275–83.

106. Stewart, **Impeached,** 278.

107. Ibid., 279.

108. Smith, **High Crimes and Misdemeanors,** 265–65.

109. Stewart, **Impeached,** 225.

110. Ibid., 303.
111. Foner, **Reconstruction,** 335.
112. Ross, **Johnson Impeachment,** 165.

RICHARD NIXON BY TIMOTHY NAFTALI

1. Angelo Lano, interview by Timothy Naftali, May 28, 2009, Richard Nixon Oral History Project, Richard Nixon Library and Museum (hereafter RNL), Yorba Linda, California.

2. Ibid.; Stanley I. Kutler, **The Wars of Watergate** (New York: W. W. Norton, 1990), 406.

3. Lano, Richard Nixon Oral History Project, May 28, 2009.

4. Alexander M. Haig, Jr., interview by Timothy Naftali, Douglas Brinkley, and John Powers, November 30, 2007, Richard Nixon Oral History Project, RNL.

5. On Richardson's role in this drama, see Michael Koncewicz, **They Said No to Nixon: Republicans Who Stood Up to the President's Abuses of Power** (Oakland: University of California Press, 2018).

6. Arthur M. Schlesinger, Jr., journal entry, October 21, 1973, box 513, Arthur M. Schlesinger, Jr., Papers, Manuscripts and Archives Division, New York Public Library.

7. John F. Kennedy, **Profiles in Courage** (New York: Harper Perennial, 2000), 114.

8. Kutler, **Wars of Watergate,** 412.

9. Timmons to Haig, October 22, 1973, White House Central Files, Timmons Staff Member & Office Files, box 40, RNL.

10. Andrew Kohut, "How the Watergate Crisis Eroded Public Support for Richard Nixon," Pew Research Center, August 8, 2014, http://www.pewresearch .org/fact-tank/2014/08/08/how-the-watergate -crisis-eroded-public-support-for-richard-nixon/.

11. Walter Flowers, oral history [June 1975], box 3, folder 10, "Fragile Coalition" series, William S. Cohen Personal Papers, Raymond H. Fogler Library, University of Maine in Orono.

12. John A. Farrell, **Richard Nixon: The Life** (New York: Doubleday, 2017), 474–75; White House Tapes, Conversation 505–18, May 28, 1971, RNL; Dwight Chapin, interview by Timothy Naftali, April 2, 2007, Richard Nixon Oral History Project, RNL.

13. See the documentary evidence assembled for the RNL's Watergate gallery, https://www.nixonlibrary .gov/mu seum/watergate-exhibit-evidence.

14. Ibid.

15. John J. Sirica, **To Set the Record Straight: The Break-in, the Tapes, the Conspirators, the Pardon** (New York: Norton, 1979), 48.

16. See the documentary evidence assembled for the RNL's Watergate gallery, https://www.nixonlibrary .gov/mu seum/watergate-exhibit-evidence.

17. D. Todd Christofferson, interview by Timothy Naftali, July 15, 2008, Richard Nixon Oral History Project, RNL.

18. Sirica, **To Set the Record Straight**, 96.

19. Ultimately, the House had formed a special committee to deal with Johnson. Stanley Kutler speculates that in October 1973 the House did not form

a special committee because at the time Gerald Ford had yet to be confirmed as vice president and as the next in line, House Speaker Carl Albert might have been perceived as selecting a committee to put himself in the White House. As a result, Albert relied on an existing, permanent committee. Kutler, **Wars of Watergate**, 440.

20. Jimmy Breslin, **How the Good Guys Finally Won: Notes from an Impeachment Summer** (New York: Viking, 1975), 71–76. Breslin, a brilliant reporter and raconteur, chose Tip O'Neill's office as the principal perch from which to watch the impeachment drama unfold. As it turned out, it was an excellent place to see how it started but not the way it ended.
21. Ibid., p. 74.
22. Ibid.
23. Ibid.
24. Albert Jenner, interview by Scott Armstrong, December 23, 1974, Bob Woodward and Carl Bernstein Watergate Papers, Harry Ransom Center, Univeristy of Texas in Austin.
25. Timmons to Haig, October 22, 1973, "Congressional Contact Update," Timmons SMOF, box 40, RNL.
26. Robert Bork, interview by Timothy Naftali, December 1, 2008, Richard Nixon Oral History Project, RNL.
27. Francis O'Brien, telephone interview by Timothy Naftali, July 30, 2018.
28. Breslin, **How the Good Guys Finally Won**, 73.

29. Francis O'Brien, interview by Timothy Naftali, September 29, 2011, Richard Nixon Oral History Project, RNL.

30. Taylor Branch, **At Canaan's Edge: America in the King Years 1965–68** (New York: Simon & Schuster, 2006), 645–47; John Doar, "The Work of the Civil Rights Division in Enforcing Voting Rights Under the Civil Rights Acts of 1957 and 1960," **Florida State University Law Review** 25, no. 1 (1997): 9.

31. John Doar, interview by Timothy Naftali, January 19, 2014, Richard Nixon Oral History Project, RNL.

32. Francis O'Brien, telephone interview by Timothy Naftali, August 1, 2018.

33. Thomas Railsback, "John Doar Briefing, January 7, 1974," box 3, "Railsback Personal Notes" folder, Thomas Railsback Collection, Western Illinois University in Macomb (hereafter WIU).

34. Railsback, "Briefing, January 29, 1974."

35. Sirica, **To Set the Record Straight**, 208–9.

36. Christofferson, Richard Nixon Library Oral History Project, July 15, 2008.

37. Leon Jaworski, **The Right and the Power: The Prosecution of Watergate** (New York: Reader's Digest Press, 1976), 45.

38. Henry Ruth, interview by Timothy Naftali, November 12, 2011, Richard Nixon Oral History Project, RNL. "I don't [think] there was anyone on the staff," Ruth recalled, "who thought there was a legal impediment to indicting a president."

39. Richard Ben-Veniste and George Frampton, Jr.,

Stonewall: The Real Story of the Watergate Prosecution (New York: Simon & Schuster), 223. His deputy, Henry Ruth, concluded that some of Jaworski's legal judgments—on whether he could indict Nixon in office, for example—were a product of his not wanting to have to stay in Washington, D.C., longer than a year. Ruth, Richard Nixon Oral History Project, November 12, 2011.

40. Jaworski, **Right and the Power,** 53–54.

41. Sirica, **To Set the Record Straight,** 215.

42. Ruth, Richard Nixon Oral History Project, November 12, 2011.

43. Robert L. Doar, "With Thoroughness and Honor: The Work of the Impeachment Inquiry Staff of the House Judiciary Committee, 1974" (unpublished thesis, Princeton University), p. 40, M. Caldwell Butler Papers, Lewis F. Powell, Jr., Archives, Washington and Lee University School of Law, Lexington, Va. (hereafter W&L). John Doar's son quoted from a document in his family's private collection.

44. Doar, Richard Nixon Oral History Project, January 24, 2014.

45. Ibid.; Francis O'Brien, telephone interview by Timothy Naftali, July 30, 2018; Doar, "With Thoroughness and Honor," 22, 45.

46. Kenneth W. Thompson, ed., **The Nixon Presidency: Twenty-Two Intimate Perspectives of Richard M. Nixon,** Portraits of Amerian Presidents, vol. 6 (Lanham, Md.: University Press of America, 1987), 21.

47. Harlow to Haig, "Impeachment," January 24, 1974, box 27, "Important Procedural Details January

1974," Alexander Meigs Haig Papers, Library of Congress (hereafter LOC).

48. Railsback, "John Doar Briefing, January 7, 1974," box 3, "Railsback Personal Notes" folder, Railsback Collection, WIU.

49. Richard E. Israel, "Grounds for Impeachment: Summaries of the Reports of the Department of Justice, the House Judiciary Committee Staff and White House Staff on the Grounds for the Impeachment of the President," Congressional Research Service, April 17, 1974, box 1, folder 3, "Fragile Coalition" series, Cohen Personal Papers, University of Maine.

50. Ibid.

51. Doar to St. Clair, February 25, 1974, Railsback papers, Box 1, Folder 15, (Impeachment Committee Actions #5), WIU.

52. "Points," March 8, 1974, Impeachment/Judiciary Committee—through April 74 (4 of 8), Timmons SMOF, Box 38, RNL.

53. Richard Nixon, Question-and-Answer session at the Executive's Club of Chicago, March 15, 1974, http://www.presidency.ucsb.edu/ws/index.php?pid=4386.

54. Jaworski, **Right and the Power**, 101–2.

55. Francis O'Brien, telephone interviews by Timothy Naftali, July 29 and July 30, 2018.

56. M. Caldwell Butler audio diary, tape 2B [March 19, 1974], Butler Papers, W&L.

57. Vern Loen to Timmons, "Carlos J. Moorhead's conversation," March 8, 1974, Timmons SMOF, box 38,

Impeachment/Judiciary Committee Through April 74 (4 of 8), RNL.

58. Republicans on the committee shared their frustration regarding the White House's stonewalling with Rhodes on March 19. Railsback, "Meeting of Republican House Judiciary Committee with Republican Leadership in John Rhodes' Office," March 19, 1974, box 3, "Railsback Personal Notes" folder, Railsback Collection, WIU; Rhodes conveyed this frustration to the president. See Richard Nixon, **RN: The Memoirs of Richard Nixon** (New York: Grosset & Dunlap, 1978), 992–93.

59. Railsback, "Telephone Call with Bill Hewitt, March 27, 1974, [3:00 P.M.]" box 3, "Railsback Personal Notes" folder, Railsback Collection, WIU. William Hewitt was chairman of the board of John Deere.

60. Nixon, **RN**, 990.

61. Raymond Thornton, "Article 2," Thornton autobiographical fragment, box 73, folder 18, Ray Thornton Papers, University of Arkansas in Fayetteville.

62. Thornton, "Judiciary Notes," April 4, 1974, box 1, folder 3, "Fragile Coalition" series, Cohen Personal Papers, University of Maine.

63. The description of the meeting comes from "Article 2," Thornton autobiographical fragment, Thornton Papers, University of Arkansas. Thornton cites Doar referring to the appearance of running a "fishing expedition" at the April 8 Democratic caucus. See "April 8, 1974," box 75, folder 14.

64. Woodward and Bernstein, **Final Days**, 106–9.

65. See Carl Bernstein's 1975 interviews with Bryce Harlow, Woodward and Bernstein Watergate Papers, University of Texas.

66. Railsback, "Memo to the File: Meeting of Republican Members of the Judiciary Committee Members in Ed Hutchinson's office on April 10th at 10:00 A.M.," box 3, "Railsback Personal Notes" folder, Railsback Collection, WIU.

67. Railsback, "Full Committee Meeting, April 11, 1974," ibid.

68. Butler audio diary, tape 5B [April 11, 1974], Butler Papers, W&L.

69. St. Clair offered to transmit materials on four out of six of the requests. He was referring to Doar's letter of February 25, 1974. For the letter, see box 1, folder 16, "Actions of the Judiciary Committee," Railsback Collection, WIU.

70. Butler audio diary, tape 5B [April 11, 1974], Butler Papers, W&L.

71. Ibid., tape 5A [April 8, 1974].

72. Ibid., tape 5B [April 11, 1974].

73. Thornton, Article 2, Thornton autobiographical fragment, Thornton Papers, University of Arkansas.

74. J. Fred Buzhardt, interviews by Bob Woodward, 1975, box 1, folder 10; box 4, folder 16, Woodward and Bernstein Watergate Papers, University of Texas.

75. Jeffrey Banchero, interview by Timothy Naftali, October 28, 2011, Richard Nixon Oral History Project, RNL.

76. Railsback, "Two Telephone Conversations on

April 29th, with John Doar at About 12:15 P.M. and Another with Bert Jenner at About 5:00 P.M.," box 1, "Railsback Personal Notes" folder, Railsback Collection, WIU.

77. Richard Nixon, "Address to the Nation Announcing Answer to the House Judiciary Committee Subpoena for Additional Presidential Tape Recordings," April 29, 1974. www.presidency.ucsb.edu/ws/?PID=4189, accessed August 22, 2018.

78. Butler audio diary, tape 6A [May 1, 1974], Butler Papers, W&L.

79. Railsback, "Telephone Conversation with Bert Jenner, at 9:45 A.M., April 9," box 3, "Railsback Personal Notes" folder, Railsback Collection, WIU.

80. William Cohen, oral history, June 17, 1975, box 2, folder 6, "Fragile Coalition" series, Cohen Personal Papers, University of Maine; Thornton, "May 8, 1974," box 75, folder 14, Thornton Papers, University of Arkansas.

81. Ben-Veniste and Frampton, **Stonewall,** 277–79; Alexander M. Haig, Jr., **Inner Circles: How America Changed the World** (New York: Warner, 1992), 455.

82. Bob Woodward and Carl Bernstein, **Final Days** (New York: Simon & Schuster, 1976) 155–60.

83. Butler audio diary, tape 10B [May 15, 1974?], Butler Papers, W&L.

84. Barber Conable interview, box 75, folder 8, Woodward and Bernstein Watergate Papers, University of Texas.

85. Woodward and Bernstein, **Final Days,** 175.

86. Thornton, "Article 3," Thornton autobiographical fragment, box 73, folder 19, Thornton Papers, University of Arkansas.

87. O'Brien, Richard Nixon Library Oral History Project, September 29, 2011.

88. Breslin, **How the Good Guys Finally Won,** 154–55.

89. Howard Fields, **High Crimes and Misdemeanors: Wherefore Richard M. Nixon . . . Warrants Impeachment: The Dramatic Story of the Rodino Committee** (New York: Norton, 1987), 186; Doar, "With Thoroughness and Honor," 177.

90. Fish, Cohen, and Butler discuss how their fellow Republicans "rationalized away" the March 21, 1973, conversation, on tape 1 of the "Fragile Coalition" oral history, July 11, 1975, box 2, folder 7, "Fragile Coalition" series, Cohen Personal Papers, University of Maine.

91. Railsback, "Meeting in Ed Hutchinson's office on April 2nd at 4 p.m." Railsback papers, Box 3, Folder "Railsback Personal Notes," WIU.

92. Railsback, "Republican Meeting of Judiciary Committee Members in Ed Hutchinson's Office at 3:00 p.m. on June 12, 1974," Railsback papers, Box 3, Folder "Railsback Personal Notes," WIU.

93. See Fish, Flowers, Mann, and Railsback discussing how they made their decision to impeach on tape 4 of the "Fragile Coalition" oral history, July 11, 1975, box 2, folder 8, "Fragile Coalition" series, Cohen Personal Papers, University of Maine.

94. Railsback, "Attitudes at This Time, June 14, 1974," box 3, "Railsback Personal Notes" folder, Railsback Collection, WIU.

95. Butler audio diary, tapes 12B [June 11 and June 12, 1974] and 15B [June 20, 1974], Butler Papers, W&L.

96. Ibid., tape 17B [June 14, 1974].

97. Francis O'Brien, telephone interview by Timothy Naftali, August 1, 2018.

98. Ibid., July 30, 2018.

99. Thornton dictation, June 28, 1974, box 75, folder 14, Thornton Papers, University of Arkansas.

100. Nixon, **RN**, 1041.

101. Raymond Thornton, oral history, June 13, 1975, box 2, folder 17, "Fragile Coalition" series, Cohen Personal Papers, University of Maine.

102. Thornton, "June 4, 1974," box 75, folder 14, Thornton Papers, University of Arkansas.

103. Flowers discusses how "the center coalesced" on tape 1 of the "Fragile Coalition" oral history, July 11, 1975, box 2, folder 7, "Fragile Coalition" series, Cohen Personal Papers, University of Maine.

104. Butler audio diary, tape 19B [July 10, 1974], Butler Papers, W&L.

105. Ibid.

106. Railsback, oral history, June 11, 1975, box 2, folder 13, "Fragile Coalition" series, Cohen Personal Papers, University of Maine.

107. Railsback, "Meeting in Bob McClory's Office at 9:00 A.M. on July 12th," box 3, "Railsback Personal Notes" folder, Railsback Collection, WIU.

108. "Testimony of Herbert Kalmbach," excerpt in box 1,

folder 5, "Fragile Coalition" series, Cohen Personal Papers, University of Maine.

109. James Mann, oral history [June 1975], "Fragile Coalition" series, Cohen Personal Papers, University of Maine.

110. "Comparisons: HJC Transcripts with White House Transcripts," box 73, folder 19, Thornton Papers, University of Arkansas.

111. Butler audio diary, tape 18A [evening of July 18, 1974], Butler Papers, W&L.

112. Kutler, **Wars of Watergate**, 496. Butler, on the other hand, was not angered by this release. He noted that it just showed "we ought to have these tapes." Butler audio diary, tape 18A [evening of July 18, 1974], Butler Papers, W&L. For what Flowers and some of the others thought about St. Clair's reveal in his rebuttal, see tape 1 of the "Fragile Coalition" oral history, July 11, 1975, box 2, folder 7, "Fragile Coalition" series, Cohen Personal Papers, University of Maine.

113. Butler audio diary, tape 20A [July 19, 1974], W&L.

114. Mann and Flowers discuss the sway they thought they might have with other Southern Democrats on tape 1 of the "Fragile Coalition" oral history, July 11, 1975, box 2, folder 7, "Fragile Coalition" series, Cohen Personal Papers, University of Maine.

115. Mann, Flowers, Fish, Cohen, and Railsback discuss the informal July 18, 1974, meeting in a joint oral history done a year later on tape 1, "Fragile Coalition" oral history, July 11, 1975, Cohen Personal Papers, University of Maine.

116. Hamilton Fish, Jr., oral history, June 26, 1975, box

2, folder 9, "Fragile Coalition" series, Cohen Personal Papers, University of Maine.

117. O'Brien, Richard Nixon Oral History Project, September 29, 2011.

118. Evan Davis, interview with Timothy Naftali, September 29, 2011, Richard Nixon Oral History Project, RNL.

119. Railsback, "The Series of Events That Led to the Establishment of the So-Called Fragile Bipartisan Coalition," August 6, 1974, box 3, "Railsback Personal Notes" folder, Railsback Collection, WIU.

120. Railsback, oral history, June 11, 1975, "Fragile Coalition" series, Cohen Personal Papers, University of Maine.

121. Doar, Richard Nixon Oral History Project, January 19, 2018.

122. Richard Nixon, "Address to the Nation Announcing Answers to the House Judiciary Committee Subpoena for Additional Presidential Tape Recordings," April 29, 1974. www.presidency.ucsb.edu /ws/?PID=4189, accessed August 22, 2018.

123. James Mann, oral history, June 19, 1975, "Fragile Coalition" series, Cohen Personal Papers, University of Maine. See also tape 2 of the "Fragile Coalition" oral history, July 11, 1975, box 2, folder 10, "Fragile Coalition" series, Cohen Personal Papers, University of Maine.

124. O'Brien, Richard Nixon Oral History Project, September 29, 2011.

125. Elizabeth Holtzman, interview by Timothy Naftali,

April 5, 2017, Richard Nixon Oral History Project, RNL.

126. Railsback, "Series of Events."

127. See Butler, Cohen, Fish, Flowers, Mann, Railsback, and Thornton oral histories, "Fragile Coalition" series, Cohen Personal Papers, University of Maine.

128. Railsback, "Series of Events"; Lou Cannon, telephone interview by Timothy Naftali, July 31, 2018.

129. Elizabeth Drew, **Washington Journal: Reporting Watergate and Nixon's Downfall** (New York: Overlook Duckworth, 2014), 328–29.

130. Dan T. Carter, **The Politics of Rage: George Wallace, the Origins of the New Conservatism, and the Transformation of American Politics,** 2nd ed. (Baton Rouge: Lousiana State University Press), 454–55.

131. Before coming to the White House, J. Fredrick Buzhardt had been a lawyer at the Pentagon, where he earned the respect and friendship of Secretary of Defense Melvin Laird. In 1973, after Laird came to the White House as a political counsel after leaving the Pentagon, Buzhardt informed him of what he had learned about the president on the tapes. See Dale Van Atta, **With Honor: Melvin Laird in War, Peace, and Politics** (Madison: University of Wisconsin Press, 2008). This authorized biography contains Laird's telling of learning the truth of Nixon's guilt from Buzhardt and how this affected Laird's decision to stay in the White House. In 1985, Laird told this story to scholar Stanley Kutler. See Kutler, **Wars of Watergate,** 386.

132. Alexander M. Haig, Jr., interview by Bob Woodward, box 72, folder 7; box 76, folder 5, Woodward and Bernstein Watergate Papers, University of Texas. Haig's actual schedule of meetings with Nixon and the timing of his telephone calls conflicts with the versions both Buzhardt and Nixon tell. See Haig schedule, July 23, 1974, Haig Papers, LOC.

133. J. Fred Buzhardt, interview by Bob Woodward, box 1, folder 10; box 4, folder 16, Woodward and Bernstein Watergate Papers, University of Texas.

134. Nixon, RM, p. 1050; Haig Telephone Log, July 23, 1974, Haig papers, Box 5, LOC.

135. Nixon, RN, 1051–52.

136. In June, Jaworski had appealed the decision, and Sirica had decided that the section was now relevant, given the start of the impeachment process. Transfer of the transcript, however, had been blocked by the White House.

137. The material leaked to Railsback is the document Eugene V. Risher, "Threat (Friday ams)" in box 3, "Opinions on Impeachment," folder 4, Railsback Papers, WIU.

138. Butler audio diary, tape 17B [June 14, 1974], Butler Papers, W&L.

139. Railsback, oral history, June 11, 1975, "Fragile Coalition" series, Cohen Personal Papers, University of Maine; Butler audio diary, tape 21B [July 27, 1974], Butler Papers, W&L.

140. Butler audio diary, tape 21B [July 27, 1974], Butler Papers, W&L.

141. Time, August 5, 1974.

142. Ibid.
143. See Railsback's comments on tapes 2 and 3 of the "Fragile Coalition" oral history, July 11, 1975, box 2, folder 7, "Fragile Coalition" series, Cohen Personal Papers, University of Maine.
144. M. Caldwell Butler, "Washington & Lee University Speech," July 6, 1987, Butler Papers, W&L.
145. Cohen oral history, June 17, 1975, "Fragile Coalition" series, box 2, folder 6, Cohen Personal Papers, University of Maine.
146. Haig, **Inner Circles**, 484.
147. Lou Cannon, telephone interview with Timothy Naftali, July 21, 2018.
148. Trent Lott, interview with Timothy Naftali, December 8, 2008, Richard Nixon Library Oral History Project, RNL.
149. Julie Nixon Eisenhower, **Pat Nixon: The Untold Story** (New York: Simon & Schuster, 1986), 421.
150. Railsback, "Telephone Call from Chairman Pete Rodino at 10:05 A.M. August 6th," box 3, "Railsback Personal Papers" folder, Railsback Collection, WIU.
151. Barbara Bush, conversation with Timothy Naftali, October 2, 2015.
152. Butler audio diary, tape 22A [July 31 or August 1, 1974], Butler Papers, W&L.

BILL CLINTON BY PETER BAKER

1. **Referral to the United States House of Representatives, Submitted by the Office of the Independent**

Counsel, September 9, 1998 (The Starr Report), *The Washington Post*, https://www.washingtonpost .com/wp-srv/politics/special/clinton/icreport/6narritxiv .htm#L138.

2. Peter Baker, **The Breach: Inside the Impeachment and Trial of William Jefferson Clinton** (New York: Scribner, 2000), 45. Much of this treatment of Clinton's impeachment and trial draws from my coverage of the events for **The Washington Post** in 1998 and 1999, as well as my subsequent book on the episode.

3. A survey by CNN, **USA Today,** and Gallup from March 20 to 22, 1998, found that 33 percent of respondents considered Clinton "honest and trustworthy" while 66 percent approved of the way he handled his job. Keating Holland, "Most Americans Think Their Moral Standards Are Higher Than Clinton's," CNN.com, March 23, 1998.

4. Sam Tanenhaus, "How Richard Nixon Created Hillary Clinton," Bloomberg, November 5, 2015.

5. Hillary Rodham Clinton, **Living History** (New York: Simon & Schuster, 2003), 68.

6. Sam Roberts, "John Paul Hammerschmidt, 92, Dies; Congressman Defeated Clinton," **The New York Times,** April 2, 2015.

7. David Maraniss, **First in His Class: A Biography of Bill Clinton** (New York: Simon & Schuster, 1995), 327.

8. Bill Clinton, "Remarks at the Funeral Service for President Richard Nixon in Yorba Linda, California," April 27, 1994, American Presidency Project, http://www.presidency.ucsb.edu/ws/?pid=50052.

9. **Referral to the United States House of Representatives, Submitted by the Office of the Independent Counsel, September 9, 1998** (The Starr Report), **The Washington Post,** https://www.washingtonpost.com/wp-srv/politics/special/clinton/icreport/6narritxiv.htm #L132.

10. Susan Schmidt, Peter Baker, and Toni Locy, "Clinton Accused of Urging Aide to Lie," **The Washington Post,** January 21, 1998.

11. Dan Balz, "President Imperiled as Never Before," **The Washington Post,** January 22, 1998.

12. Bill Clinton, interview with Jim Lehrer, **The NewsHour with Jim Lehrer,** PBS, January 21, 1998.

13. John F. Harris and Dan Balz, "Clinton Forcefully Denies Affair, or Urging Lies," **The Washington Post,** January 27, 1998.

14. Baker, **Breach,** 27.

15. Peter Baker, "When the President Testified: People in the Room Recall Clinton's 1998 Interrogation," **The New York Times,** May 29, 2018.

16. **Referral to the United States House of Representatives, Submitted by the Office of the Independent Counsel, September 9, 1998** (The Starr Report), Document Supplement A, 460–61.

17. Ibid., 510.

18. Baker, **Breach,** 33.

19. Bill Clinton, "Address to the Nation on Testimony Before the Independent Counsel's Grand Jury," August 17, 1998, American Presidency Project, http://www.presidency.ucsb.edu/ws/?pid =54794.

20. Ibid.

21. Keating Holland, "Poll: Most Americans Think Clinton Lied, but Don't Want Impeachment," CNN.com, August 24, 1998.

22. Baker, **Breach**, 34.

23. Ibid., 42.

24. Charlie Savage, "Can the President Be Indicted? A Long-Hidden Legal Memo Says Yes," **The New York Times,** July 22, 2017.

25. 28 U.S. Code, chap. 40, section 595 (c), https://www.law.cornell.edu/uscode/text/28/part-II/chapter-40.

26. **Referral to the United States House of Representatives, Submitted by the Office of the Independent Counsel, September 9, 1998** (The Starr Report), **The Washington Post,** https://www.washingtonpost.com/wp-srv/politics/special/clinton/icreport/icreport.htm.

27. Baker, **Breach**, 108.

28. Ibid., 120.

29. David Stout, "Hyde Acknowledges 'Indiscretion' Following Report of an Affair," **The New York Times,** September 17, 1998.

30. "Seats in Congress Gained/Lost by the President's Party in Mid-Term Elections," American Presidency Project, http://www.presidency.ucsb.edu/data/mid-term_elections.php.

31. Michael Kranish and Brian McGrory, "Democrats Show Spunk, Blunting Republican Gains," **The Boston Globe,** November 4, 1998.

32. Baker, **Breach**, 143.

33. **Impeachment Inquiry: William Jefferson Clinton,**

President of the United States, Hearing Before the Committee on the Judiciary, House of Representatives, 105th Cong. (November 19, 1998), https://www.gpo.gov/fdsys/pkg/GPO-CDOC-106sdoc3/pdf/GPO-CDOC-106sdoc3-9.pdf.

34. Baker, **Breach,** 181–82.

35. Ibid., 123.

36. "Senate Censures President," March 28, 1834, Senate Historical Office, https://www.senate.gov/artandhistory/history/minute/Senate_Censures_President.htm.

37. Baker, **Breach,** 236.

38. "Excerpts from Impeachment Debate," December 18, 1998, **The Washington Post,** http://www.washingtonpost.com/wp-srv/politics/special/clinton/stories/excerpts121898.htm.

39. Ibid.

40. Baker, **Breach,** 241–42.

41. Ibid., 16–17.

42. Robert Livingston, speech to the House, December 19, 1998, The History Place, http://www.historyplace.com/speeches/gephardt-livingston.htm.

43. Baker, **Breach,** 247.

44. Livingston speech, December 19, 1998.

45. The House voted 228 to 206 to approve article one largely along party lines, with five Democrats breaking from their colleagues to vote yes and five Republicans defecting from their caucus to vote no, http://clerk.house.gov/evs/1998/roll543.xml. Article two was rejected 229 to 205, with twenty-eight Republicans joining a nearly unanimous Democratic

caucus, http://clerk.house.gov/evs/1998/roll544.xml. Article three was approved 221 to 212, http://clerk .house.gov/evs/1998/roll545.xml. Article four was rejected 285 to 148, with eighty-one Republicans voting no, http://clerk.house.gov/evs/1998/roll546 .xml.

46. John F. Harris, "Clinton Vows to Finish Term," **The Washington Post,** December 20, 1998.

47. Ibid.

48. Baker, **Breach,** 261.

49. Ibid., 301.

50. Charles F. C. Ruff, speech to the Senate, January 19, 1999, **The Washington Post,** https://www.washing tonpost.com/wp-srv/politics/special/clinton/stories /rufftext011999.htm.

51. Dale Bumpers, speech to the Senate, January 21, 1999, **The Washington Post,** https://www.washing tonpost.com/wp-srv/politics/special/clinton /stories/bumperstext012199.htm.

52. Baker, **Breach,** 373.

53. The senator was Charles Grassley of Iowa. Baker, **Breach,** 397.

54. Ibid., 389.

55. All forty-five Democrats were joined by ten Republicans in voting against the first article of impeachment, February 12, 1999, https://www.senate.gov /legis lative/LIS/roll_call_lists/roll_call_vote_cfm.cfm ?congress=106&session=1&vote=00017.

56. Five Republicans joined the Democrats in rejecting the second article of impeachment, February 12, 1999, https://www.senate.gov/legislative/LIS/roll_call

_lists/roll_call_vote_cfm.cfm?congress=106 &session=1&vote=00018.

57. Baker, **Breach**, 411.

58. John F. Harris, "President Responds with Simple Apology," **The Washington Post**, February 13, 1999.

59. Ibid.

60. Baker, **Breach**, 417.

61. Bill Clinton, "Interview with Dan Rather of CBS News," March 31, 1999, American Presidency Project, http://www.presidency.ucsb.edu/ws/?pid=57340.

62. Baker, **Breach**, 417.

63. Jennifer Steinhauer, "Bill Clinton Should Have Resigned Over Lewinsky Affair, Gillibrand Says," **The New York Times**, November 16, 2017.

64. Peter Baker, "'What About Bill?' Sexual Misconduct Debate Revives Questions About Clinton," **The New York Times**, November 15, 2017.

CONCLUSION

1. For "going to happen," see "Giuliani Likens Clintons to Crime Family," **The Gazette** (Cedar Rapids, Iowa), November 2, 2016; and Tessa Berenson, "Donald Trump Raises Specter of Hillary Clinton Impeachment," **Time**, November 2, 2016. See also Mike DeBonis, "Some Republicans Are Discussing Their Plans for President Clinton—Starting with Impeachment," **The Washington Post**, November 3, 2016.

2. Peter W. Stevenson, "'Prediction Professor' Who Called Trump's Big Win Also Made Another Forecast: Trump Will Be Impeached," **The Independent**, November 11, 2016.

3. Berenson, "Donald Trump Raises Specter of Hillary Clinton Impeachment."

4. "Obama Blasts Republicans for Clinton Impeachment Talk," **Politico,** November 2, 2016.

5. Madison's Notes, July 20.

6. Ibid.

7. Ibid.

8. David Greenberg, "Andrew Johnson: Saved by a Scoundrel," **Slate,** January 31, 1999.

9. John Farrell's masterful new biography examines this statement and its context clearly and insightfully. See **Richard Nixon: The Life** (New York: Vintage Books, 2017), 550.

10. I credit Joshua Adam Engel for this insight.

11. John M. Naughton et al., "Nixon Slide from Power: Backers Give Final Push," **The New York Times,** August 12, 1974.

12. Ibid.

13. Ibid.

14. Unless one weighs less than a duck.

15. Note that a supermajority of popular support is not required to prevent calamity. The Constitution is clear on how to impeach and if necessary convict a president. It is silent on how to physically remove an unwilling ex-president from office. Force may be required, of the sort likely to enrage his or her most intractable supporters. Sixty-seven senators may be required to convict, but a far smaller number of determined loyalists, willing to deploy deadly force to defend their champion against charges and a conviction they deem illegitimate, could wreak havoc in

Washington in a way unseen since the trampling of the 1932 Bonus March encampment. In this awful scenario, Tiananmen on the national mall would prove a more fitting analogy.

16. Andrew Arenge et al., "Poll: Republicans Who Think Trump Untruthful Still Approve of Him," NBC News, May 2, 2018.

17. " 'Truth Isn't Truth': Trump Lawyer Rudy Giuliani Worries Mueller Interview Could Lead to Perjury Charge," USA Today, August 19, 2018.

INDEX

ABOUT THE AUTHORS

JEFFREY A. ENGEL is founding director of the Center for Presidential History at Southern Methodist University and a Senior Fellow of the John Goodwin Tower Center for Political Studies. Educated at Cornell University, Oxford University, and the University of Wisconsin–Madison, from which he received his PhD in American history in 2001, he has taught history and international affairs at Yale University, the University of Pennsylvania, and Texas A&M University, where he was the Verlin and Howard Kruse '52 Founders Professor. A frequent lecture and media commentator on historical and contemporary affairs, Engel has also authored or edited twelve books on American foreign policy, including his latest, **When the World Seemed New: George H. W. Bush and the End of the Cold War.**

JON MEACHAM is a Pulitzer Prize–winning biographer. The author of the **New York Times** bestsellers **The Soul of America: The Battle for Our Better Angels,**

Thomas Jefferson: The Art of Power, American Lion: Andrew Jackson in the White House, Franklin and Winston, and Destiny and Power: The American Odyssey of George Herbert Walker Bush, he is a distinguished visiting professor at Vanderbilt University, a contributing writer for The New York Times Book Review, and a fellow of the Society of American Historians. Meacham lives in Nashville with his wife and children.

TIMOTHY NAFTALI teaches at New York University, where he is a clinical associate professor of public service at the Robert F. Wagner Graduate School of Public Service and a clinical associate professor of history. From 2006 to 2011, Naftali was the last director of the Nixon Presidential Materials Project at the National Archives and Records Administration in College Park, Maryland, and then was the founding director of the federal Richard Nixon Presidential Library and Museum in Yorba Linda, California, where he curated a new, nonpartisan Watergate gallery and interviewed more than 110 former Nixon officials and others from the era for the library's oral history project. His books include "One Hell of a Gamble: Khrushchev, Castro, and Kennedy, 1958–1964," a study of the Cuban missile crisis (with Aleksandr Fursenko), and George H. W. Bush.

PETER BAKER is the chief White House correspondent for The New York Times and a political analyst for MSNBC. He was coauthor of the original Washington **Post** story in January 1998 that broke the news of the investigation into Bill Clinton's efforts to cover up his affair with Monica Lewinsky that led to his impeachment. Baker has covered four presidents for the **Post** and the **Times,** including Clinton, George W. Bush, Barack Obama, and Donald J. Trump. He and his wife, Susan Glasser, served as Moscow bureau chiefs of the **Post** and covered the opening months of the wars in Afghanistan and Iraq. Baker is author of four previous books, including **The Breach: Inside the Impeachment and Trial of William Jefferson Clinton,** a **New York Times** bestseller. He lives in Washington with Glasser and their son, Theodore.